THE
LIKE
SWITCH

An Ex–FBI Agent's Guide to Influencing,
Attracting, and Winning People Over

JACK SCHAFER, Ph.D.,
with MARVIN KARLINS, Ph.D.

A TOUCHSTONE BOOK
Published by Simon & Schuster

New York   London   Toronto   Sydney   New Delhi

Touchstone
A Division of Simon & Schuster, Inc.
1230 Avenue of the Americas
New York, NY 10020

First Touchstone trade paperback edition January 2015

TOUCHSTONE and colophon are registered trademarks of Simon & Schuster, Inc.

For information about special discounts for bulk purchases, please contact Simon & Schuster Special Sales at 1-866-506-1949 or business@simonandschuster.com.

The Simon & Schuster Speakers Bureau can bring authors to your live event. For more information or to book an event contact the Simon & Schuster Speakers Bureau at 1-866-248-3049 or visit our website at www.simonspeakers.com.

Interior design by Ruth Lee-Mui
Cover design by David High
Cover art by ArtBitz/Shutterstock
Photographs by Dave and Lynda Mills of Dave Mills Photography, Lancaster, California

Manufactured in the United States of America

10 9 8 7 6 5 4 3 2 1

Library of Congress Cataloging-in-Publication Data
Schafer, Jack.
   The like switch : an ex–FBI agent's guide to influencing, attracting, and winning people over / Jack Schafer, Marvin Karlins.
        pages   cm.—(A Touchstone book)
1. Friendship. 2. Interpersonal attraction. 3. Influence (Psychology)
4. Interpersonal relations. I. Karlins, Marvin. II. Title.
   BF575.F66S33 2015
   158.2'5—dc23
                                            2014009121
ISBN 978-1-4767-5448-2
ISBN 978-1-4767-5450-5 (ebook)

To my wife, Helen, a woman overflowing with love, strength of character, and, above all, patience for enduring my antics for over three decades of marriage.

JACK SCHAFER

To my wife, Edyth, and daughter, Amber: for who you are, for what you've accomplished, for your love that has enriched so many lives.

MARVIN KARLINS

CONTENTS

THE LIKE SWITCH

How to Turn People On to You

When you hear "FBI," you likely don't think the Friendly Bureau of Investigation. But my twenty years as an agent specializing in behavioral analysis enhanced my ability to quickly read people and gave me a unique understanding of human nature and shared human behaviors. And my work, which ranged from convincing people to spy on their own country to identifying perpetrators and convincing them to confess, allowed me to develop many incredibly powerful methods for getting people to trust me, often without me saying a word. In my role as behavioral analyst for the FBI's Behavioral Analysis Program, I developed strategies to recruit spies and make friends out of sworn foes. In other words, I developed specific skills and techniques that could turn an enemy of the United States into a friend who was willing to become a spy for America.

My profession boiled down to getting people to like me. My work with "Vladimir" (I have changed the names and identifying characteristics of those I discuss and have created some composites to best illustrate what my work has demonstrated) illustrates this point well.

Vladimir had illegally entered the United States to commit espionage. He was caught in possession of classified defense documents. As an FBI Special Agent, I was assigned to interview Vladimir. At our first meeting he made a vow not to speak to me under any circumstances. I then began the process of countering his defiance by simply sitting opposite him and reading a newspaper. But at a carefully planned time, I deliberately folded the newspaper and left without saying a word. Day after day and week after week I sat across from him and read the newspaper while he remained mute, handcuffed to a nearby table.

Finally, he asked why I kept coming daily to see him. I folded the newspaper, looked at him, and said, "Because I want to talk to you." I immediately returned the newspaper to the upright position and continued reading, ignoring Vladimir. After a while, I got up and left without saying another word.

On the following day, Vladimir again asked me why I came every day and read the newspaper. I again told him that I came because I wanted to talk to him. I sat down and opened the newspaper. A few minutes later, Vladimir said, "I want to talk." I put the newspaper down and said, "Vladimir, are you sure you want to talk to me? When we first met, you told me that you would never speak to me." Vladimir replied, "I want to talk to you, but not about spying." I agreed to this condition but added, "You will let me know when you are ready to talk about your spying activities, won't you?" Vladimir agreed.

Over the next month, Vladimir and I talked about everything except his spying activities. Then, one afternoon, Vladimir announced, "I'm ready to talk about what I did." Only then did we finally speak in great detail about his espionage activities. Vladimir spoke freely and honestly not because he was forced to talk, but because he liked me and considered me his friend.

The interrogation techniques I used with Vladimir may, at first glance, seem to make little sense . . . but everything I did was carefully orchestrated to achieve Vladimir's eventual confession and cooperation. In *The Like Switch,* I will reveal the secrets of how I won Vladimir over and how, using the same techniques, you can get anyone to like you for the moment or for a lifetime. I can do this because it turns out that the same social skills I developed to befriend and recruit spies are equally effective in developing successful friendships at home, at work, or anywhere else that personal interactions take place.

At first, I did not see this one-to-one crossover from my fieldwork to everyday life. In fact, it was initially brought to my attention near the end of my career with the FBI. At that time I was teaching classes to young intelligence officers on how to recruit spies. On the first day of a new class I arrived a half hour early to set up the room for a group exercise. To my surprise, two students were already there. I didn't recognize them. They sat quietly in the front row with their hands folded on their desks and a look of anticipation on their faces. Considering the time of day and the fact that most students were not known for arriving early to class, I wondered what was going on. I asked them who they were and why they had decided to show up at such an early hour.

"Do you remember Tim from your previous class?" one of the students asked.

"Yes," I said.

"Several weeks ago the two of us went to a bar with Tim. He told us about your lecture on influence and rapport building."

"And . . . ?" I still didn't see where this was leading.

"Tim bragged that he learned in class how to pick up ladies."

"Obviously, we were skeptical," said the second student.

"So we put him to the test," the first student continued. "We picked a random woman who was in the club and challenged Tim to get her to come to our table and have a drink with us, without saying a word."

"What did he do?" I inquired.

"He took us up on the challenge," the student exclaimed. "We thought he was nuts. But then, about forty-five minutes later, the woman came over to our table and asked if she could join us for a drink. We still find it hard to believe, and we saw it happen."

I gave the students a quizzical look. "Do you know how he did it?"

"No!" exclaimed one of them. And then, in unison, both of them said, "That's what we came here to learn!"

My first reaction to their comments was to assert the professionalism expected of me, and I told them the purpose of the classroom training was to teach students to be effective intelligence officers, not pickup artists. It was my second reaction that took me by surprise, an epiphany of sorts. Thinking of Tim's antics, I suddenly realized that the same techniques used to recruit spies could be employed to become a victor in the so-called dating game. Even more important, in a broader sense, these techniques could be used whenever a person wants to win anyone over in virtually any personal interaction. It was that realization that served as the launchpad for this book and all the information contained within it.

After retiring from the FBI, I went on to get my doctorate in psychology and a university teaching position. It was during this phase of my life that I fleshed out my Like Switch strategies to help you achieve successful interpersonal relationships at home, at work, or anywhere else person-to-person interaction is involved. For example:

- New salespeople can use the techniques presented in this book to establish a clientele list from scratch.
- Experienced salespeople can also benefit from learning how to maintain or enhance existing relationships as well as from developing additional clients.
- All levels and types of employees, from managers at Wall Street firms to restaurant waitstaff, can use these tactics to interact more effectively with their supervisors, colleagues, subordinates, and customers.

- Parents can use the strategies to repair, maintain, and strengthen their relationships with their children.
- Consumers can use this information to get better service, better deals, and better personalized attention.
- And, of course, people seeking friends or romantic relationships can use these social skills to overcome this inherently difficult experience (made even more challenging in our digitally focused society).

The Like Switch is for anyone seeking to make new friends, to maintain or enhance existing relationships, to make brief encounters with people more enjoyable, or to get better tips and bonuses.

CONQUERING THE FRIENDSHIP CHALLENGE

Human beings are social animals. As a species, we are hardwired to seek out others. This desire is rooted in our primitive beginnings, when togetherness gave us the best chance to move up the food chain as we emerged from our caves and struggled for survival in a hostile and unforgiving world. Thus, one would assume that making friends would be easy, even automatic. Sadly, this isn't so. In poll after poll, study after study, an increasing number of people report feeling isolated and incapable of developing rudimentary, let alone meaningful, long-lasting relationships. This problem has grown worse with the introduction of social media, which further distances us from face-to-face, meaningful social interaction.

Dealing with people, particularly with individuals you don't know, can be a challenging, even scary, experience. Whether you are a man or a woman doesn't seem to matter. The fear is there: fear of embarrassment, fear of rejection, fear of causing hurt feelings, fear of making a bad impression, even the fear of being used or taken advantage of. The good news is that relationships don't have to be an invitation to disaster. If you are struggling with friendship issues or just want to improve the friendships you already have, take heart. You are not alone and your situation is not hopeless. This book is designed to allay your concerns about interacting with others at work, at home, with strangers, or with loved ones.

The techniques presented in this book provide you with the best possible chance, based on the latest scientific evidence, to get people to like you, without saying a word. Eventually, though, you have to speak to people. Words translate the initial feelings of goodwill into friendships and, in some cases, lifelong relationships. This book presents the nonverbal cues along with the verbal prompts that can get anyone to like you instantly.

Rewarding personal relationships are within your reach. It's not a matter of guesswork or luck. It is the result of using proven scientific knowledge and techniques in dealing with other individuals. The opportunity to make friends is three steps away:

1. **You must be willing to learn and master the techniques presented in this book.** The techniques are similar to the power tools used by construction workers. The key is to let the tools do the work. When I was young, I routinely used a handsaw to cut wood. One day my father let me use his newly purchased circular saw. I took the power saw in hand and began to cut a piece of wood. I applied the same pressure to the power saw that I would have applied to a hand saw. My father tapped me on the shoulder and told me to ease up on the pressure and let the saw do the work. The techniques in this book are based on similarly sound principles. Simply apply the techniques and relax, be yourself, and let the techniques do the work. You will be amazed at the results.

2. **You must actually use this new knowledge in dealing with people in your everyday life.** Knowing the best way to do something is great, but only when you actually utilize what you have learned. *Always remember that knowledge without action is knowledge wasted.*

3. **You need to constantly practice what you have learned.** Friendship skills are like skills in general. The more you use them, the more proficient you become; the less you use them, the quicker you lose them. If you are willing to take these three steps, you will find that making friends becomes as automatic as breathing.

The Like Switch is within your reach. To flip it on, just utilize the information you'll be learning in the following pages and watch your LQ (Likability Quotient) soar.

1

THE FRIENDSHIP FORMULA

I've learned that people will forget what you said,
people will forget what you did, but people will
never forget how you made them feel.
—MAYA ANGELOU

OPERATION SEAGULL

His code name was Seagull.

He was a highly placed foreign diplomat.

He could be a valuable asset if he became a spy for the United States.

The problem was, how do you convince somebody to pledge their allegiance to an opposing country? The answer was to befriend Seagull and make him an offer too tempting to refuse. The key to this strategy involved patience, painstaking intelligence gathering about every facet of Seagull's life, and a way to foster a relationship with an American counterpart he could trust.

A background investigation of Seagull revealed that he had been passed over for promotion several times and was overheard telling his wife that he liked living in America and would consider retiring there if that were possible. Seagull was also concerned his country's small pension would be insufficient to provide him with a comfortable retirement. Armed with this knowledge, security analysts believed Seagull's allegiance to his country could be compromised if he was offered the proper financial incentives.

The challenge became how to get close enough to Seagull to make him a financial deal without "spooking" him. The FBI operative, Charles, was told to slowly and systematically grow a relationship with Seagull, like aging a fine wine to bring out its best flavor, to a point where the time was ripe to approach him with an offer. The agent was told if he moved too fast it was likely that Seagull would go "shields up" and avoid him completely. Instead, he was instructed to orchestrate his approach, using behavioral strategies designed to establish friendships. The first step was to get Seagull to like Charles before they exchanged a single word. The second step was to use the appropriate verbal prompts to translate that goodwill into a lasting friendship.

The preparation for the critical first encounter with Seagull started many months before the actual meeting took place. Surveillance had determined that Seagull routinely left his embassy compound once a week and walked two blocks to the corner grocery store to shop. Armed with this information, Charles was instructed to station himself at various locations along Seagull's route to the store. He was warned never to approach Seagull or threaten him in any way; instead he was to simply "be there" so Seagull could see him.

As a trained intelligence officer, it was not long before Seagull took notice of the FBI agent, who, by the way, made no effort to conceal his identity. Because Charles made no move to intercept or speak with his target, Seagull did not feel threatened and became accustomed to seeing the American on his trips to the store.

After several weeks of being in the same vicinity together, Seagull made eye contact with the American operative. Charles nodded his head, acknowledging Seagull's presence, but showed no further interest in him.

More weeks passed and, as they did, Charles increased his non-verbal interaction with Seagull by **increasing his eye contact, raising**

his eyebrows, tilting his head, and **jutting out his chin,** which are all nonverbal signs that scientists have discovered are interpreted by the human brain as "friend signals."

Two months elapsed before Charles made his next move. He followed Seagull into the grocery store he routinely visited, but kept his distance from the foreign diplomat. With each new trip to the store, Charles continued to enter the grocery as well, still maintaining space between himself and Seagull but increasing the number of times he passed the diplomat in the aisles and increasing the duration of visual contact with him. He noted that Seagull bought a can of peas on each of his shopping excursions. With this new information, Charles waited a few additional weeks and then, on one occasion, followed Seagull into the store as he usually did, but this time to introduce himself to Seagull. As the foreign diplomat reached for a can of peas, Charles reached for the can next to it, turned to Seagull, and said, "Hi, my name is Charles and I'm a Special Agent with the FBI." Seagull smiled and said, "I thought so." From that first innocuous meeting, Charles and Seagull developed a close friendship. Seagull eventually agreed to assist his new FBI friend by regularly providing him with classified information.

A casual observer, watching the many months' wooing of Seagull, might wonder why it took so long for the first meeting to take place. It was not by accident. In fact, the entire Seagull recruitment strategy was a carefully choreographed psychological operation designed to establish a bond of friendship between two men who would, under normal circumstances, never contemplate such a relationship.

As a member of the FBI's Behavioral Analysis Program, I was assigned, along with my colleagues, the task of orchestrating the recruitment scenario for Seagull. Our objective was to get Seagull comfortable enough with Charles, our FBI operative, so that a first meeting could take place and, hopefully, would be followed by future meetings if Charles could make a good impression on Seagull. Our task was made more difficult because Seagull was a highly trained intelligence officer who would be constantly on the alert for any person who might arouse his suspicion, and which would result in his avoidance of that individual at all costs.

For Charles to have a successful face-to-face first meeting with Seagull, the foreign operative would have to be psychologically comfortable with his American counterpart. And for that to happen, Charles would have to take specific steps, which, it turned out, he successfully achieved. The steps Charles was required to follow in winning Seagull over are the same ones you must take if you want to develop either short- or long-term friendships.

Using the Seagull case as a backdrop, let's examine the steps Charles successfully completed to recruit his target using the Friendship Formula.

THE FRIENDSHIP FORMULA

The Friendship Formula consists of the four basic building blocks: proximity, frequency, duration, and intensity. These four elements can be expressed using the following mathematical formula:

$$\text{Friendship} = \text{Proximity} + \text{Frequency} + \text{Duration} + \text{Intensity}$$

Proximity is the distance between you and another individual and your exposure to that individual over time. In the Seagull case, Charles didn't simply walk up to Seagull and introduce himself. Such behavior would have resulted in Seagull's rapid departure from the scene. The conditions of the case required a more measured approach, one that allowed Seagull time to "get used" to Charles and not view him as a threat. To achieve this end, the friendship factor of **proximity** was employed. Proximity serves as an essential element in all personal relationships. Just being in the same vicinity as your recruitment target is critical to the development of a personal relationship. Proximity predisposes your recruitment target to like you and promotes mutual attraction. People who share physical space are more likely to become attracted to one another, even when no words are exchanged.

The key to the power of proximity is that it must take place in a nonthreatening environment. If a person feels threatened by someone being too close, they go "shields up" and take evasive action to move away from that person. In the Seagull scenario, Charles was proximal to his target, but he kept a safe distance to prevent him from perceiving Charles as a potential danger and consequently triggering a "fight or flight" response.

Frequency is the number of contacts you have with another individual over time and Duration is the length of time you spend with another individual over time. As time passed, Charles employed the second and third friendship factors: **Frequency** and **Duration.** He did this by positioning himself on Seagull's shopping route in a manner that increased the number of instances (frequency) where the foreign diplomat saw him. After several months, he added duration to the mix by spending longer periods of time around Seagull. He did this by following his target into the grocery store, thereby extending the contact time between them.

Intensity is how strongly you are able to satisfy another person's psychological and/or physical needs through the use of verbal and nonverbal behaviors. The final factor in the Friendship Formula, **Intensity,** was achieved gradually over time as Seagull became more and more aware of Charles's presence and the FBI agent's seemingly unexplainable reluctance to approach him. This introduced one type of intensity, *curiosity,* into the mix. When a new stimulus is introduced into a person's environment (in this case a stranger enters Seagull's world), the brain is hardwired to determine if that new stimulus presents a threat or a perceived threat. If the new stimulus is judged to be a threat, the person will attempt to eliminate or neutralize it by employing the fight or flight response. If, on the other hand, the new stimulus is not perceived as a threat, then it becomes the object of curiosity. The person wants to learn more about the new stimulus: What is it? Why is it there? Can I use it to my benefit?

Charles's activities were conducted at a safe distance and, over time, became the object of Seagull's curiosity. This curiosity motivated Seagull to discover who Charles was and what he wanted.

Seagull later told Charles that he knew he was an FBI agent the first time he saw him. Whether this was true or not, Seagull received the nonverbal "friend" signals the FBI agent was sending him.

Once Seagull determined that Charles was an FBI agent, his curiosity increased. He certainly knew he was a target of recruitment, but for what purpose and at what price? Since Seagull was already unhappy with his career advancement and looming retirement, he no doubt thought about different scenarios involving Charles, including working as a spy for the FBI.

The decision to become a spy is not made overnight. Potential spies need time to develop their own rationalization strategies and time to grow accustomed to switching their allegiance. The recruitment strategy for Seagull included a length of time for the seed of betrayal to germinate. Seagull's imagination provided the necessary nutrients for the idea to mature and bloom. This latency period also provided time for Seagull to convince his wife to join him. As Charles moved physically closer to Seagull, the diplomat did not see the FBI agent as a pending threat but rather as a symbol of hope—hope for a better life in the years to come.

Once Seagull made up his mind to assist the FBI, he had to wait for Charles to approach him. Seagull later told Charles that the wait was excruciating. His curiosity peaked. "Why wasn't the American operative making a move?" In fact, the second thing Seagull said to Charles when he finally introduced himself at the grocery store was "What took you so long?"

FREQUENCY AND DURATION

Duration has a unique quality in that the more time you spend with a person, the more influence they have over your thoughts and actions. Mentors who spend a lot of time with their mentees exercise a positive influence over them. People who have less than honorable intentions can negatively influence the people they spend time with. The best example of the power of duration is between parents and their children. The more time parents spend with their children, the more likely the parents will be able to influence them. If parental duration is lacking, the children tend to spend more time with their friends, including, in extreme cases, gang members. These people now have a greater influence on children because they spend most of their time with them.

Duration shares an inverse relationship with frequency. If you see a friend frequently, then the duration of the encounter will be shorter. Conversely, if you don't see your friend very often, the duration of your visit will typically increase significantly. For example, if you see a friend every day, the duration of your visits can be low because you can keep up with what's going on as events unfold. If, however, you only see your friend twice a year, the duration of your visits will be greater. Think back to a time when you had dinner in a restaurant with a friend you hadn't seen for a long period of time. You probably spent several hours catching up on each other's lives. The duration of the same dinner would be considerably shorter if you saw the person on a regular basis. Conversely, in romantic relationships the frequency and duration are very high because couples, especially newly minted ones, want to spend as much time with each other as possible. The intensity of the relationship will also be very high.

RELATIONSHIP SELF-EVALUATION

Think back to the beginning of your current relationship or a relationship you had in the past; you should now be able to see that it developed in accordance with the elements of the Friendship Formula. The Formula can also be used to identify the parts of a relationship that need improvement. For example, a couple who has been married for several years senses that their relationship is deteriorating, but they don't know how to fix it. Their relationship can be self-evaluated by looking at the interaction of each of the elements of the Friendship Formula. The first element to look at is proximity. Does the couple share the same space or are they separately pursuing their own goals and rarely sharing physical space together? The second element is frequency. Do they frequently share time together? The third element is duration. How much time do they spend together when they do see each other? The fourth element is intensity, the glue that holds relationships together. The couple may have proximity, frequency, and duration, but lack intensity. An example of this combination is a couple who spends a lot of time at home watching television together, but do not interact with any emotion. This relationship can be improved if the couple increases the intensity of their relationship. They could go out on "date nights" to rekindle the feelings they felt for each other when they first met. They could shut the television off for a few hours each night and talk to each other, thus intensifying their relationship.

The combinations of the four elements of the Friendship Formula are seemingly endless, depending on how couples interact with each another. In many instances, one member in the relationship travels on business most of the year. The lack of proximity can adversely affect the relationship because it often leads to reduced frequency, duration, and intensity. The lack of proximity can be overcome with technology. Frequency, duration, and intensity can be maintained with the help of email, chatting, texting, Skyping, and social media.

Once you know the basic elements of all relationships, you will be able to evaluate existing ones and nurture new ones by consciously regulating the four relationship elements. To practice relationship self-evaluations, examine the relationships you are in right now and see how the four basic elements are playing a role in affecting them. If you want to strengthen a relationship, think of ways to regulate the Friendship Formula to achieve the desired outcome.

You can also extricate yourself from unwanted relationships by slowly decreasing each of the basic elements of the Friendship Formula. This gradual decrease will let the unwanted person down incrementally without hurting their feelings and without seeming like an abrupt break in the relationship. In most cases, the unwanted person will naturally come to the conclusion that the relationship is no longer viable and seek more rewarding interactions.

RECRUITING SPIES USING A SILENT PARTNER

Imagine you are a scientist, with a top-secret clearance, working as a contractor for the Department of Defense. One day, seemingly out of nowhere, you receive a telephone call from a government official from the Chinese embassy. He invites you to come to China to give a lecture on some of your unclassified research. All your expenses will be paid by the Chinese government. You report this invitation to your security officer, who tells you that you can give a lecture in China as long as you don't discuss classified information. You call to confirm your attendance and the Chinese official invites you to come a week earlier so you can do some sightseeing. You agree. You are very excited because this is a once-in-a-lifetime opportunity.

You are met at the airport by a representative from the Chinese government, who informs you that he will be your guide and translator for your entire trip. Each morning the translator meets you at your hotel and has breakfast with you. You spend all day sightseeing. The translator buys all your meals and arranges some evening social activities. The translator is friendly and shares information about his family and social activities. You reciprocate by sharing information about your family, nothing important, just the names of your wife and children, their birthdays, your wedding anniversary, and the holidays you and your family celebrate. As the days go by, you are amazed that you and your translator have so much in common despite stark cultural differences.

The day of the lecture arrives. The lecture hall is filled to capacity. Your lecture is well received. At the end of the lecture, one of the participants approaches you and says he is very interested in your research. He comments that your research is fascinating and innovative. He poses a question relating to the work he has been doing that relates to your research. The answer requires you to reveal sensitive but not classified information. You gladly provide the information along with a lengthy explanation even though it borders on the classified realm.

While you are waiting to board your plane back to the United States, your translator informs you that your lecture was a tremendous success and the Chinese government would like to invite you back next year to present another lecture. Since the small lecture hall was filled to capacity, you will be speaking in the Grand Ballroom next year. (The Chinese translator presented an opportunity for the scientist to flatter himself, which is the most powerful form of flattery. This technique of flattery will be discussed later.) Oh, and by the way, your wife is invited to accompany you, all expenses paid.

As an FBI counterintelligence officer, I was required to debrief scientists who went overseas to determine if they were approached by foreign intelligence officers seeking classified information. I interviewed many scientists who described similar stories to the one above. All the scientists reported that the Chinese were impeccable hosts and never asked about any classified information. No foul play. Case closed.

The one thing that bothered me was the scientists' comments that they had so much in common with their translators. Given the cultural differences, this piqued my curiosity. I knew that establishing "common ground" was the quickest way to develop rapport. (This "common ground" technique to build rapport will be discussed in Chapter 2.)

I then used the Friendship Formula to further evaluate the scientists' visits to China. Certainly, proximity was present. Frequency was low, for the scientists only went to China once a year. If frequency is low then duration must be high in order to develop a personal relationship. Duration was high. The same translator met the scientists early every morning and spent the entire day and evening with them. Based on the topics of the translators' discussions with the scientists, intensity was high. It finally dawned on me. The scientists were being recruited but they didn't know it and neither did I up to that point.

The scientists and, for a while, I myself, did not see the recruitment effort. The Chinese, knowingly or unknowingly, used the Friendship Formula, which describes the way people naturally develop friendships. Because it is a natural process, the brain does not attend to this subtle recruitment technique. From that time forward, I interviewed scientists using the Friendship Formula to determine if any recruitment attempts by foreign intelligence services took place. I specifically asked the scientist to describe the proximity, frequency, duration, and intensity with any people they met during their trips. I also briefed the scientists before they went to China to be aware of the subtle techniques the Chinese use to steal our secrets.

THE FRIENDSHIP FORMULA AND YOU

Throughout the rest of this book, the Friendship Formula will be used as the foundation upon which friendships are built. Regardless of what type of friendship you desire (short, long, relaxed, or intense) it will always be influenced by **proximity, frequency, duration,** and **intensity**. Think of the Friendship Formula as the concrete foundation upon which a house is built. The home can take many different forms, just like friendships can, but the foundation remains basically the same.

APPLYING THE FRIENDSHIP FORMULA IN EVERYDAY LIFE

I met Phillip, the son of a close friend, at a local coffee shop. Phillip had recently graduated from a small-town college and landed his first job in Los Angeles. He was single and wanted to make new friends. He had lived his entire life in small towns but suddenly found himself in a big city, where making friends seemed like a daunting task.

I advised him to routinely frequent a bar near his apartment and display friend signals as he entered to send the message he was not a threat (friend signals are introduced in the next chapter), and to sit alone at the bar, a table, or a booth.

His daily visits to the bar would allow proximity to take hold, and his constant appearances would allow for frequency and duration to be established. With each visit, he could gradually increase intensity, the final component of the Friendship Formula, by looking at other customers a little longer and smiling. Phillip needed a curiosity hook to draw people to him. Phillip told me he was an antique marble collector. I instructed him to bring a magnifying glass and a bag of marbles with him each time he visited the bar. I further instructed him to set the marbles on the bar and thoughtfully examine each one with the magnifying glass. This activity would serve as a curiosity hook. I also told him to build good rapport with the bartender and servers because they would become his ambassadors to the members in the community. Because the bartender and servers had direct contact with Phillip, other customers would naturally ask them who the new person was. When they did, they would say nice things about Phillip, which in turn would form a primacy filter through which the other customers would view Phillip. (Primacy filters will be discussed in the next chapter.)

Several weeks later, Phillip telephoned me and reported that I was right. The first time he visited the bar he ordered a drink, laid out the marbles, and examined them one by one with the magnifying glass. A few minutes after the bartender served Phillip his drink, he asked him about his unusual activity. Phillip told the bartender briefly about his marble collection and noted the differences in size, color, and texture of each marble. After several visits to the bar, Phillip and the bartender became better acquainted.

The bartender liked Phillip and introduced him to several people who were obviously interested in his quirky hobby. The marbles served as a conversation starter and made the transition to other topics effortless.

The Friendship Formula looks like magic, but it is not. It just mirrors the way people normally form relationships. And knowing the basic elements of friendship development makes building friendships easy.

HOW VLADIMIR WAS INFLUENCED BY THE FRIENDSHIP FORMULA

Remember that Vladimir had initially vowed to not speak to me. The first thing I did was to establish **proximity**. Every day I sat with him and read the newspaper, not saying a word, virtually ignoring him. This silent activity established proximity, but, more important, did not pose a threat. Once Vladimir determined that I was not a threat, he became curious. Why does this agent come each day? What is his purpose? Why doesn't he say anything to me? My daily visits and silent reading activity served as a curiosity hook. Overcome with curiosity, Vladimir eventually broke his silence and made the first move to establish contact. Speaking with me was no longer my idea; it became his. Vladimir took the initiative. Even then, I did not immediately begin talking with him; instead, I reminded him that when we first met, he vowed never to talk. In addition to the Friendship Formula, this introduced two psychological principles that will be discussed later in the book, "the principle of scarcity" and the "principle of increased restraint increases drive."

In simple terms, I did not readily make myself available to Vladimir, which heightened his curiosity, causing an increase in his motivation to talk. Once Vladimir opened his personal and psychological space to me, I was able to use the rapport-building techniques discussed throughout this book to bring him to the point where he willingly provided me with information.

To effectively use the Friendship Formula, you have to keep in mind what kind of relationship you are looking to establish and the time you will be required to spend with your person of interest. Obviously, the formula will not play a major role in getting someone to like you if you are only going to see them once or sporadically. To illustrate: Say you're in Cleveland, Ohio, for a one-day conference and you meet this particularly attractive man or woman (you choose which is appropriate) and want to spend the evening with him or her. When you give the person a friend signal, it is not reciprocated; in fact, the person goes "shields up." At this point, you're not going to get anywhere with this individual; not tonight, anyway. But, according to the Friendship Formula, if you end up moving to Cleveland, you might still be able to win this person over using proximity, frequency, duration, and intensity to develop a relationship.

THE FRIEND-FOE CONTINUUM

Friend	Stranger	Foe

When two people meet each other for the first time (assuming neither person knows anything about the other person), they are **strangers.** Imagine yourself walking down the street in a town where you don't know anybody and people are moving around you as they head toward their destinations. Or think of yourself in a bar or restaurant or other public building where you are among dozens of people unfamiliar to you. In these cases, you are in the "stranger" zone of the continuum. You are a stranger to those around you, as they are strangers to you.

Most human interactions remain in the stranger zone. We hardly take notice of the hundreds, even thousands, of personal contacts we experience in our daily lives as we go about our business. Yet, sometimes a stranger does something that makes us take notice of his or her presence; we become *aware* of this individual. It doesn't have to be something obvious. In fact, at first we might not even understand why a particular person has "caught our attention."

So, what makes a stranger suddenly stand out and become a person of interest? They have been picked up by, for lack of a better name, your brain's *territory scan*. Scientists have discovered that as we go about our daily lives, our senses are constantly sending messages to our brain, which, in turn, processes the information to assess, among other things, if any given individual in our range of observation can be ignored, is worthy of approach, or is someone to avoid. This process is automatic or "hardwired" into our brains and is based on the brain's capacity to interpret specific nonverbal and verbal behaviors as either "friend," "neutral," or "foe" signals.

The function of the "territory scan" can be described using the following analogy. A woman is walking up and down a stretch of oceanfront beach. As she moves, she holds a metal detector in front of her, sweeping it left to right, side to side. Most of her walk is uninterrupted; the metal detector has not "picked up" anything of interest lying beneath the sand. But, every so often, the machine will beep and the woman will stop and dig in the sand to discover what is buried there. What she finds might be treasure . . . an expensive watch or a valuable coin. Or it could be trash . . . a discarded can or tin foil. If she is extremely unlucky, it could be some long-forgotten land mine just waiting to be detonated.

Your brain is like the metal detector, constantly evaluating your environment for signals that indicate things you should approach or avoid, or that are irrelevant and can be ignored. Behavioral scientists have spent decades discovering, cataloging, and describing the kinds of human behaviors the brain interprets as "friend" or "foe" signals. Once you know what the signals are, you will be able to use them to make friends and, as a collateral benefit, keep people away from you that you would like to avoid.

FOR RENT, FOR LEASE, OR NOT FOR SALE SIGNS

One of my students reported to the class that she started picking up interesting nonverbal signals at her local bar. She frequently observed that men in exclusively committed relationships sent out different signals than those men in committed relationships who were seemingly seeking extra-relationship affairs. The student commented that she could sense strong nonverbal foe signals from some of the married men that discouraged unwanted personal attention. But other supposedly committed men were sending out strong friend signals that they were seeking something extra. The student noted that these friend signals were more subtle than the friend signals transmitted by unattached men.

THE URBAN SCOWL

Have you ever wondered why one individual seems to have the "knack" when it comes to attracting others, making a good impression, and getting people to like him or her, while another person, who is equally attractive and successful in life, can't seem to duplicate that "magnetic appeal"? It often comes down to unconsciously sending off "foe" signals. Another student presented me with (unfortunately for her) a great example of this. She mentioned that she was having trouble making friends at the Midwestern college where I teach. She said that people often remarked that she appeared cold, aloof, and unapproachable, but that once they got to know her, she had little difficulty developing close relationships with them.

As we talked, I found out she grew up in a tough and dangerous neighborhood in Atlanta, where she had to learn from a young age to have a very thick skin. I told her that she didn't need to improve her communication skills, but instead, all she had to do was change the way she presented herself to people. She hadn't stopped showing her "urban scowl" to the world. This is not uncommon for people who grow up in rough neighborhoods or even just large cities. The urban scowl sends a clear, nonverbal signal to others that you are a foe, not a friend. It is a warning to stay away and "don't screw with me." Predators are less likely to target people who project this urban scowl, so it becomes a valuable survival tool in tough neighborhoods. Once she makes a concerted effort to send out more "friend" than "foe" signals she will have little trouble connecting with other students.

An urban scowl.

Would you want to approach the person who is pictured wearing an urban scowl? Keep in mind that many people who exhibit this expression are totally unaware they are displaying foe signals that discourage others from interacting with them. That is why an understanding of what constitutes appropriate verbal and nonverbal friend signals is so critical.

WHEN TO SEND FOE SIGNALS

Street people are constantly seeking handouts, especially in big cities. They can be persistent. Their persistence is not random, though. They target people who are most likely to give them money, and aggressively pursue them. How do they know who is a soft touch and who is not? Easy: They look for friend and foe signals. If their targets make eye contact, the odds go up. If their targets smile, the odds go up. If their targets show pity, the odds go up.

If you are constantly being targeted by beggars and panhandlers, it is most likely because you are unwittingly sending them nonverbal signals that invite personal contact. Without personal contact, the chances of receiving money are nonexistent. Beggars know this and pursue targets who are more likely to give them a return on their efforts. So, in this case, an urban scowl could come in quite handy.

Once, as a teenager, I was walking in a neighborhood I was unfamiliar with, which turned out to be quite dangerous. I was very much a fish out of water. An older man who recognized that I was out of my comfort zone came to my rescue. He offered me some unsolicited but extremely helpful advice in order to get me safely out of the neighborhood: "Walk like you have somewhere to go. Swing your arms and take purposeful steps. And if anyone talks to you, talk like you've got something to say. If you can do that, you won't be seen as a potential victim and [will] be less likely to be victimized." It was good advice then, and it is good advice now.

Your nonverbal (how you behave) and verbal (what you say) communications send signals to those around you. Moving with purpose has a purpose. To a potential predator, you are less likely to be seen as prey, just as a healthy, speedy, alert antelope is not likely to be the target of first choice for a lion who is chasing a herd of the beasts across the African savanna.

Cullen Hightower has been credited with this very insightful observation: "Strangers are what friends are made of." Every time you encounter another person for the first time, that individual starts out as a stranger and, at the moment of contact, occupies the exact middle position on the friend-foe continuum. If you use the nonverbal and verbal signals discussed in this book, you can turn strangers into friends.

THE HUMAN BASELINE

Picture yourself driving home from work when all of a sudden you notice that another car is right on your tail. Your brain, which is constantly taking in information from your five senses and scanning the data for possible danger, has detected a threat. Another automobile has done something abnormal. It has intruded into the bubble of space that separates "safe distance" from "unsafe distance" and it now poses a risk to your well-being. Here is what's interesting: You have been "automatically" monitoring the traffic behind you, not even aware you are doing it so long as other vehicles do not penetrate your bubble of protection. It is only when a trailing vehicle violates the boundaries of normal following distance that you take notice.

What is true with your driving is also true with making friends. Your brain is automatically monitoring verbal and nonverbal communication. When the inputs are assessed as normal and non-threatening, you respond to them automatically; they don't arouse suspicion or a sense of danger. This is the reason the techniques you'll learn in this book work; they all fall within the human baseline. Even though you might *think* a person would "pick up" on what you are doing, they won't because the brain perceives these behaviors as normal and, like the cars following at a safe distance, they don't arouse attention.

Throughout this book, we will emphasize friend and foe signals. They all fall within the human baseline and can be used to enhance your relationships. Each of you has the capacity to use these signals;

in fact, we all have used them during our lives. Unfortunately, many people don't know all of the signals available to use, and/or how to use them most effectively. This is even truer today than in the past, due to technological advances that have stifled the development of our "emotional intelligence."

MAKING FRIENDS IN A THUMB-TALKING WORLD

I once invited two students to the front of the room at the beginning of a lecture and had them sit face-to-face in chairs. I asked them to talk to each other for five minutes. They looked puzzled and asked what they should talk about. I told them to talk about anything they wanted to. They couldn't come up with a single subject! They just sat there and stared at each other. I then instructed them to turn their chairs back to back, and text each other about anything. Amazingly, they had no problem conversing with each other via text for the five minutes.

And therein lies a problem. In the days before cell phones and video games, kids would learn basic social skills during face-to-face interactions on the playground. They learned all about making friends and how to deal with conflict and interpersonal differences; that's where social skills were picked up. Along the way, kids learned how to read and transmit subtle nonverbal signals, even if they were not consciously aware of it.

In today's "thumb-talking" world, nobody plays ball like generations of pre–cell phone children used to. Kids stay home and play video games and text one another. Sure, there are some organized sports and school activities, but face-to-face social interaction has been drastically reduced in our tech-savvy world. That's bad. It's not that "tech-raised" kids lack the capacity to pick up on social skills and signals; it's that they don't have enough practice to hone these skills and become effective in handling face-to-face relations.

A visual demonstration that face-to-face
communication is more difficult than texting.

In the photo on the top of page 21, note the signals of disinterest between the two individuals who are trying to carry on a conversation. The man has his hands in his pockets and is looking away. The woman is looking down. There are no head tilts, no smiles, no positive gestures, no mirroring of each other. The photo on the bottom shows the ease and positive body language associated with young people in the midst of texting.

The Like Switch is designed to bring out the best in you when it comes to making friends and enjoying successful relationships—in real life, not just in digitally enhanced life.

2

GETTING NOTICED BEFORE A WORD IS SPOKEN

You never get a second chance to make a good first impression.
—WILL ROGERS

Perhaps you were fortunate enough as a child to spend a lazy summer evening watching nature's light show. Maybe you even grabbed a Mason jar from the kitchen and tried to capture the pinpoints of luminescence that appeared and disappeared in the gathering darkness, moving like tiny lanterns adrift on a gentle breeze.

Fireflies are one of earth's most fascinating creatures. For our purposes, *how* fireflies light up isn't really that relevant; you'd need to be half biologist and half physicist to understand the process. What is interesting is *why* they light up.

It turns out fireflies light up for a number of reasons. Some scientists believe their flashing is a warning to potential predators that they taste bitter and would make a lousy meal. How the predators would leap to that conclusion (*leap* is a good word, since frogs seem to devour them in serious numbers) is not explained. Others point to the fact that different species of fireflies have different flash patterns that help them identify members of their own species and also determine the sex of the flasher. The reason that is of interest here involves the firefly's use of light as a mating signal. Here "flashing" takes on a whole new meaning. It has been determined that male fireflies have specific flash patterns that are used to attract their female counterparts. In case you need a conversation starter, it might interest you that Marc Brown observed that "higher male flash rates, as well as increased flash intensity, have been shown to be more attractive to females in two different firefly species."

FIREFLIES AND FRIENDS

The behavior of the firefly is a great metaphor for how to be more attractive to other people and predispose them to see us as potential friends. Because people often *see* you before they *hear* you, the nonverbal signals you send them can influence their opinion. This is particularly true when you are meeting a person for the first time and that individual has no prior knowledge of you. Like the firefly, you can transmit "friend" or "foe" signals to individuals around you in an attempt to encourage or discourage interaction. Or you can "turn your light off" and remain relatively anonymous.

Remember that in any setting where two or more strangers are in line-of-sight proximity to each other, there is the chance that one person will observe the other. What he or she sees will be automatically processed by the observer's brain for potential "friend" or "foe" signals. In most cases, that's as far as it goes because the person's visual appearance is "neutral," and the brain, assessing the person as neither a threat nor an opportunity, chooses to dismiss it entirely. Think of it like a person trying to hail a cab in New York City. As dozens of cabs move along the street the individual's attention is on the dome light atop the taxi. If the light is off, it is quickly ignored, but if the light is on, the person's attention and actions are directed to that specific vehicle.

I am sure that at some point you have been a part of a group of guys or a group of girls who have gone to a nightclub, bar, or some other public gathering place to try to meet members of the opposite sex. Ever notice how some people seem to attract attention while others are hardly noticed? Sometimes it is because of differences in physical attractiveness or outward manifestations of wealth, but, just as often, if not more often, it is because the "popular" person is sending out "friend" signals that gets them moved from the "neutral" (stranger) point on the friend-foe continuum toward the positive (friend) point on the continuum, increasing the chances of social interaction.

Remember, our brains are continually scanning the environment for friend or foe signals. People who give off foe signals are perceived as a threat to be avoided. People who transmit friend signals are viewed as nonthreatening and approachable. When you meet people, especially for the first time, ensure that you send the right nonverbal cues that allow others to see you in a positive rather than neutral or negative light.

THE "BIG THREE" FRIEND SIGNALS

What exactly are these nonverbal friend signals you can use to enhance your chances of other people taking positive notice of you and laying a positive groundwork for a friendship, whether for a night or a lifetime? There are numerous signals to choose from, but, for our purposes, three critical cues are essential to use if you want to encourage others to see you as a likable person and worthy of possible friendship. They are the "eyebrow flash," "head tilt," and the real, as opposed to fake, "smile" (yes, the human brain can detect the difference!).

THE EYEBROW FLASH

The eyebrow flash is a quick up-and-down movement of the eyebrows that lasts for about one-sixth of a second and is used as a primary, nonverbal friend signal. As individuals approach one another they eyebrow-flash each other to send the message they don't pose a threat. Within five to six feet of meeting someone, our brains look for this signal. If the signal is present and we reciprocate, our nonverbal communication is telling the other person we are not a foe to be feared or avoided. Most people do not realize that they eyebrow flash because the gesture is almost an unconscious one. Experiment for yourself: watch individuals as they meet each other for the first time and, if possible, in subsequent interactions. When people greet people for the first time in an office or social setting, they use a verbal greeting along with the eyebrow flash. Verbal greetings could include "How are you?" "What's up?" or "How's it going?" The second time people see each other, they don't have to say anything, but they do exchange eyebrow flashes, or in the case of males, display chin juts. A chin jut is a forward and slightly upward movement of the chin. The next time you meet someone, pay close attention to what you do and to what the other person does. You will be amazed at the flurry of nonverbal activity that takes place when people meet. You will be even more amazed that you went through your entire life and never recognized the nonverbal cues you have displayed.

Eyebrow flashes can be sent over long distances. If you are interested in meeting someone who is across a crowded room, send an eyebrow flash and watch for a return signal. If a reciprocating eyebrow flash is sent, further involvement is possible. No return signal could indicate a lack of interest. Therefore, you can use eyebrow flashes as a kind of early warning system to help you determine if the person you are interested in is interested in you. The lack of a return eyebrow flash might save you from an awkward moment, or outright rejection, and

A natural eyebrow flash. In real-life situations, it doesn't appear so exaggerated because it occurs very quickly . . . thus the term eyebrow *flash*.

indicate that your best course of action is to look elsewhere for a more receptive individual to approach.

If you are still interested in meeting someone who doesn't reciprocate your eyebrow flash, it doesn't guarantee that person is "off-limits" but you might want to use (and look for) other friend signals before you decide to actually try to meet that individual.

"Friendly" eyebrow flashes involve *brief* eye contact with other persons, particularly if you don't know the person or are a passing acquaintance. Prolonged eye contact between two people indicates intense emotion, and is either an act of love or hostility. Prolonged eye contact ("staring") is so disturbing that in normal social encounters we avoid eye contact lasting more than a second or two. Among a crowd of strangers in a public setting, eye contact will generally last only a fraction of a second, and most people will avoid making any eye contact at all.

Not all eyebrow flashes are friend signals. An example of an "unnatural" eyebrow flash is pictured on the next page. In real time, an unnatural eyebrow flash occurs when a person displays an eyebrow flash with extended "hang time" of the upward movement of the eyebrows. An unnatural eyebrow flash will be perceived as unfriendly at best and creepy at worst. If you see or display an unnatural eyebrow flash, it will be perceived as a foe signal and, like the urban scowl, will not be conducive to social interaction or making friends.

THE HEAD TILT

A head tilt to the right or to the left is a nonthreatening gesture. The tilted head exposes one of the carotid arteries, which are positioned on either side of the neck. The carotid arteries are the pathways that supply the brain with oxygenated blood. Severing either carotid artery causes death within minutes. People who feel threatened protect their carotid arteries by tucking their neck into their shoulders. People expose their carotid arteries when they meet people who do not pose a threat.

A head tilt is a strong friend signal. People who tilt their heads

Unnatural Eyebrow Flash

Head tilts

when they interact with others are seen as more trustworthy and more attractive. Women see men who approach them with their head slightly canted to one side or the other as more handsome. Likewise, men see women who tilt their heads as more attractive. Furthermore, people who tilt their heads toward the person they are talking with are seen as more friendly, kind, and honest as compared with individuals whose heads remain upright when they talk.

Women tilt their heads more often than men do. Men tend to communicate with their heads upright to present themselves as more dominant. This gesture in the business world may be an advantage; however, in a social context, the absence of head tilting could send the wrong message. In dating environments, such as nightclubs and bars, men should make a conscious effort to cant their heads to one side or the other when approaching women or else they may be perceived as predators. In such cases, you might be a "heads up" guy and your intensions may be friendly, but your actions will cause women to go "on the defensive" and make meaningful contact difficult, if not impossible, to achieve.

It seems that the head tilt has universal "friend" appeal throughout the animal kingdom.

THE SMILE

A smile is a powerful "friend" signal. Smiling faces are judged to be more attractive, more likable, and less dominant. A smile portrays confidence, happiness, and enthusiasm and, most important, signals acceptance. A smile telegraphs friendliness and increases the attractiveness of the person who is smiling. The mere act of smiling will put people in a better, more receptive mood. For the most part, people smile at individuals they like and do not smile at those they do not like.

A smile releases endorphins, which give us a sense of well-being. When we smile at other people, it is very difficult for them not to smile back. This return smile causes the target of your smile to feel good about themselves, and, as we will learn in a later chapter, if you make people feel good about themselves, they will like you.

The only problem with the smile is what scientists and observant members of the general population have long recognized: There is the "real" or "genuine" smile and then there is the "fake" or "forced" smile. The "real" smile is used around people we really want to make contact with or already know and like. The fake smile, on the other hand, is often used when we are forced by social obligation or the requirements of our job to appear friendly toward another individual or group.

Can you tell which smile is the "real" smile and which one is "fake"? If you can't, don't despair. Actually, they're *both* real smiles!

If you want people to like you, your smiles should be genuine. The telltale signs of a genuine smile are the upturned corners of the mouth and upward movement of the cheeks accompanied by wrinkling around the edges of the eyes. As opposed to sincere smiles, forced smiles tend to be lopsided. For right-handed people a forced smile tends to be stronger on the right side of the face, and for left-handed people, it tends to be stronger on the left. Fake smiles also lack synchrony. They begin later than real smiles and taper off in an irregular manner. With a real smile, the cheeks are raised, bagged skin forms under the eyes, crow's feet appear around the corners of the eyes, and with some individuals, the nose may dip downward. In a fake smile, you can see that the corners of the mouth are not upturned and the

The smile on the top left is fake, the expression on the top right is neutral, and the smile on the bottom is real.

cheeks are not uplifted to cause wrinkling around the eyes, the telltale sign of a genuine smile. Wrinkling around the eyes is often difficult to see in young people, whose skin is more elastic than older folks. Nonetheless, our brains can spot the difference between a real smile and a fake smile.

SMILES FOR EFFECT

The way you smile will influence the way people perceive you and encourage or discourage friendship formation. Women in particular often use smiles to regulate the initiation of first encounters and to set the pace of the subsequent personal interactions. Men more readily approach women who smile at them. A sincere smile gives men permission to approach. A forced smile or no smile at all sends the message that a woman is not interested in a man's overtures. Likewise, a woman can send the message that she is open to male approaches by regulating the frequency and intensity of her smile, in conjunction with other friend signals.

Learning how to produce a "real" smile at will, particularly when you don't feel in the mood to display it, takes practice. Study the pictures in the book and think about smiles you have seen in your everyday life. Then stand in front of a mirror and actually produce fake and real smiles. It won't be that difficult. Just think about the times you have genuinely wanted to show appreciation to someone you loved or were forced to smile at some unwanted houseguest at a family dinner or at an obnoxious business associate. Practice the real smile until it becomes automatic. Then you can choose to use it when you wish.

EYE CONTACT

Eye contact works in concert with other friend signals. Eye contact can be attempted from a distance and, therefore, like other nonverbal signals in this chapter, it is a way to get noticed before a word is spoken. Also, like the other nonverbal signals, it is designed to give the signal receiver a positive impression of you, as someone who will be perceived as a potential friend.

To send a friend signal via eye contact, pick out your person of interest and establish eye contact by holding your gaze for no longer than a second. Holding an eye gaze for longer than that can be perceived as aggression, which is a foe signal. As mentioned earlier, when you stare at someone, especially in a dating environment, you are invading his or her personal space. If you do not have permission to enter that individual's personal space, your actions will be perceived as predatory behavior at best, creepy at worst. You should end the eye gaze with a smile. If you cannot manage a genuine smile, make sure that the corners of your mouth are upturned and wrinkle the outer edges of your eyes. A return smile indicates interest. If your person of interest meets your gaze, looks down and away briefly, and then reestablishes eye contact, you can approach this person with a high degree of confidence that your overtures will be well received.

EXTENDED EYE GAZE

Extended eye gaze is a powerful rapport builder. This nonverbal behavior should not be confused with staring. Typically, when you make contact with another person, your eyes lock for a second or less and then you break eye contact. Eye contact lasting more than a second or two will be perceived as threatening. Staring at people, especially strangers, is considered a foe signal. However, when two people know and like each other, they are permitted to make eye contact for longer than a few seconds. People who are romantically involved often stare into each other's eyes for extended periods of time. With the following technique the power of this mutual gaze can be safely used on strangers to enhance rapport building.

After you make eye contact with your person of interest, hold your gaze for one second and then slowly turn your head, holding your gaze for another second or two. The person you are looking at will see your head turning away, giving the illusion of broken eye contact, and your actions will not be perceived as staring. This technique allows you to intensify the emotional content of your friend signal. Increased eye contact should not be used to force premature intimacy. Men often overuse this technique and sabotage potential relationships.

PUPIL DILATION

Pupil dilation expresses interest. When an individual sees another person they like, their pupils, the black portion of their eyes, expand. The wider the dilation, the more the attraction the person feels. This is obviously a cue for positive attraction, although it is difficult to spot in everyday personal interactions. Thus its value as a friend signal is very limited.

Pupil dilation is most noticeable in people with blue eyes. People who have dark eyes appear more exotic because their eyes appear to be dilated all the time. In the last century BC, Cleopatra, the most beautiful woman of her time, used atropine, a naturally occurring drug, to dilate her pupils to make herself appear more sensual. Pupil dilation can occur with changes in ambient light, so care should be taken when interpreting this autonomic response.

GETTING CONSENT TO GO TO PRISON: USING FRIEND SIGNALS TO ENCOURAGE A CONFESSION

In one particular case, while I was at the FBI, we had identified a suspected child molester. We knew of one victim, but signs pointed to many more. It was believed that the suspect used his computer to target victims. I wanted to arrest him immediately but lacked the necessary probable cause to obtain the arrest warrant.

I decided to interview the suspect to seek his consent for the FBI to examine his personal computer. If the interview had any chance of success, I had to create a nonthreatening environment, quickly build rapport, and, when the time was right, ask for consent. I invited the suspect to meet me at the FBI office. I did this to give him a sense of control (he could determine his course of action) and to demonstrate that the interview was voluntary (he wasn't being forced to participate in the interview).

I met the suspect at the door with a manufactured eyebrow flash, a slightly tilted head, and a simulated real smile complete with crow's feet around my eyes. Displaying real friend signals was not possible because I found the suspect's behavior reprehensible. I warmly shook his hand and invited him into the interview room. I offered him a cup of coffee, for two reasons. First, I wanted to tap into the psychological principle of reciprocity. When people receive things, even trivial things, they feel a need to reciprocate. In exchange for coffee I wanted consent. Second, I wanted to use the suspect's placement of the cup to determine when rapport had been established (cup placement will be discussed in a later chapter). When I handed the suspect the cup of coffee, he stated, "How could you treat me with such respect after what I did?" This was an admission, albeit a small one, even before the interview began. I was able to establish sufficient rapport with the suspect using mimicked friend signals to give the suspect the illusion that I was not a threat, but a person he could trust with a secret. A secret that put him in jail for the rest of his life.

THE BOTOX PARADOX

When it comes to friend signals, sometimes the best of intentions have unforeseen negative consequences. Consider, for example, the sad story of the aging wife who wanted to look younger and more attractive for her spouse. She decided to get Botox treatments for her face, a bit of sculpting to get the lines and wrinkles out. She couldn't wait to show off the results to her husband.

So, what happened when he saw his "new" wife? Because the Botox paralyzes certain muscles around the eyes for about two months, she couldn't display eyebrow flashes and full, real smiles, including the

All examples of safe touching. At the beginning of a relationship, touching should be limited to touching between the elbow and shoulder and hand to hand.

crow's feet he was used to seeing. The woman looked more attractive but because her husband wasn't getting the friend signals he was accustomed to, he suspected his wife didn't love him anymore and that she had gotten the procedure to look more appealing for someone else. Unless the husband is aware of *why* the wife is not sending the friend signals he has come to expect, the results of trying to be pretty could turn out quite ugly!

TOUCH: A FRIENDSHIP SIGNAL . . . BUT PROCEED WITH CAUTION

Touching is a powerful, subtle, and complex form of nonverbal communication. In social situations, the language of touch can be used to convey a surprising variety of messages. Different touches can be used to express agreement, affection, affiliation, or attraction, to offer support, emphasize a point, call for attention or participation, guide and direct, greet, congratulate, establish or reinforce power relations, and negotiate levels of intimacy.

For our purposes, touch is important in making friends, as studies have concluded that even the most fleeting touch can have a dramatic influence on our perceptions and relationships. Experiments have shown that even a light, brief touch on the arm during a brief social encounter between strangers has both immediate and lasting positive effects. Polite requests for help or directions, for example, produce more positive results when accompanied by a light touch on the arm.

But proceed cautiously: Even the most innocuous of touches can produce a negative reaction in the person being touched. These negative reactions include pulling the arm away, increasing distance, frowning, turning away, or other expressions of displeasure or anxiety. Negative reactions indicate that the person will be unlikely to see you as a potential friend.

Unless the individual is exceptionally shy and reserved, negative reactions to a simple arm touch probably indicate dislike or distrust.

With the exception of a traditional handshake, touching another person's hand is more personal than touching his or her arm. Hand touching serves as a barometer for romantic relationships. Movies often focus on hand touching to signal that a relationship is cold, growing, or in full bloom. If you touch a person's hand and they pull away, even slightly, the person being touched is not yet ready to intensify the relationship. Pulling away does not necessarily signal rejection. It means that you will have to build more rapport with your person of interest before advancing the relationship. Touch acceptance signals that the person is ready for hand holding, a more intense form of touching. Interlocking of the fingers during hand holding is the most intimate form of hand holding. A risk-free way to measure the strength of a new relationship is to "accidentally" touch or brush against the hand of your person of interest. Most people will tolerate an accidental touch, even if they don't like the person touching them, but they will unconsciously send nonverbal signals indicating the acceptance or rejection of the touch. Watch for these nonverbal displays and proceed accordingly.

ISOPRAXISM (MIRRORING THE BEHAVIOR OF ANOTHER PERSON)

Isopraxism is the fancy term for "mirroring," a nonverbal practice that can be used to make friendship development easier and more effective. Mirroring creates a favorable impression in the mind of the person you are mirroring. When you first meet someone and want to gain their friendship, make a conscious effort to mirror their body language. If they stand with their arms crossed, you stand with your arms crossed. If they sit with their legs crossed, you sit with your legs crossed. In some situations, mirroring is impractical. A woman who is wearing a short dress or skirt cannot be expected to assume an open leg cross to mirror the person she is talking with. In this instance, cross matching will suffice. Instead of an open leg cross, a woman could assume a closed leg cross at the ankles or knees.

The other person will not consciously notice your mirroring behavior because it falls within the human baseline and the brain considers it "normal." However, the absence of mirroring is a foe signal and the brain will take notice when two people are out of synchrony during personal interactions. The person not being mirrored may not be able to specifically articulate why they are uncomfortable, but this foe signal will trigger a defensive response, which discourages attempts at friendship.

Isopraxism (mirroring) gestures

Mirroring takes practice. Fortunately, you can rehearse mirroring in any professional or social setting. When you casually talk to a group of friends at work or in a social setting, you will notice that the members of the group will mirror one another. To practice the mirroring technique, change your stance or posture. Within a short period of time, other members of the group will mirror your posture. The first few times you do this, you may feel as though everybody in the group knows what you are doing. I can assure you they will not know. What you are experiencing is the spotlight effect described later in this chapter. Another way to practice isopraxism is to mirror random people when you meet them. After a few sessions, you will master the mirroring technique and will be able to use it as an additional tool in establishing friendships.

THE INWARD LEAN

People tend to lean toward individuals they like and distance themselves from people they don't like. Occasionally during my FBI career, I was asked to attend embassy parties and diplomatic functions. I spent most of my time observing the other guests to determine which relationships were well established, which relationships were developing, and which guests were receptive to relationship building.

An inward lean is receptive to relationship building. Inward leaning between people conversing indicates a positive relationship has already been established. Inward leaning in association with other friend signals such as smiles, head nodding, head tilts, whispering, and touching indicates an even closer relationship between the parties involved.

People tilt their heads slightly backward to increase distance from another person, which signals that relationship building is not going well. The same thing applies when individuals turn their torsos away from another person during interaction. People will also reposition their feet away from unwanted visitors. These subtle, nonverbal cues can mean the difference between acceptance and rejection.

I often use nonverbal signals to monitor the effectiveness of my lectures. Students who are interested in the material will lean forward in their seats, tilt their heads to the right or the left, and periodically nod their heads in agreement. Students who are not interested, or who have lost interest, will lean back in their seats, roll their eyes, or in extreme circumstances, tilt their heads backward or forward as they doze off.

This focus on nonverbal cues can also be used in business settings. If you are making a sales pitch to a group of people, you can learn who you have won over, who is on the fence, or who is in opposition by monitoring the nonverbal gestures displayed by your audience.

THE TABLES ARE TURNED . . . OR TURN THOSE WHO ARE AT THE TABLE

Back in my days at the FBI, I had to do many presentations. In one particular presentation I was trying to obtain the necessary funds for an operation that I had been planning for months. The operation was complex and somewhat expensive. Getting funding came down to convincing the people at the meeting that the benefit from the operation was worth the amount of resources expended.

As I made my presentation, I monitored the nonverbal displays of the people who were sitting around the table. I immediately identified the ones who were on my side. They were leaning forward and occasionally nodding their heads. I also identified those who were skeptical about the merits of the operation or the expenditure of resources. My immediate inclination was to talk to the people who agreed with me (preaching to the choir) because I would find acceptance and comfort from those people who thought the same way I did. I resisted this temptation. I didn't have to convince the people who I had already won over. I had to win over those people who did not agree with me.

I focused my attention on them. On several occasions, I walked around the room moving closer to my detractors, looked directly at them, and made personal appeals. Ever so slowly, I could see that the tide was turning. Those individuals originally aligned against me began leaning forward by increments and their heads tilted more and more to either side.

After my presentation, I received approval for my operation. Monitoring nonverbal cues and knowing what they meant gave me an enormous advantage in presenting my case. I was able to tailor my presentation to the people who disagreed with me and win them over.

WHISPERING

Whispering is an intimate behavior and positive friend signal. Not everyone can whisper in your ear with impunity. When you see whispering taking place between two individuals, you can be relatively certain a close personal relationship exists.

FOOD FORKING

Imagine sitting in a restaurant and some stranger comes over to your table and picks food off your plate with a fork! You would certainly feel uneasy, and be most unlikely to ask the individual to join you for dinner. Now imagine you are having a pleasant meal with your family and a son or sister reaches over and picks a piece of food off your plate with a fork. The probability is your reaction would be radically different from when the stranger did the same thing. The difference is that you have a close relationship with your family members and, under these conditions, food forking is considered appropriate. Food forking, then, is a friend signal and, if permitted, indicates a close relationship between the person possessing the food and the person reaching for it.

EXPRESSIVE GESTURES

The amount and intensity of gestures people use vary from one culture to another and even within cultures. Some people are naturally more expressive than others, even in more socially restrained cultures. None-theless, people who like one another tend to display more expressive gestures. Expressive gestures signal interest in what the other person is saying and keeps the focus of the conversation on the speaker.

Speakers can emphasize a point with a sharp downward movement of the hand at the end of a sentence, or express openness and sincerity with extended open palms. Expressive gestures reinforce verbal com-munication and mutual interest.

You can encourage potential friends to continue speaking (and like you more because of it) by additional head nodding, smiles, and fo-cused attention (when you lean forward, cock your head slightly and appear to be listening intensely to what is being said). Be aware that nonverbal gestures can also signal discomfort, dislike, or disinterest.

HEAD NODDING

One way we signal to a speaker that we are engaged with them and that they should continue is with a head nod. It tells the speaker to keep talking. A double nod tells the speaker to increase the tempo of the speech. Multiple head nods or a single slow nod tend to cause a disruption in the speakers cadence. Excessive head nodding can rush a response. Rapid head nodding sends a nonverbal cue for the speaker to hurry his or her response, usually because the listener wants to say something or is disinterested. Inappropriate rapid head nodding can be perceived as rude behavior or an attempt to dominate the conversa-tion. This behavior takes the focus off the speaker and turns the spot-light onto the listener, which is a clear violation of the Golden Rule of Friendship, and will be discussed in the next chapter. Used correctly, head nodding allows the speaker to fully express his or her thoughts in a satisfying manner. If you use appropriate head nods, you will be perceived as a good listener, and viewed in a positive light.

VERBAL NUDGES

Verbal nudges reinforce head nodding and encourage the speaker to continue talking. Verbal nudges consist of speech confirmation indicators such as "I see" and "Go on" plus word fillers such as "Ummm" and "Uh-huh." Verbal nudges let the speaker know that you are not only listening but are also validating the speaker's message with verbal confirmation.

FOCUSED ATTENTION

Don't let distractions interrupt your attentive listening to the speaker. You want to send the message that what the speaker is saying is important to you. That message will ring hollow if you answer your cell phone and put the speaker on hold. If your cell phone rings while you are in a conversation, fight the urge to answer. For reasons unknown, most people feel compelled to answer a ringing phone. Just because your cell is ringing doesn't mean you are obligated to answer it. Rarely are telephone calls urgent. If no message is left, that is clearly the case. And if a message is left, you can listen to it, usually in a matter of minutes, once your conversation has finished. Even in today's tech-savvy world, texting and answering telephone calls during a conversation is disrespectful.

The best way to handle a ringing phone is to take it out of your pocket or purse, send the caller to voice mail, put it back into your pocket or purse, and return your attention to the speaker. This action sends a deliberate message to the speaker that he or she is more important than a telephone call and they have your undivided attention. Plus, you will make a positive impression on them . . . making any relationship easier to achieve.

SEVEN TIPS TO GET HIGHER TIPS

Getting people to like you, even for a onetime encounter, can be beneficial. You are more likely to have complaints addressed properly, you are more likely to get people to assist you, even when they don't have to go the extra mile, and—if you're a waiter or waitress—you can predispose people to show their appreciation for personal service in the form of higher tips.

The key to receiving higher tips is to create an environment that predisposes customers to like the server.

Tip 1: Lightly Touch Customers (Female Servers)

Research shows that female servers who touch customers, male or female, lightly on the shoulder, hand, or arm receive higher tips than from customers who are not touched. Males, in particular, drank more alcohol than customers who were not touched, creating more opportunities to tip the server. Touch when interpreted properly produces a feeling of friendliness and, therefore, predisposes customers to tip more generously.

A word of warning: Touching can have a negative effect if it is perceived as flirtatious or dominating and could reduce the amount of tips rather than increase them. Female servers should be careful when touching male customers who are in the company of involved females because any touching could produce jealousy.

Tip 2: Wear Something in Your Hair (Female Servers)

Female servers who wear ornamentation in their hair such as flowers, real or fake, barrettes, or other similar objects receive higher tips from both male and female customers. One explanation for this finding is that customers may perceive servers who wear ornaments in their hair as more attractive, which thus predisposes customers to give higher tips. Interestingly, attractiveness has no effect on tip amounts for male servers from either male or female customers.

Now, let's tackle the eight-hundred-pound gorilla in the room. Yes, research shows that more attractive female servers get higher tips than less attractive servers do, regardless of the level of service. Servers with larger breasts get higher tips. Servers with blond hair get higher tips. Tips increase as a server's body size decreases. Servers who wear makeup receive higher tips from male customers but not from female customers. That is just the way it is. Enough said.

Tip 3: Introduce Yourself by Name (Male and Female Servers)
When servers introduce themselves by name, they receive higher tips. Personal introductions make the servers appear friendlier. Customers tip servers who appear friendly and likable. Servers who introduced themselves by name received an average tip of two dollars more than servers who did not. Mundanely providing customers your name is not sufficient. Your introduction should be accompanied by a wide smile as it makes you appear friendlier and more personable and thus predisposes customers to leave higher tips.

Tip 4: Create Reciprocity (Male and Female Servers)
When people receive something from somebody, they are predisposed to reciprocate. Customers who receive something, even small items, will typically reciprocate by leaving a larger tip. Servers can induce reciprocity through several techniques; even just writing "Thank you" on the back of the check will produce higher tips.

Reciprocity can also be induced in a more subtle fashion. Just prior to the time when the customers' orders are complete, tell one of the customers that the manner in which the food was prepared was not up to your standards and that you sent the meal back to the chef to have it cooked correctly. Then apologize for the delay and, after a few minutes, serve the food as it was originally prepared. The customers perceive that you have done them a favor, although no favor was actually performed, thus predisposing the customers to reciprocate by means of a higher gratuity. Caution should be used when using this technique. You should select imperfections that do not question the taste or quality of the food or discredit the restaurant. Reciprocity can also be induced by bringing mints along with the check.

Tip 5: Repeat the Customer's Order (Male and Female Servers)
People like people who are like them. When you repeat orders, customers subconsciously feel that you are more like them than not. People who are in good rapport

mirror each other's gestures and speech. By repeating the customers' orders, they experience sameness with you, like you more, and tend to leave bigger tips.

Tip 6: Provide Good Service (Male and Female Servers)

At the heart of a good tip is good service. Greet customers with a warm, friendly smile, introduce yourself by name, repeat the customers' order, refill drink glasses without being asked, and periodically check in on the customers to see if they need anything. Each customer is different and you should learn to speed-read them. Some customers want to be pampered, some customers require minimal service, and some customers just want to be left alone to enjoy their meal. The quicker you learn to read your customers, the higher your tips will be.

Tip 7: Apply the Golden Rule of Friendship

The Golden Rule of Friendship (see Chapter 3) applies to everyone: "Make the customers feel good about themselves and they will like you." The more customers like their servers, the higher the tips they are likely to leave.

FOE SIGNALS

As you'll recall from the beginning of the chapter, fireflies can light up as a friend signal to attract members of the opposite sex or as a foe signal to stave off would-be predators. The same is true with each of us. We have the capacity to transmit friend or foe signals to those around us. Obviously, in a book about making friends, one would hope that your focus would be on sending out friend signals and avoiding nonverbal cues that encourage others to perceive you as a foe. The problem is (as the student with the "urban scowl" discovered) we are not always aware we are sending out foe signals, oftentimes because we don't realize what they are. When the goal is to make people you do not know view you favorably, whether it be for a onetime interaction or a lasting friendship, you want to use "firefly" tactics (nonverbal signals) to make your intentions known and predispose the targeted individual to like you. Thus, foe signals are nonverbal signals you *don't* want to send or see when you attempt interactions with strangers.

If you are having trouble making friends you might want to study your gestures and facial expressions to see if you are the unwitting transmitter of any or all of the following nonverbal behaviors.

THE ELONGATED GAZE (STARE)

Eye contact, in concert with other friend signals, can have a positive impact on both parties involved as long as the gaze doesn't last longer than a second. As pointed out earlier, gazing that continues beyond a second is often perceived as aggression, which turns the nonverbal communication into a foe signal. The human brain perceives such behavior as predatory in nature and sends a "shields up" warning to the person at the receiving end of the eye contact.

ELEVATOR EYES

Elevator eyes consist of a sweeping head-to-toe gaze. As a nonverbal gesture, it is highly offensive in fledgling relationships. This form of eye gaze is perceived as intrusive because the person doing the looking has not yet earned the right to invade personal space, which can be violated psychologically as well as physically. Invading personal space with your eyes can be perceived as being offensive, sometimes even more offensive than the physical invasion of personal space. In some cases, the behavior can also be viewed as threatening and/or aggressive, causing a defensive response from the person being looked at. In contrast, a head-to-toe gaze will be accepted or even be seen as complimentary in a close, established relationship.

THE BOYFRIEND BODY SCAN

Long before the tolerated but unpleasant full body scans became a necessity at airports around the world, they were being done by individuals using "elevator eyes" to size up persons of interest. I routinely used the full body scan when my daughter's boyfriends would appear at the front door. I would open the door, stare deeply into the suitor's eyes, and very slowly scan his body from head to toe. I would finish my introduction with a stern, "What do you want?" The young man would stammer and stutter to find words to say. I knew then that my message was received loud and clear. That nonverbal message was more effective than any verbal threats I could have issued.

UNCOVERED

During my post-FBI career, I trained undercover police officers in how to behave during operations to avoid being identified. Eye gaze is one of the nonverbal cues that exposes undercover officers. As stated earlier, people have to earn the right to enter your personal space physically or with their eyes. Police officers, by virtue of their authority, have the right to look into places and at people in a way normal people can't. Have you ever been stopped in traffic at a red light next to a police car? You take sneak peeks into the officer's car. If the officer happens to turn and meet your gaze, you quickly break eye contact and look forward again. The opposite is not true. If the police officer looks into your car and you meet his gaze, he does not break eye contact, he just continues to look. You would likely be the one who quickly breaks eye contact and hope he doesn't find a reason to stop you. The police officer has the right to look at you and into your car by virtue of his authority; you can't do the same thing without risking social repercussions.

The freedom to look in forbidden spaces is one of the most common nonverbal "tells" that expose undercover officers. For example, an undercover officer is assigned to go to a bar where known drug dealers hang out, to make friends with them and buy drugs. When the under-cover officer walks into the bar for the first time, he will, out of habit, pause for a moment, make a slow scan of the room looking for possible threats, walk to the bar, and order a drink. The undercover officer feels comfortable invading other people's space with his eyes (making direct eye contact) because of his authority as a law enforcement officer. The problem is that normal people don't act this way when they enter a bar for the first time, especially a shady establishment. When people enter a bar for the first time, they typically walk directly to the bar or a table and sit down without making direct eye contact with anyone. Once they are seated and have a drink in hand, they then are permitted to take furtive looks around the bar. Conversely, people who routinely frequent the bar have earned the right to invade personal space and are permitted to look around the bar for friends when they enter. This nonverbal tell, albeit subtle, is easily picked up by criminals, who, for fear of getting caught, are very adept at reading people.

An eye roll

EYE ROLLS

Rolling your eyes at someone is a "foe signal" that discourages further interaction. It sends the message you think the individual is stupid or that his or her actions are inappropriate. If, for instance, you are in a large group and spot someone saying something you think is dumb, you might roll your eyes in response. If the person who made the comment sees you doing this, it predisposes them to respond negatively to you in any future interactions. This holds true whether you are a stranger or are known to that individual.

WATCH FOR EYE ROLL

Watching for eye rolls at meetings can be an entertaining way to pass the time, and can provide information about where people stand on specific issues. When people disagree with a comment or proposal, they will often roll their eyes when the person who made the comment or proposal turns away or looks at his or her notes. This nonverbal signal identifies who is not receptive to what is being said.

If you make a comment and catch somebody rolling their eyes, focus your attention on that person to try to convince them your idea has merit. Remember: You don't have to spend time trying to convince the choir, the ones who are nodding their approval, leaning forward, and smiling.

SQUINTING OF THE EYES

This foe signal is not as powerful as other foe cues are, but can still have a chilling effect on personal relationships. If the squinting is due to factors such as looking into bright illumination, it might be wrongly interpreted.

FURROWED EYEBROWS

This is another common foe signal, assuming it is not due to someone being in deep concentration. This nonverbal cue is often associated with disapproval, uncertainty, or anger.

FACIAL TENSION

Tightened jaw muscles, narrowing of the eyes, and furrowed eyebrows are a cluster of nonverbal foe signals that can be seen from a distance and serve as early warning indicators to alert you

Furrowed eyebrows

to the possibility that the person you are about to meet may pose a threat. Displaying foe signals makes meaningful communication difficult, especially in new relationships. Facial tension can be easily misinterpreted because people often carry over tensions from their jobs or home lives to social situations, causing new friends or even old ones to take note and become unnecessarily guarded and apprehensive.

AGGRESSIVE STANCE

A wide stance with arms akimbo (hands on hips) is a foe signal. A wide stance lowers the body's center of gravity and is used by a person preparing for a fight. Arms akimbo widens a person's profile in an attempt to display dominance.

ATTACK SIGNALS

People who are about to attack telegraph nonverbal signals such as clenching their fists and widening their stance for stability. A wide stance lowers the body's center of gravity in preparation for a fight. A wide stance with arms akimbo (hands on hips) signals dominance. Arms akimbo widens a person's profile in an attempt to display dominance. Oftentimes, an angry person's nostrils "flare" (widen) in an attempt to enhance oxygen intake. They are also likely to give anger signs such as redness of the face. Obviously, these foe signals alert the scanning brain to potential danger and prepare the recipient of these attack signals for the "fight or flight" response, hardly a prelude to a positive friendship.

An Attack Stance

INSULTING GESTURES

Numerous gestures are offensive to others and antithetical to developing good relationships. Some of them are almost universally recognized: for example, the upraised middle finger. It is doubtful anyone intent on establishing a positive interaction with another person would transmit this gesture. The problem is that certain gestures that are "harmless" (have no negative connotation) in one culture might be highly offensive in another. Just as the same words have different meanings across different cultures, so, too, do nonverbal communications. If you note that somebody reacts negatively toward you for no "apparent" reason you might want to consider if any gesture you just made might have been perceived as offensive to them.

SCRUNCHED NOSE

Like other foe signals, a scrunched nose makes anyone observing it less likely to see you in a positive light and less open to any further overtures you send their way.

CLOTHING, ACCESSORIES, AND OTHER ITEMS WORN ON THE BODY

The old saying "one man's floor is another man's ceiling" is applicable to this particular foe signal (or cluster of signals). For example, if you're sporting a leather jacket with a skull and crossbones, have numerous tattoos on your arms, and are wearing a spike necklace, it might be interpreted by someone who doesn't know you as a person to avoid at all costs. In that sense, your appearance is a foe signal. On the other hand, if you happen to be at a death metal concert, the same outfit might be seen as a friend signal worthy of notice. Thus you will need to determine, using common sense, whether the way you are clothed and accessorized will likely be perceived as a friend or foe signal by a

A Scrunched Nose

person you might want to approach. Just because someone is dressed differently than you doesn't guarantee that your appearance will automatically be a "turnoff," but the adage "birds of a feather flock together" should be considered when it comes to interactions between individuals with significantly different ways of adorning their bodies.

My son, Bradley, inadvertently taught me a valuable lesson about assessing people by the clothes they wear. In high school, he went through a phase where he was all about men's fashion, which included spending every penny he earned at his part-time job after school on clothes and accessories. I accompanied Bradley to the shopping mall one day to buy a wallet. He looked at the most expensive wallets in an exclusive clothier shop. The one he bought cost $150. I was shocked. I pulled out my three-fold wallet and reminded him that my wallet only cost about $20 including tax. "No, Dad," he replied. "It's the details that make the difference. You can wear expensive clothes and shoes but people will know you are a 'poser' if you pull out a twenty-dollar, three-fold wallet." My son eventually passed through that phase in his life and is back to wearing faded blue jeans and sweatshirts, but I still carry the lesson he taught me.

From that day forward I paid closer attention to the details. I look at stitch count in shirts. The more stitches per inch, the higher the quality of the shirt. Four-millimeter buttons are sewn on higher-quality shirts. If a man wears an expensive suit and a cheap watch, he is pretending to be someone he is not. Unshined shoes are another sign of a poser. People who engage in perception management often overlook the details, a tell that exposes who they really are.

WHO WAS THAT MASKED MAN?

Although it is usually worn by individuals who require it due to a medical condition, a face mask, particularly the "surgical" kind that covers the mouth and nose of the user, acts as a foe signal even when that is not its intended purpose.

A masked individual sends out such a powerful foe signal that one person I know used it to increase the space around him on the notoriously crowded commuter trains that service the New York City area. His modus operandi was to occupy the window seat where the aisle seat next to him was open. Then, when anyone approached the unoccupied seat, he would turn his head so that his masked mouth and nose were clearly visible. Many times the seat remained open until *all* other available seats in the car were taken.

And he didn't stop there. If someone *did* sit next to him, he would begin to twitch and mutter under his breath. This was usually sufficient to dislodge the newly arrived seatmate. If that didn't work, he would reach in his pocket, pull out a pill bottle that obviously was issued from a drugstore, take out a pill, lift up his mask, and pop the pill in his mouth. Very few people can sit through such an experience and remain in place.

It turns out that karma has its moments. On one particular trip, the masked individual glanced up at a man moving toward him in the aisle, shifted in his seat to be sure the stranger saw the white surgical mask on his face, and then turned back to the window. A moment later, he caught a glimpse of the stranger sitting down next to him. So he went into his twitch-and-mutter scenario. The stranger remained rooted in his chair. Finally, the masked passenger took out his trusty pill bottle and went through his pill-taking routine. The person next to him remained, without unmoving.

The masked passenger couldn't believe his ruse had failed. He turned his head to see what kind of person could remain in such a threatening environment. What he saw was a seatmate who was now also wearing a face mask, twitching, and holding a prescription bottle in *his* hand! That was *all* he needed to see. Without any hesitation, he bolted from his window seat and moved down the aisle into the next passenger car.

TERRITORIAL (PERSONAL SPACE) INVASION

There seem to be definite consistencies in the ways humans govern the space around them, that is, the manner in which they regulate the distance between themselves and other people. The term for such spatial regulation is *territoriality*, and the territorial imperative is practiced by humans and lower animals alike. The underlying principle of territoriality is that many species of life desire and attempt to maintain a specified amount and *quality* of space for themselves. If you don't believe that the territorial imperative exists, get on a bus or subway car occupied by only one other passenger and plop yourself down next to him. In some instances, people will tolerate an invasion of their personal space if the invasion occurs in a side-by-side encounter such as in crowded elevators or at sporting events.

"Invading" another person's territory—whether through intrusive eye contact or actual physical closeness—is a powerful foe signal.

The purpose of using friend signals when first meeting a stranger is to encourage them to allow you into their territory without them feeling threatened or under siege. If a person you wish to meet judges you as friendly, then he or she will be more willing to allow you to enter their personal space.

Territorial boundaries are, of course, invisible and can vary from person to person and from culture to culture. For example, a person who has been physically abused will typically have a larger personal space to protect himself or herself from anyone who poses a physical threat. Similarly, an individual who has been emotionally hurt may be very cautious about who they allow into their personal space, for fear of being emotionally hurt again. In extreme cases, physically and/or emotionally abused persons build walls around themselves that are too high to climb over and too thick to penetrate in an attempt to protect themselves against any further physical or psychological pain.

Territorial boundaries are also affected by where people live. In societies where people live in close quarters, they establish smaller personal boundaries out of necessity. Conversely, people who are accustomed to wide-open spaces create larger personal spaces. Mental health can also affect personal space. Ted Kaczynski, the Unabomber, lived in an isolated cabin in Montana. He perceived anyone who came within half a mile of his cabin as a threat and prepared to defend himself against those who encroached on his personal space.

Because people have such wide variations in what they consider "their" territory and personal space, it is important that you take this into consideration when attempting to make friends with someone you do not know. After sending out friend signals, and receiving like signals in return, approach the individual carefully and observe their body language as you do. If the individual shows signs of stress or negative reactions, such as backing away or disapproving facial expressions, stop your forward progress and do not move closer to that person until he or she gives you verbal or nonverbal clues that they are ready for that.

People tend to be slow to yield personal territory, especially when it comes to parking spaces. When you have been driving circles in a crowded parking lot, looking for a spot, and finally see someone getting ready to leave, you immediately activate your turn signal to mark your turf. You are effectively telling other drivers to back off because this is your parking space. Now the waiting game begins. The driver who is about to pull out of the space fidgets and fiddles with various gadgets mounted on the dashboard, painstakingly taking his or her time to properly adjust the seat belt and mirrors. You ask yourself, "What's taking this person so long to pull out?" The answer is that they are masters of their space and will not surrender it until they are good and ready. Interestingly, people leave parking spaces sooner if no one is waiting to pull in.

DOGMATIC VIEW OF TERRITORIAL FOE SIGNALS

Pets, particularly dogs, provide interesting examples of territorial behavior. For example, two people enter a friend's house for the first time. One person is an avid dog lover and the other individual hates dogs. The dog lover immediately focuses his or her attention on the dog, looks the dog directly in the eyes, and bends down to pet the animal. To the dog lover's surprise, the canine growls and bares its teeth. The dog hater, on the other hand, limits physical and visual contact with the dog. To the dog hater's chagrin, the animal approaches, sniffs, and eagerly seeks his attention.

The dog's reaction to the two strangers seems counterintuitive, but when viewed from a territorial perspective, it makes perfect sense. The dog lover violated the animal's physical space by moving toward it and further challenged the animal by looking directly into its eyes at ground level. Both dogs and humans perceive staring as a threatening (foe signal) gesture. The dog viewed the canine lover's presence as a threat or a potential threat; therefore, the dog presented an aggressive threat to protect its territory. With familiarity, the dog lover will eventually be accepted. Conversely, the dog hater ignored the animal and consequently posed no territorial threat. Without an actual or perceived threat, the dog became intrigued by the stranger. In an effort to satisfy natural curiosity (the same "hook" that got Vladimir to talk to me and Seagull interested in Charles, the FBI agent), the dog approached the person who hated it.

BEFORE YOU START WALKING, LET THEIR FEET DO THE TALKING

All right, you've got a working knowledge of friend and foe signals, and you know which ones to display and look for when dealing with strangers you want to either approach or avoid—maybe you've even practiced your nonverbal signals in front of a mirror. There's one more thing to consider before you actually start *speaking* with anybody, and that has to do with situations where your person of interest is not alone but already interacting with others. How do you break in and start a conversation? *When* should you break in and begin talking?

There are times when you won't be able to answer such questions. For example, at business meetings or social events where people are seated at tables or when they are moving about the room, seamlessly integrating into ongoing conversations can be difficult. However, if two or more people are standing together and socially interacting, then you can use *foot behavior* to help determine whether it is a good time to approach the group or, conversely, if it is a better idea to delay your effort to make contact. This is because observing foot positions offers clues as to which group will accept a new member and which will be reluctant or unwilling to do so.

Members of a large group who form a semicircle with their feet pointing toward the open side of the circle are signaling that they are willing to accept new members. Members of a large group who form a closed circle are signaling they are not going to be receptive to adding new individuals to their gathering.

If you see two people who are facing each other—each with their feet pointing toward the other person—they are telegraphing the message that their conversation is private. Stay away. They do not want outsiders to interrupt. On the other hand, if two people are facing each other with their feet askew, this leaves an "opening" and sends the message that they are willing to admit a new person to their group.

Feet telegraphing a private conversation.

Feet askew invites other people to join the conversation.

When three people face each other and their feet are pointed in-ward forming a closed circle, they are nonverbally communicating an unwillingness to accept new members.

Conversely, when three people face each other and assume a wider circle, opening up space, they are signaling they are willing to have others join their group.

Closed conversation

The members of this group are standing with their feet askew, which sends the message that they are willing to admit a new person to their group.

Your job is to identify groups that are open to new members and make your approach. Purposefully walk toward the group and display friend signals either before or during the approach. Recall that our brains are constantly scanning the environment for friend or foe cues. If you exhibit foe signals, the people in the group you are approaching are going to defend themselves against a possible threat and be hostile to your intrusion. If these same individuals see you exhibiting eyebrow flashes, head tilts, and a smile, they are going to interpret these friend signals as positive and are more likely to welcome you into their gathering.

When you reach the group you have chosen, confidently step into the empty space. Confident people are more liked than people who are not self-assured. Even if you don't feel confident, fake it as best you can. A fine line exists between self-confidence and arrogance. Don't cross it!

When you enter the once-empty space, listen to the conversation thread and wait for a pause before saying anything. While you are listening, you should slightly nod your head. Nodding signals approval and interest in what the other individuals are saying and also sends the message that you are confident, not arrogant. Arrogant people are typically not good listeners. The group may be willing to accept new members, but no one likes a newcomer who rudely interrupts an ongoing conversation. When a natural pause in the conversation occurs, this is your cue to introduce yourself or add to the conversation you have been listening to.

Try to find common ground with the other members of the group. Finding common ground (similar interests, backgrounds, jobs, etc.) is the quickest way to develop rapport and kick your friend-making process into high gear. Techniques to quickly build rapport will be discussed in detail in a later chapter. If you are at a trade show or conference, you have instant common ground because everybody at that event shares common interests or else they wouldn't be there in the first place.

If common ground cannot be readily established, default to the topic of music. Almost everyone likes music. Even if people do not like the same music, the similarities and differences between music genres can foster lively and usually noncontroversial conversations. You don't want to discuss topics that have the potential to create strong feelings and potential conflicts, as these can prove divisive and are antithetical to nurturing budding friendships.

When you see these people later in the event, call them by their names. It will mean a lot to them. How much? In the words of Dale Carnegie: "Remember that a person's name is to that person the sweetest and most important sound in any language." People like to be remembered. Remembering a person's name assigns them value and recognition and shows that you care. Things remembered are things cherished.

CONVERSATIONAL BRIDGE-BACKS

When encountering individuals you met earlier, you can employ a conversational *bridge-back*. This refers to your use of portions of earlier discussions at a later time. Conversational bridge-backs can be comments, jokes, gestures, or other things unique to the earlier conversation. Using a conversational bridge-back sends the subtle message that you are not a newcomer to the person's circle of friends and acquaintances. You are a familiar person with mutual interests. Conversational bridge-backs also allow you to pick up the friend-building process where it left off at the end of the first conversation. That, in turn, allows you to move forward in your friendship building without having to start out from scratch.

FOOT BEHAVIORAL CUES WHEN A PERSON IS ALONE

If you see a person standing alone and his or her feet are pointed toward the exit, there's a good chance that they are thinking about leaving but haven't yet made the move. This provides you with an opening to approach that person. Give friend signals as you approach and then make an empathic statement (discussed in the next chapter) like "Oh, I see you're ready to leave" or "Oh, you find the party boring." You can use such a statement because you are just describing the physical stance you have observed, which reflects that individual's inner feelings. Or you might walk up and simply say, "Oh, I see you're here by yourself today. What do you think of the place (or event)?" Hopefully, the person will respond to your inquiry, and you can use the response to continue the conversation and see how things go from there.

OUT OF THE FIREFLY AND INTO THE FRIENDSHIP: THE NEXT STEP

The making of a friend or foe begins at the first moment of contact, usually visual, and moves forward from there. This chapter has focused almost exclusively on the nonverbal signals we send out to others and the impact they have on personal relationships. Because people normally see us before they hear us, our nonverbal signals are like "coming attractions" or "trailers" for movies, giving the viewer advance notice of what they can expect from the main attraction and helping them decide if it's worth their time to pursue or avoid.

DON'T BASK IN THIS SPOTLIGHT!

If you use your friend signals effectively, you will have set the stage for a successful interaction to follow. Getting another person's attention and, at the same time, encouraging them to see you in a positive light is a critical first step on the path to making friends, but you need to be careful to not bask in the spotlight. Intentionally sending friend (or foe) signals takes practice. Subconsciously, people are very adept at transmitting these nonverbal communications. However, now that you have read about these signals and are aware of them, you will begin to notice other people sending and receiving them and, from time to time, you will catch yourself in the act of signaling others.

In order to *consciously* imitate the same signals you *subconsciously* send with ease and authenticity, you must overcome *the spotlight effect*. The spotlight effect triggers when you do something surreptitiously and, because you are making a conscious effort to influence people's behavior, you think that everybody is aware of what you are doing. This, in turn, makes it difficult for you to make your behavior appear natural and appropriate, resulting in an inability to perform your actions in a convincing manner. The end result: Your actions are not believable or believed.

An example of the spotlight effect in action involves someone who lies. The liar thinks that the person he is lying to can see right through the lie, even when that individual is totally unaware of the deception. This, in turn, causes the liar to display verbal and nonverbal cues that actually indicate deception, allowing the person on the receiving end of the lie to detect the deception or, at least, become suspicious of what is being said.

The same thing happens when you first attempt to consciously imitate friend signals. You've been successfully sending these signals throughout your life; yet, the first few times you approach people and consciously attempt to tilt your head and display an eyebrow flash, you will think they know you're socially awkward. The spotlight effect takes hold. This causes you to "force" the behavior—your head tilts and eyebrow flashes become awkward—and your intentions *are* revealed, leaving you as the victim of your own self-fulfilling prophecy . . . and a failed attempt to make a friend. If you want to avoid the spotlight effect, you first have to know of its existence.

Now you do.

THE NONVERBAL TWO-STEP

During my FBI career, I attended many conferences and parties. On one occasion, I attended a pre-conference "get-to-know-you party" with a fellow member of the Behavioral Analysis Program. The party became boring, so my friend and I amused ourselves by playing "nonverbal footrace."

The game worked like this: We each selected partygoers who were at an equal distance from the door. The object of the game was to see who could get their selected target to cross the threshold of the door without them realizing what they were doing. We initially engaged each of our targets in casual conversation at an acceptable physical distance. Knowing that people unconsciously try to maintain a comfortable distance from the person they are talking to, we took imperceptible steps closer to our targets. As the space between us and our targets closed, they unconsciously stepped backward to maintain their personal space. We repeated this maneuver until our targets passed the doorjamb. The first person to accomplish this was declared the winner. In one instance, I backed my target into the lobby of the hotel without his conscious awareness. When he realized where he was, he exclaimed, "Whoosh! How did we get out here?" I just smiled and shrugged my shoulders.

The first step in successfully imitating friend (or foe) signals is to watch how other people naturally display these signals and, also, to monitor your own signals. When you imitate a friend signal, try to duplicate the same sensation you feel when you catch yourself automatically displaying these nonverbal communications.

A good place to hone these skills is walking down the street, in shopping malls, and in other public places. When a person approaches, tilt your head, make eye contact, and smile. Watch the person's reaction. If the individual returns an eyebrow flash along with a smile, you have successfully transmitted a friend signal. If the person gives you a goofy look or a "get away from me, you creep" expression, you might have chosen a sourpuss or need more practice. Over time, you should see an improvement in how people respond to your friend signals. Further, with practice, you won't have to consciously think about sending the signals or how they look; they will become automatic.

Acquiring new skills, or making old skills look authentic when we use them "in the spotlight," takes lots of practice. While working to perfect these signals, you might become discouraged and give up for various reasons, including embarrassment, lack of immediate mastery of the new skills, or frustration. This is normal. In studying how people acquire new skills, scientists have discovered that many novices experience a period of "free fall" early in the learning experience. During this time, individuals are not comfortable using the new skills and become frustrated or embarrassed when the skills do not work as advertised. Instead of continuing to practice the skills, they give up.

Don't you be one of those people! Persevere through this free-fall phase, confident in the knowledge that you *will* achieve skill mastery with time and effort. The frustration and discomfort of acquiring new skills will be well worth the effort because you will be rewarded with superior results in achieving successful relationships.

That should make smiling *very* easy to do, consciously or otherwise!

TO ERR IS HUMAN . . . AND MAKES THAT HUMAN MORE LIKABLE, TOO

At the beginning of my lectures, I intentionally make several mistakes that don't damage my credibility, such as mispronouncing a word or misspelling a word on the whiteboard. The participants immediately correct my small errors. With a show of embarrassment, I graciously accept the correction and credit the participants for being attentive.

This technique accomplishes several objectives. First, the participants making the corrections feel good about themselves, which builds rapport and friendship. Second, participants are more likely to spontaneously interact during the lecture without the fear of looking stupid in front of the instructor. After all, they reason, it's okay to make mistakes because the instructor already has made several himself. Third, minor mistakes make me look human. People like lecturers who are subject matter experts yet at the same time possess human qualities similar to the seminar participants (the Law of Similarity, discussed in Chapter 5).

OBSERVE AND LEARN

Tapping on a cell phone keyboard and having earbuds in place shuts you out of the sending or receiving of friendship signals. And the lack of personal interaction with other people reduces the opportunity for you to sharpen your social skills or learn from observing others.

Learning from others doesn't even take much effort. All you need to do is go to a restaurant and people-watch. People feel comfortable communicating when they are eating or drinking. See if you can determine the status and intensity of relationships by observing the non-verbal signals of nearby couples.

ROMANTIC RELATIONSHIPS

When two people walk into a restaurant you can tell if they are a couple or not by observing their nonverbal behaviors. Hand holding is a sign of romantic interest. Couples who hold hands without interlacing their fingers indicate a less intimate relationship than if they hold hands with their fingers interlaced. The following sequence of actions typically takes place after the couple sits at a table or booth: 1) the centerpiece, menu stand, or condiment rack is moved to one side of the table, 2) the couple exchange eyebrow flashes, 3) the couple look at each other for a longer time than they would look at strangers, 4) they smile, 5) they tilt their heads to one side or the other, 6) they lean in toward each other, 7) they mirror each other's posture, 8) they hold hands, 9) they freely use gestures when they communicate, 10) they whisper, or lower their voices, to signal to others that the conversation is private and intruders are not welcome, and 11) they share food. This sequence of activity may not take place in the exact order listed or may be interrupted by waitstaff, but you will observe some or all of these nonverbal cues at some point during the course of dinner.

BROKEN RELATIONSHIPS

Relationships that are strained will become obvious because the normal nonverbal cues present in a good relationship will be absent. For example, the couple will not look at each other. Their smiles are forced. One or both will often look at their plates when they speak. Heads are erect, not tilted. Their eyes are sweeping across the restaurant looking for other stimuli. They don't mirror each other's postures. They don't lean toward one another; in fact, they are usually leaning backward, away from each other.

SPLIT RELATIONSHIPS

A nonverbal sequence that indicates that one member of the couple is interested in the other person but the other person is not interested in them is not hard to spot. The interested person displays all the nonverbal cues present in a romantic relationship as previously described; however, the other person is displaying negative nonverbal cues (foe signals).

The man is displaying nonverbal cues indicating interest; the female is not.

QUIET COMFORT

Couples who have spent many years together often display nonverbal cues that signal a bad or broken relationship, but this is not always the case. People who spend a long time in each other's company are confident that the other person is committed to the relationship. They don't need constant reminders. They are relaxed and comfortable in each other's company without the fear of betrayal or abandonment.

Watching couples interact with one another when they reach this stage in their relationship is a wonder to behold.

These same observational relationship evaluations can be made with businesspeople making deals, people trying to pick someone up, or just friends out for a casual meal or drink. The point of people-watching is to sharpen your observation skills, allowing you to become more aware of how people naturally interact with one another and enhance your ability to accurately interpret what you see. If you practice enough, your observations and skills in evaluating human behavior will become automatic, thus making you a more effective communicator.

3

THE GOLDEN RULE
OF FRIENDSHIP

You can make more friends in two months by becoming
genuinely interested in other people than you can in two
years by trying to get other people interested in you.
—DALE CARNEGIE

The nonverbal friend signals you learned in the previous chapter are
designed to set the stage for the start of a positive relationship with
another person. They function like a comedian whose warm-up act
is designed to get the audience in the right frame of mind before the
headliner makes his appearance. Used correctly, these signals will make
your person of interest more receptive to interacting with you, should
you choose to approach and speak with them. So let's assume you *do*
choose to make contact with somebody. What now? You have reached
your "moment of truth" with them.

MAKING YOUR "MOMENT OF TRUTH" A SUCCESS

Many years ago, a businessman named Jan Carlzon was named CEO
of a struggling European airline company, Scandinavian Airlines System (SAS), and given the formidable task of making it profitable. He

accomplished this objective with such speed that his feat became the focal point of management cases and literature highlighting business turnarounds.

How did he achieve such success? By giving his frontline staff the power to solve customer service problems on the spot, without having to check with their supervisors first. This greatly improved customer satisfaction, employee morale, and corporate profit . . . a win-win situation for all involved.

What was interesting about Carlzon's philosophy and business strategy, as it relates to this book, is the importance he put on the point of contact between two individuals. In fact, he called it a "moment of truth" because it was these moments that shaped a customer's view of the company and helped determine if they would purchase SAS services. Carlzon observed: "Last year each of our ten million customers came in contact with approximately five SAS employees. These 50 million 'moments of truth' are the moments that ultimately determine whether SAS will succeed or fail as a company. They are the moments when we must prove to our customers that SAS is their best alternative."

When you meet another person for the first time, it is a defining moment of truth in how that relationship will develop. Will that person treat you like a friend or shun you like a foe? *The Golden Rule of Friendship—If you want people to like you, make them feel good about themselves*—can be a deciding factor in which side the person puts you on.

Unlike some of the techniques that will be presented later, which only become relevant when you are looking for long-term relationships rather than brief or sporadic interactions, the Golden Rule of Friendship serves as the key to all successful relationships, whether they are of short, medium, or long duration.

Do not underestimate the power and importance of this rule in making friends. As an FBI Special Agent, I was required to meet people from every station in life and convince them to provide sensitive information, become spies, or confess to a variety of crimes. The key to the successful completion of these daunting tasks was my ability to get people to not only like me but to trust me and, in many cases, trust me with their lives. The most difficult task facing new Special Agents bent on getting people to like them is developing this vital skill. Agents often approached me and asked me to teach them the techniques to get people to like them instantly. And I gave them the exact same instruction: *If you want people to like you, make them feel good about themselves.* You must focus your attention on the person you are be-friending. It sounds easy, but it takes practice even for trained agents. If you make someone feel good about themselves, they will credit you with helping them attain that good feeling. People gravitate toward individuals who make them happy and tend to avoid people who bring them pain or discomfort.

If every time you meet a person you make them feel good about themselves, he or she will seek out every opportunity to see you again to experience those same good feelings. The stumbling block many of my fellow agents confronted in achieving this objective is the same one we all encounter: our own ego. People's egos get in the way of prac-ticing the Golden Rule of Friendship. Most people think the world revolves around them and they should be the center of attention. But if you want to appear friendly and attractive to others, you must forgo your ego and pay attention to the other person and his or her par-ticular needs and circumstances. Other people will like you when you make *them* (not you) the focus of attention.

Think about it: It is unfortunate that we seldom use this powerful rule for making ourselves more attractive to others while, at the same time, making those individuals feel better about themselves. We are too busy focusing on ourselves and not on the people we meet. We put our wants and needs before the wants and needs of others. The irony of all this is that other people will be eager to fulfill your wants and needs if they like you.

TECHNIQUES TO MAKE PEOPLE FEEL GOOD ABOUT THEMSELVES: EMPATHIC STATEMENTS

Empathic statements keep the focus of the conversation on the person you are talking with rather than on yourself. They are one of the most effective ways to make people feel good about themselves. Keeping the focus on the other person is difficult because we are, by nature, egocentric and think the world revolves around us. Nevertheless, if every time you talk to people they feel good about themselves, you will have successfully achieved the objective of the Golden Rule of Friendship and people will like you as a result.

Empathic statements such as "You look like you are having a bad day" or "You look happy today" let people know that someone is listening to them and cares to some degree about their well-being. This kind of attention makes us feel good about ourselves and, more important, predisposes us to like the person who gave us the attention.

Empathic statements also close the discourse cycle. When a person says something, they want feedback to know if their message was received and understood. Mirroring back what a person says using parallel language closes the communication circle. People feel good about themselves when they successfully communicate a message.

Constructing empathic statements requires you to carefully listen to the other person. Concentrated listening demonstrates that you are really interested in the other person and understand what they are saying.

The basic formula for constructing empathic statements is "So you . . ." There are many ways to form empathic statements but this basic formula gets you in the habit of keeping the focus of the conversation on the other person and away from you. Simple empathic statements might include "So you like the way things are going today," or "So you are having a good day." We naturally tend to say something to the effect of "I understand how you feel." The other person then automatically thinks, *No, you don't know how I feel because you are not me.*

The basic "So you . . ." formula ensures that the focus of the conversation remains on the other person. For example, you get on an elevator and see a person who is smiling and looks happy. You can naturally say, "So, things are going your way today," mirroring back their physical nonverbal cues.

When using empathic statements to achieve the objective of the Golden Rule of Friendship, avoid repeating back word for word what the person said. Since people rarely do this, when it occurs the repetition is processed by the brain of the listener as abnormal behavior and causes a defensive reaction. This is the exact opposite effect of what you are trying to achieve by using empathic statements. Parroting another person's statement can also sound patronizing and condescending. Don't do it!

Empathic statements keep the focus of the conversation on the other person and make them feel good about themselves. And using empathic statements is a simple yet effective technique that will have people seeking you out to be their friend, because every time they converse with you, you make them feel good about themselves. And, best of all, people will not know you are using this technique, because they naturally think they deserve the attention and will not see your actions as being out of the ordinary (it will pass their territory scan without arousing any attention). Once you have mastered constructing empathic statements using the basic formula, you can construct more sophisticated empathic statements by dropping the "So you . . ."

BEN AND VICKI'S EMPATHIC STATEMENT ADVENTURE

Let's look at how a conversation might work using the techniques discussed thus far. Using the standard friend signals, Ben sends a nonverbal invitation to Vicki, who is standing near the bar with several friends. Vicki nonverbally accepts Ben's invitation. As Ben approaches Vicki, he notes that she is smiling and laughing with her friends.

BEN: Hi, my name is Ben? What's yours?

VICKI: Hi, my name is Vicki.

BEN: So you look like you are really having fun tonight. (basic empathic statement)

VICKI: I sure am. I really needed a night out.

Once you have mastered constructing empathic statements using the basic formula, you can construct more sophisticated empathic statements by dropping the "So you . . ." Let's revisit Ben's conversation with Vicki using sophisticated empathic statements instead of the basic formula.

BEN: Hi, my name is Ben. What's yours?

VICKI: Hi, my name is Vicki.

BEN: You look like you're really having fun tonight. (sophisticated empathic statement)

VICKI: I sure am. I really need a night out.

BEN: Then you've been really busy lately. (sophisticated empathic statement)

VICKI: Yeah, I worked sixty hours a week for the last three weeks getting a project done.

With either approach, Ben recognized that Vicki was smiling and laughing, two physical signs that she was enjoying herself. Ben constructed an empathic statement that reflected her emotional status. Ben achieved several things. First, he communicated to Vicki that he took an interest in her feelings. Second, he focused the conversation on her. Third, Vicki's response lets Ben know in which direction to steer the conversation. Her response, "I sure am. I really need a night out," indicates that Vicki experienced some type of stress during the week or in the recent past. Ben does not know what that stress was, but he can construct another empathic statement to explore the reasons for her stress in a noninvasive way. By doing so, he continues to keep the focus of the conversation on Vicki and lets her know that he is still interested in her and her emotional feelings. Vicki will not recognize that Ben is using a series of empathic statements because this kind of behavior is perceived by the brain as "normal behavior" and doesn't arouse suspicion or a defensive reaction. Further, Vicki subconsciously thinks she should be the center of attention (we all do!) and she is delighted that Ben is giving her his undivided attention. This makes her feel good about herself and increases the probability that she will like Ben, according to the Golden Rule of Friendship.

USING EMPATHIC STATEMENTS TO KEEP CONVERSATIONS GOING

Empathic statements also serve as effective conversation fillers. The awkward silence that comes when the other person stops talking and you cannot think of anything to say is devastating. When you are struggling for something to say, fall back on the empathic statement. All you have to remember is the last thing the person said and construct an empathic statement based on that information. The speaker will carry the conversation, giving you time to think of something meaningful to say. It is far better to use a series of empathic statements when you have nothing to say than to say something inappropriate. Remember: The person you are talking to will not realize that you are using empathic statements because they will be processed as "normal" by the listener's brain and will go unnoticed.

FLATTERY/COMPLIMENTS

A fine line separates flattery from compliments. The word *flattery* has a more negative connotation than the term *compliment*. Flattery is often associated with insincere compliments used to exploit and manipulate others for selfish reasons. The purpose of compliments is to praise others and acknowledge their accomplishments. As relationships grow and develop, compliments play an ever-increasing role in the bonding of two individuals. Compliments signal that the other person is still interested in you and what you do well.

One of the pitfalls of using compliments in fledgling relationships is that you do not know the person well enough to be sincere. Insincere compliments and flattery are one and the same and will give the person receiving the false accolade a negative impression of you. After all, no one likes to feel they are being manipulated or lied to. People know what they are good at and where they are weak. If you tell someone that they are good at something and they know they aren't, they are likely to question your motive because they recognize the discrepancy between your assessment of them and the way they *really* perform.

An alternate, and vastly superior, method of using compliments exists. This approach avoids the pitfalls inherent in complimenting another person and instead allows others to compliment themselves. This technique avoids the problem of appearing insincere. When people compliment themselves, sincerity is not an issue, and people rarely miss an opportunity to compliment themselves if given the opportunity (which you conveniently provide).

The key to allowing people to compliment themselves is to construct a dialogue that predisposes people to recognize their attributes or accomplishments and give themselves a silent pat on the back. When people compliment themselves, they feel good about themselves, and according to the Golden Rule of Friendship, they will like you because you provided the opportunity to make them feel good about themselves.

Referring back to Ben's fledgling relationship with Vicki, he can set the stage for Vicki to compliment herself.

BEN: Then you've been really busy lately. (sophisticated empathic statement)

VICKI: Yeah, I worked sixty hours a week for the last three weeks getting a project done.

> **BEN:** It takes a lot of dedication and determination to commit to a project of that magnitude. (a statement that provides Vicki the opportunity to compliment herself)
>
> **VICKI:** (Thinking) I sacrificed a lot to get that mega project done and I did a very good job, if I may say so myself.

Note that Ben did not directly tell Vicki he thought she was a dedicated and determined person. However, it was not hard for Vicki to recognize those attributes in herself and apply them to her circumstances at work. In the event Vicki does not see herself as a dedicated and determined person, no damage will be done to the fledgling relationship. What Ben said is true regardless of Vicki's self-assessment, so his comment at worst will go unnoticed, and at best will provide the impetus for Vicki to feel good about herself (and Ben). Based on human nature, even if Vicki was in reality not a dedicated and determined person, she would likely apply those favorable attributes to herself. Few people would admit in public, much less to themselves, that they are not dedicated, determined people.

THIRD-PARTY COMPLIMENTS

You can use a third party to compliment a person you want to befriend—*without doing it yourself*—and still get the "credit" for making the target of your compliment feel good about themselves and, by extension, feel good about you. When you directly compliment other people, particularly anybody who suspects you might want something from them (for example: your date, your boss, or a friend), they tend to discount your efforts because they suspect you are intentionally trying to influence them through flattery. A third-party compliment eliminates this skepticism.

To construct a third-party compliment you will need to find a mutual friend or acquaintance who knows both you and your person of interest. Further, you should be relatively certain that the third-party individual you choose will be likely to pass along your compliment to the person for whom it was intended. If this transmission of information is successful, the next time you meet your person of interest, he or she will see you from a positive perspective. Consider the following exchange and assume you are Mark.

> **MIKE:** I met Mark the other day. He told me he thinks you're really
> bright. In fact, he said you're one of the most capable problem
> solvers he has ever met.
> **SONJA:** Oh, really? He said that?
> **MIKE:** That's what he told me.

Sonja will more readily accept this compliment as related by Mike than if you (Mark) directly told her the same thing. Additionally, Mike feels free to tell Sonja exactly what you said, which you may or may not be socially allowed to say at the beginning stages of a relationship. Indirectly you, through Mike, allowed Sonja to compliment herself, which makes her feel good about herself, thus predisposing her to like you before you meet her for the first time or at the point in your relationship when she receives Mike's third-party compliment.

CASHING IN ON THIRD-PARTY COMPLIMENTS AT WORK

Beyond the dating landscape, I found third-party compliments to be very effective in the workplace. A case in point: Money to fund operations within the FBI is competitive; consequently, not every proposal gets funded. To improve the probability that my proposals would be approved I would employ the third-party-compliment strategy.

Several weeks before my proposal was scheduled to be reviewed by the newly appointed assistant director, I sought out the most notorious gossip in the office and casually mentioned to him that it was about time our field office got an assistant director who finally knew what he was doing. I also commented that the new assistant director was a clever man with keen insights into operational strategies. For gossips, the coin of the realm is information. In their eyes, they gain value by spreading information they hear to the individuals who would have interest in hearing it. Sure enough, the boss soon heard of my comments "through the grapevine." The assistant director was more likely to accept this compliment as sincere from a third-party individual than directly from me. Besides, I did not have access to the assistant director, as I was in the field at the time.

When the assistant director reviewed my proposals, he was predisposed to look at them more favorably because of his knowledge of how I viewed him. I had made him feel good about himself, a fulfillment of the Golden Rule of Friendship, and I had done it in a way that didn't arouse his suspicions. Third-party compliments are within normal behavioral parameters and pass a person's "territory scan" without arousing an alert. So I had nothing to lose. If my strategy failed, the downside risk was zero, because I would have lost the funding anyway. If the technique worked, the upside is successfully achieving what I wanted. As it turned out, most of my proposals were funded.

THIRD PARTY AND THE "PRIMACY EFFECT"

Words cannot change reality, but they can change how people *perceive* reality. Words create filters through which people view the world around them. A single word can make the difference between liking and disliking a person.

Consider this example: Your friend Calvin tells you about your new neighbor, Bill, whom you are meeting for the first time. Calvin says, "Your new neighbor, Bill, is not very trustworthy; in fact, when you shake hands, check your fingers to make sure he hasn't taken any." How are you going to view Bill when you first are introduced? The problem is you have already been encouraged to *prejudge* him as untrustworthy through what behavioral scientists refer to as the "primacy effect." If a friend describes the person you are about to meet for the first time as untrustworthy, you will be predisposed to view that person as untrustworthy, regardless of the person's actual level of trustworthiness. Thereafter, you will tend to view everything that person says or does as untrustworthy.

Conversely, say your friend Calvin tells you that your new neighbor, Bill, "is very friendly, gregarious, and has a great sense of humor . . . you're going to love him." How are you going to view Bill now? You will likely see Bill as friendly, regardless of his degree of friendliness.

Overcoming negative or positive perceptions you might have toward a specific individual because of what you were told by someone else (particularly if you respect and/or like that person) is difficult, but not impossible to achieve. The more times you meet the "untrustworthy" Bill and do not experience instances of untrustworthiness, the more likely you are to see him as trustworthy, thus overcoming the original negativity created by the primacy effect. However, you are less likely to give a person labeled "untrustworthy" a chance to prove the label wrong because your desire to see the person a second time will be reduced.

If you meet the "friendly" Bill several times and do not experience friendliness, then you will tend to excuse away the unfriendly behavior. Such excuses might include "He must be having a bad day" or "I must have caught him at a bad time." An unfriendly person initially described as friendly gains an advantage from the primacy effect because people tend to allow the unfriendly person multiple opportunities to demonstrate friendliness despite numerous displays of unfriendly behavior.

It is precisely because the primacy effect can be so powerful that we can use it as one of our tools for shaping friendships or getting people to see us as we want to be seen. What you are doing with the primacy effect is sending a message that will predispose somebody to see someone else in a way that you want them to be perceived.

TAKING THE PRIMACY EFFECT TO THE BANK

I often employed the primacy effect during interrogations of people suspected of committing crimes. I remember one case where we were interviewing a possible bank robber. There were two of us and the suspect sitting in the interrogation room. Early in the interview, my partner excused himself, saying he had to make a telephone call. Actually, his departure was part of our plan that allowed me to be alone with the suspect so I could speak with him privately.

I told the suspect, "You're lucky to have my partner on the job. He's honest and fair. He'll listen without prejudice to your side of the story." Then I sat back, waiting for my partner to return. A few moments later, before he actually returned, I added, "The thing about my partner—I guess he can afford to be fair. The guy's a human lie detector. I don't know how he does it, but he knows when someone is lying. No matter what the subject is or who is talking, the man can tell if someone is being dishonest." What I did through my last comment was to create a filter through which I wanted the suspect to view my partner. I employed the primacy effect to shape his assessment of my partner's skills.

When my partner returned to the room, he already knew that he was to remain silent until I asked the suspect, "Did you rob the bank?" If the man said, "No," my partner was instructed to look at the suspect like "You've got to be kidding" and give him a skeptical look.

So, what happened? I asked the guy, "Did you rob the bank?" and he said, "No." My partner responded by saying, "What?" with a skeptical look. And—this is the truth—the suspect took his hand, slapped it on the table, and said, "Damn, he's good!" and went on to confess to the crime.

BEWARE OF THE PRIMACY EFFECT IN BIASING YOUR OWN BEHAVIOR

Using the primacy effect is a great idea when you're using it to influence others, but be aware that it can cut both ways. If you're not careful, the primacy effect can cause you to be prejudicial in your own behavior toward others, leading to inaccurate and misleading beliefs about their behavior.

In my early days as an FBI agent, I fell victim to the primacy effect. I was given the task of interviewing a suspect who, my colleague informed me, had kidnapped a four-year-old girl. Before talking to the suspect, my thoughts were already filtered through my colleague's statement, and by the time I actually met the man, I had already made up my mind that he was the kidnapper. Consequently, everything the suspect said or did I viewed through my "filter" as an indication of guilt . . . despite ample evidence to the contrary.

The more pressure I put on the suspect, the more nervous he became, not because he was guilty, but because I did not believe him and he thought he would go to prison for something he didn't do. The more nervous the suspect became, the more it reinforced my initial belief that he was the kidnapper, and the more pressure I applied. It was no surprise that the interview spiraled out of control. In the end, I was embarrassed when the real kidnapper was caught.

The next time you conduct an interview, meet a new colleague, or buy a new product, think about how you came to form your opinion about that person or product. Chances are high that your opinions were formed by primacy.

The acceptance of employees who transfer from one office to another often depends on the reputation that precedes their arrival . . . just as you are convinced that the new brand of toothpaste you purchased has to be good because four out of five dentists recommended it.

The primacy effect is powerful. Use it wisely.

ASKING A FAVOR

Good old Ben Franklin, the guy on the hundred-dollar bill, observed that if he asked a colleague for a favor, the colleague liked him more than if he hadn't made the request. This phenomenon became known as (no surprise here) the Ben Franklin effect.

At first glance, this finding seems counterintuitive. Shouldn't you like the person more for doing you the favor than the other way around? It turns out, such is not the case. When a person does someone a favor, they feel good about themselves. The Golden Rule of Friendship states that if you make a person feel good about themselves, they will like you. Thus, asking someone to do you a favor is not all about you. It is also about the person doing you the favor.

A warning, however: Do not overuse this technique, because Ben Franklin also observed that "guests, like fish, begin to smell after three days." (As do people who ask too many favors!)

Returning to Ben's encounter with Vicki, he can use this "ask a favor" technique during his conversation with the young woman.

> **BEN:** It takes a lot of dedication and determination to commit to a project of that magnitude. (allowing Vicki to compliment herself)
> **VICKI:** Yeah. (thinking) I sure am dedicated and determined. I sacrificed a lot to get that mega-project done and I did a very good job if I may say so myself.
> **BEN:** Vicki, could you do me a favor and watch my drink while I go to the bathroom? (asks for a favor)
> **VICKI:** Sure, no problem.

Ben addressed Vicki by her first name (recall that people like the sound of their name and the fact that someone remembers it) and then asked her to do him a small favor. These small behaviors predispose Vicki to like Ben because people who do favors for others feel good about themselves.

COMBINING FRIENDSHIP TOOLS TO ENHANCE RELATIONSHIP EFFECTIVENESS

Depending on the circumstances, you might find yourself using one or a combination of several techniques presented in this book to make a new friend. The advantage of using several techniques together is the additional friend-making power such combined techniques provide. To illustrate, consider how using the primacy effect, Friendship Formula, and third-party introduction helped our military forces make friends out of people that might well be predisposed to be wary or downright hostile toward Americans.

Winning over the hearts and minds of civilians when you are a foreigner conducting military operations in their country can be a daunting assignment. Combat soldiers on foreign soil, by the very nature of their work, are forced to adopt a strategy voiced by General James "Mad Dog" Mattis, who said, "Be polite, be professional, but have a plan to kill everybody you meet." In other words, making friends out of potential enemies can be a trying task.

In an attempt to win over the Afghan people, I was a member of a team that was asked to "show our guys [American forces] how to be less threatening yet, at the same time, maintain their battlefield awareness."

So how do you go about making someone appear friendly when everything they wear appears threatening (battle gear, helmets, gun belts) and they are taught to scowl (their "game face") when dealing with the local populace? It's no wonder that when these soldiers come into a local village the native population takes one look, sees foe signals, and goes shields up.

This is what we told the military to do: Go into the villages with the same battle gear and a readiness to defend yourself if attacked but also do the following:

1. **Employ the Friendship Formula:** Spend some time in the village without really doing anything . . . just be there. This satisfies the

condition of proximity. Then, over time, increase the number (frequency) of visits to the village and the amount of time (duration) spent there. Finally, add intensity to the mix by giving the children of the village things they like (more on this in a moment).

2. **Send out "friend" rather than "foe" signals:** Keep your game face but put a mask over it; in other words, smile, don't scowl.

3. **Once the villagers are used to seeing you acting in a nonthreatening way, load up a truck with soccer balls and drive into the village where the children can see you.** What will happen? Because you're sending out friend signals, the children won't see you as a threat and, further, their curiosity will be aroused (intensity) and they'll approach the truck and ask, "Who are those balls all for?" The driver of the truck can tell the children, "They're for you!" Then give them away.

So, what happens? The kids like you. So when they see their parents, the kids serve as a third-party introduction on behalf of the Americans. They say, "I saw the Americans, they gave us soccer balls, and they are nice people." So now the parents see you through the primacy filter created by their children and they are more open to seeing you as a friend rather than as "the enemy."

If the Americans had simply come into the village without employing the Friendship Formula (no attempt to establish proximity, frequency, duration, and intensity), sending foe rather than friend signals and not using the primacy effect through third-party introductions, what do you think would have happened when the American forces told the village elders they weren't a threat? The Americans simply wouldn't have been believed. The soldiers would have been perceived as liars.

It is amazing how easy it is to influence people's behavior using these friendship tools. Alone or in combination, they allow you to make people feel better about themselves and, in turn, encourage them to make you feel better as well. When you employ the Golden Rule of Friendship, it encourages reciprocity: "If you make me happy, I want to make you happy." Even in onetime encounters, when you are interacting with a person you will probably never see again, you can witness this reciprocity in action.

THE CHOICE BETWEEN FLYING FIRST CLASS OR BEING GROUNDED FOR BEING GRUMPY

Several years ago, I had a layover in Frankfurt, Germany. I wasn't looking forward to the rest of my flight; I had the middle seat in coach and the scheduled flying time was eight hours. I certainly didn't want to board early, and with an hour to spare, I decided to put the time to good use. I pulled up every German word I could remember from my high school language class and walked over to the ticket agent. As I approached, I gave the major friend signals, the eyebrow flash, the smile, the head tilt. When I got to the counter, I said "Guten tag . . ." so we would have some "common ground" (see Chapter 4). He smiled at my amateur attempt to speak the language but returned the greeting, and then said in English, "Can I help you?"

I answered no but began to engage him in conversation. I used empathic statements to encourage him to speak and to make him feel good about himself. As the conversation progressed, spurred on by my brief empathic comments, he was doing almost all of the talking. He didn't notice this because people see the world as revolving around them and thus my behavior did not stray outside the human baseline and cause an "alert" reaction in his brain. I gave him an excuse to talk; in fact, I *encouraged* it and it made him feel good.

So now he likes me.

At the end of our "conversation," the agent asked me why I didn't board the plane. I told him that I had a middle seat and I wanted to spend as little time as possible jammed in there. That was it.

About twenty minutes later, the ticket agent made a final boarding call. As I walked to the air bridge, I heard the agent call out, "Herr Schafer." I stopped and the agent walked over to me. He asked if I had my boarding pass. I nodded and showed it to him. He took it and handed me a different pass.

"Enjoy your flight, Herr Schafer," he said.

I looked at the document and recognized I had been upgraded to a seat in business class. I said, "Thank you, sir, I really appreciate that."

"No problem, don't worry about it," he replied and waved me toward the plane.

Another time my plane was late and people were really angry. I was waiting in line at the boarding counter and the guy in front of me was so worked up he was yelling at the agent about how he was going to miss his connecting flight and yada, yada, yada. She told him there was nothing she could do but put him on the later flight that left at 5:30 p.m.

Then it was my turn. I walked up to the obviously flustered employee and didn't expect anything; I was only trying to make the agent's day better. She took the ticket I handed her and said, "Sorry, sir, you're going to miss your connecting flight. I can book you on a later plane leaving at five thirty p.m."

I looked her directly in the eyes and said wryly, "I don't think that's acceptable," mimicking the previous passenger. And as she looked back at me I added, "Can I yell at you now?" And she said no and mentioned the 5:30 p.m. flight again.

I repeated, "Can I yell at you now?" That's when she started giggling. I said, "When *can* I start yelling at you?" Both of us were now grinning and bantering back and forth. After about a minute of this she said, "You know what . . . I just found a seat on the two forty p.m. flight," and typed my name into the computer. I commented, "I'm just curious, I overheard you tell the previous customer that there were no seats available on the two forty p.m. flight." "There are no seats for people who yell at me. Do you want to yell at me now?" she said. "No, ma'am," I sheepishly replied. "Thank you."

The interesting thing is I didn't walk up to the agent with the idea of getting an earlier flight; I just wanted to make her feel better. But when you make other people feel good, good things often end up happening to you.

I've used this "get out your frustration" approach many times with all kinds of customer service representatives and it never fails to assuage their anger and put them in a better mood. During one of my foreign trips, a group of Chinese passengers missed their connecting flight to Hong Kong and they were giving the gate agent a hard time. She was trying to be nice to them, to no avail. Eventually, the police were called to deal with the situation because the passengers were causing such a ruckus.

I had the dubious "honor" of being the next person in line to speak with the ticket agent. So I walked up to the podium and said, "Looks like you had a little trouble here today." (empathic statement)

Her answer was short and curt, "Yeah."

"Looks like you're frustrated," I observed. (empathic statement)

"Yeah, I'm very frustrated that I can't yell at those people. I can't get rid of my frustration."

I gave the agent a sympathetic nod of the head. "Ma'am, I'll tell you what I can do. I'm going to go back to the rope at the beginning of the line and then I'm going to walk up to you again and say something about your service and I want you to let me have it. Get it out of your system."

The woman looked a bit leery but said, "Okay."

So I went back to the roped area, turned around, and walked back up to the counter. I pointed my finger at the agent and said, "I didn't like the way you treated those people. You were rude, inconsiderate and . . ." I got no further, as the agent told me to shut up and then she let me have it. I mean, all that pent-up frustration was boiling just below the surface and now she had a chance to get it out!

After she finished her tirade, I told the woman I was extremely angry and disappointed.

The agent caught her breath and asked, "What would assuage your anger, sir? Would an upgrade help?"

I nodded affirmatively. "Yes, I think that would help."

"All right, I'll give you an upgrade to first class," she declared.

I said, "Thank you." And then we both started laughing.

As my flight was boarding the agent actually came on the plane and thanked me for "making her day."

This kind of thing happens to me all the time. People do things for me. I don't ask for favors, not even a hint. What I have discovered is when you make other people feel good about themselves (the Golden Rule of Friendship) you not only get people to like you, there's also a collateral benefit; they want to make you feel good as well. I see it every day. I experience it time after time.

Here's another air travel experience to illustrate this "benefit." I was in Moline, Illinois, when my flight was canceled. This is *not* exactly a great place to get stranded. People were ranting and swearing. The woman directly in front of me in line was waving her arms and screaming at the ticket agent, who was trying her best not to lose it. She said, "The next flight I can put you on, ma'am, is tomorrow morning." Upon hearing that information, the woman swore even louder and stomped off.

It was my turn. I walked up to the still-simmering agent and said, "Wow, that lady was pretty intense." (empathic statement)

"She was," she agreed. "I didn't like her."

I replied, "Well, I couldn't help but overhear there isn't a flight until tomorrow morning."

And she said, "No, there's another flight in an hour."

I started to say something, but she interrupted, "I don't like her. She waits until tomorrow. I like you. You get on today."

UTILIZING FRIENDSHIP TOOLS: THE SKY'S THE LIMIT

I have one last flying story that should, without a doubt, confirm that the friendship tools do indeed work. I was on the last flight out of town, with a ninety-minute layover, so I decided this would be a great opportunity to interview some airline personnel and get their thoughts about the relationship between customer service and customer behavior.

There was a single employee still working the ticket counter. I headed her way, using friendship signals as I approached. I needed a "hook" that would pique her curiosity. When she asked me where I was going I said I was going to Chicago to finish up an investigation. She asked what I did for a living and I said, "I work for the FBI." That got her attention and she asked what kind of FBI work I did.

"I train people," I replied.

"Train people in what?" she asked.

"To be nice to people . . . to get things they don't deserve." (curiosity hook)

She laughed. "Like what?"

"Like an upgrade."

We were both grinning at this point. I said: "If I walked up to you and asked for an upgrade, would you do it?"

"No," she exclaimed. "People do that all the time and I say no."

"So do you ever give upgrades?"

"Yeah, to people I like."

Case closed.

Whether you're in Afghanistan or Atlanta, the techniques in this book work, alone or in combination. When you use them, you maximize your chances for making friends, even with those individuals who start out seeing you as an enemy. And, who knows, you just might get an upgrade in the process.

4

THE LAWS OF ATTRACTION

If you go looking for a friend, you're going to find they're very
scarce. If you go out to be a friend, you'll find them everywhere.
—ZIG ZIGLAR

In this chapter I will give you some additional tools for your friendship
toolbox: the "Laws of Attraction." These "laws" describe certain factors
that, when present, serve to heighten the probability that two individuals will be drawn to each other and experience a positive outcome
when they interact. Because these laws play a critical role in shaping
human relationships, if you can incorporate them into your own relationship interactions they will provide additional ways for you to make
friends with the people you meet.

Think of each Law of Attraction as a tool to enhance your relationship effectiveness. You don't have to use them all to achieve your
friendship objectives; in fact, you shouldn't, because some of the laws
are not congruent with your personal characteristics or are designed to
work with long- versus short-term relationships (a onetime encounter
with a sales clerk as opposed to the development of a lasting friendship). Pick the ones that suit you the best and go with those when
interacting with persons of interest.

THE LAW OF SIMILARITY ("COMMON GROUND")

People who share the same perspectives, attitudes, and activities tend to develop close relationships. The adage "Birds of a feather flock together" has merit. People are attracted to other people who share their interests. The need to avoid cognitive dissonance may explain why this is true. Dissonance occurs when people hold two opposing ideas or beliefs. This real or perceived difference creates anxiety.

People holding similar views reinforce one another and thereby enhance the likelihood of mutual attraction. Similarity also increases the probability that like-minded individuals will meet again. Mutual reinforcement maintains or elevates self-esteem, which leads to a greater sense of well-being and happiness.

People who share the same principles and beliefs rarely experience dissonance and feel secure in the sameness they share with each other. These individuals tend to experience less conflict because they perceive the world in similar ways. Sameness leads to the perception of greater happiness and a feeling of being understood. When people first meet, even the perception of sameness will increase mutual attraction.

CUT FROM THE SAME CLOTH

Early in my career, I noticed that most FBI agents looked alike and shared the same views. This can be explained by the psychological principle of similarity and attraction. FBI agents sitting on hiring boards tended to hire new agents who were most like themselves. When the newly hired agents gained enough seniority to participate in the hiring process, they also unconsciously selected individuals who were most like them. Over the decades, the FBI became populated by agents who shared the same views, dressed alike, and looked alike.

With the advent of affirmative action, more women and minorities were included in the FBI ranks. When these individuals gained seniority and sat on hiring boards, they tended to select applicants who were most like themselves. Based on the psychological principle of similarity and attraction, current FBI agents as well as most U.S. businesses more closely reflect the diversity of the American population today.

Commonalities connect people. Finding common ground quickly establishes rapport and a fertile environment for developing friendships. Aristotle wrote, "We like those who resemble us, and are engaged in the same pursuits. . . . We like those who desire the same things as we [do]." Developing relationships is easy if you can find common ground with another person. People automatically think that other people think like they do, especially when meeting an individual for the first time. Thus when you first meet another individual, you can build on this predisposition by seeking things you have in common.

When assessing someone from a distance, look for potential commonalities. These can be found, for example, in the way people dress. An individual wearing a shirt embossed with a sports team logo suggests that he or she has at least a passing interest in the team. Even if you don't favor the same team, you can use the information to start a conversation, particularly if you have any interest in sports.

What a person is *doing* can also serve as a basis for establishing common ground. If a person is walking a dog, reading a book, or pushing a baby carriage it provides you with valuable information for identifying potential conversation openers and/or similar interests.

Tattoos can also provide clues to people's interests. Tattoos are permanent. Most of the time when people get one, they put some thought into the type of tattoo they want and where it should be placed on their bodies. A small tattoo of a marijuana leaf placed on a prominent part of a person's body projects a strongly held attitude. If you are strongly opposed to the use of weed, it might be best to look elsewhere for a friend who shares more compatible beliefs.

The way a person interacts with others can also provide clues to their personal disposition. A person who slumps in a chair and does not easily interact with others has a different disposition than someone who sits upright and easily engages those around them. If your personality differs significantly from the person across from you, the probability of developing a close relationship significantly diminishes.

After you make initial contact with a person, listening to what they say can provide you with additional clues to their likes and dislikes. Make a conscious effort to direct the conversation toward the things you have in common. Talking about shared experiences, interests, hobbies, jobs, or any number of other common topics enhances rapport and the development of friendships. Here are a few illustrations of how quickly you can find common ground with other individuals.

CONTEMPORANEOUS EXPERIENCE

A contemporaneous experience means that you and the person you just met share the same interests or attitudes. For example, if you spot someone wearing a shirt with a Chicago White Sox logo and you are a White Sox fan, then you share a contemporaneous interest in that team. However, just because someone is wearing a White Sox shirt does not automatically mean he or she is a White Sox fan. In addition to building rapport, empathic statements can be used to explore observations or hypotheses you may develop regarding the person you just met. Consider the following conversation:

BRYAN: Hi, my name is Bryan. What's yours?
CHRISTINE: Christine.
BRYAN: So you must be a White sox fan. (empathic statement)
CHRISTINE: I've been a Sox fan all of my life.
BRYAN: Me too.

By using an empathic statement, Bryan learned that both he and Christine were passionate about the White Sox. Once common ground has been established, Bryan can now focus on that topic and the conversation will flow naturally. If Brian is not a Sox fan, he could retreat to their shared general interest in baseball, as in this exchange:

BRYAN: Hi, my name is Bryan. What's yours?

CHRISTINE: Christine.

BRYAN: So you must be a White Sox fan. (empathic statement)

CHRISTINE: I've been a Sox fan all my life.

BRYAN: I like baseball, but I'm a Cubs fan.

CHRISTINE: Oh, I don't follow minor-league baseball.

(Note: It's obvious that Christine, besides having a sense of humor, has disdain for her favorite team's crosstown rival!) Once it has been established that Christine and Bryan share an interest in baseball but root for different teams, Bryan could use that information to spark a lively conversation on the pros and cons of each ball club.

People who share the same hometowns can quickly build friendships, especially when they meet outside those geographical boundaries. Shared job interests, political positions, religious beliefs, mutual friends, and similar experiences are good topics to explore for common ground.

If you are having a difficult time finding contemporaneous common ground, talk about music. As mentioned earlier, the one thing that most people have in common with each other is music. Music is a neutral topic that most people are willing to talk about, even if their listening tastes differ.

TEMPORAL EXPERIENCES

Experiences shared across time, such as attendance at the same school, military service, or living in the same area, enhance opportunities for making friends. You may not have shared the experiences at the same time, but you can reach across time to seek common ground.

VICARIOUS EXPERIENCES

A vicarious experience occurs when you live out a lifestyle or activity through the revelations of another person. You can use vicarious experiences to establish common ground with another person even when, in reality, you know very little about the subject matter being discussed. This approach is particularly effective because it allows your person of interest to talk about themselves and something they most likely are interested in. This makes them feel good about themselves, and because you are the one providing the impetus for that feeling, you are seen in a positive light (the Golden Rule of Friendship in action). This is a favorite technique for salespeople to use because they can find common ground with a customer even when they don't know much about what the customer is talking about. Here is an example:

CAR SALESPERSON: What do you do for a living?

CUSTOMER: I'm a baker.

CAR SALESPERSON: Really? My father was a baker.

The car salesperson doesn't have to know anything about being a baker because his father was a baker. You can use the same technique to seek common ground when you meet someone for the first time.

AUDREY: Where do you work?

SUSAN: I'm a financial planner.

AUDREY: Interesting. My sister is an accountant.

Most of us have family members or extended family members who are employed in the same or similar occupations as the people we speak with. In Audrey's case, her sister is an accountant, which is a similar field to financial planning. If you don't have a family member or relative working in the same or similar field as your person of interest, think of a friend who is. Using the technique of vicarious experiences can pay dividends whenever you are trying to establish a relationship. Exercise caution, however: Do not lie to the person you are meeting for the first time. If your relationship blossoms, then the truth may be revealed. Broken trust, especially occurring at the beginning of a relationship, can quickly turn off the Like Switch.

THE LAW OF MISATTRIBUTION

Sometimes making friends is simply a matter of being in the right place at the right time. When people feel good about themselves and do not attribute the good feeling to a specific cause, they tend to associate the cause of that good feeling with the person who is physically close to them at the time. If you happen to be that person, you're going to benefit and be liked not for anything you did but because of the "misattribution." In a sense, what we have here is a case of collateral benefit rather than collateral damage.

Consider this example. When people exercise, their brains release endorphins. The release of endorphins gives these individuals a nonspecific sense of well-being. Since the effect of the endorphins is not directly attributed to exercise, the good feeling tends to be linked to another person, if one happens to be nearby. Think of it as the "collateral benefit." Since that good feeling is "misattributed" to the nearby person, he or she is subconsciously seen as the cause of the good feeling and, therefore, appears more attractive.

How can you use this information to get someone to like you? Actually, you can take advantage of this phenomenon in a number of ways. If you are in shape, you can arrange a meeting around an exercise activity, join a fitness club, or participate in sports (organized walks or runs—"fun" or otherwise—provide a great opportunity for misattribution to work).

USING MISATTRIBUTION TO GET A DATE: "EXERCISE" YOUR OPTIONS

Let's assume you want to ask a person of interest on a date and want to increase your chances of getting a positive response. Using the Law of Misattribution might do the trick. If you discover that the person you want to meet jogs or exercises regularly, arrange for a "chance meeting" during or shortly after he or she completes their exercise regimen. The encounter does not have to include a verbal exchange. Simply sharing the same space can induce misattribution and will make you appear more attractive. If both you and your person of interest work out, try to arrange your workout time to coincide with theirs. Being nearby during the exercise will produce the collateral benefits already discussed. If the person you want to meet is a coworker who exercises, be in the vicinity of their office or cubicle when they return from their physical activity. Likewise, if you know the person you are interested in goes to a coffee shop every day after his or her exercise routine, make sure you are present at the shop at the time they arrive.

What you are trying to do is take advantage of the misattribution principle and increase your attractiveness in the eyes of the other person by being associated with the good feelings that come about through the release of exercise-related endorphins. To accomplish this objective, you need to be in close physical proximity to the person during or soon after the endorphins are released.

Surprisingly, misattribution also occurs when people experience frightening events or traumatic experiences. People feel closer relationships with others with whom they share the same frightening or traumatic experiences. Soldiers who survive harrowing battles form deep bonds with their comrades in arms. Police officers develop close relationships with their partners after they share traumatic experiences. In the days when it was allowed (or tolerated), "hazing" of sorority and fraternity pledges brought those who survived the ordeal closer together and often created lasting friendships.

A scary movie can evoke the same response. If you go with some-one to a scary movie, the shared frightful experience triggers misattribu-tion, which in turn increases attraction between the moviegoers. For that reason, arranging to see a scary movie is ideal for a first date be-cause it increases the chance for mutual attraction in a new relationship. Likewise, if your long-term relationship with someone is waning, go skydiving or bungee jumping, ride a roller coaster, or pursue other ac-tivities that create the perception of danger. The shared experience will bring you closer together and reinvigorate your friendship or romance.

THE LAW OF CURIOSITY

Curiosity can be used as a "hook" to increase intensity (Friendship Formula) and pique a person's interest in you. It is an effective way to make friends. All creatures capable of more than a mere mechanical response to stimuli are curious. It is a biological imperative, driven by the need for self-preservation, reproduction, and greed. Humans want to know everything: who we are, who others are, where we came from and when, what's on the other side of the hill, and the shape, size, composition, longevity, and distance of everything from quarks to the universe.

In order to survive, animals above the primitive level must under-stand the niche in which they live. In addition, they must discover any changes in that niche to be able to respond to them appropriately and effectively. Since it is personal survival that the individual is concerned about, the changes in the immediate vicinity—those that will affect him or her personally—are the most important.

The most effective way to discover changes is to go looking for them. Thus, a noise in the bushes draws the cat's attention, followed by a slow, stealthy stalk (no sense charging into trouble). The noise might be prey, it might be a predator, or it could be the automatic sprinkler coming on. This curiosity can lead to a meal, a timely escape, or an inadvertent bath. In any case, it must be investigated.

When you behave in a manner that produces curiosity in another person, it significantly increases the chances that individual will want to interact with you in an attempt to satisfy their curiosity. Thus, a "curiosity hook" becomes an effective tool to meet a person of interest and develop a friendship. I used the Law of Curiosity regularly as an FBI agent to enhance my recruiting effectiveness of foreign nationals. At one point during my FBI career, a North Korean moved into my jurisdiction. There was reason to suspect he was an agent for his government and I was given the assignment to try to get the guy to become a double agent. I knew if I simply walked into the photo shop where he worked and said, "I'm Jack Schafer with the FBI, can we talk?" the guy would have probably panicked and bolted from the store. So I decided to use a curiosity hook to try to reel him in.

First, I went into his store when I knew he wasn't there and left him a note saying, "Sorry I missed you," and signed it, "Jack Schafer." I did this on three separate occasions. On the third visit, I added my phone number to the note I left behind. All these messages were designed to pique the North Korean's curiosity. Who is this Jack Schafer and why does he want to contact me? This was what I wanted the North Korean to be wondering, hoping that each new note would further arouse his curiosity. It worked. After receiving the note with my phone number, he called me and I was able to arrange a meeting with him later in the week.

THE LAW OF RECIPROCITY

Social norms dictate that if someone gives you something or performs a favor for you, large or small, then you are predisposed to return the gesture in like kind or in greater measure. Organizations take advantage of this law by mailing people return address labels, calendars, or other small trinkets along with a request for a donation. People are more likely to comply because they received something first and feel obligated to reciprocate in kind.

The Law of Reciprocity is a very effective tool for making friends. When you smile at someone, that person feels obligated to return the smile. A smile signals acceptance and liking. People like to be liked. The principle of reciprocity is triggered when people become aware that someone else likes them. Once a person discovers that another person likes them, they find that person more attractive. People tend to reciprocate the same feelings others extend to them. Reciprocity produces the most dramatic results when both parties to the interaction form good first impressions of or have natural feelings toward the other person.

Not "You're Welcome," But . . .

The next time someone thanks you for something, don't say, "You're welcome." Instead, say, "I know you'd do the same thing for me." This response invokes reciprocity. The other person is now predisposed to help you when you ask them for a favor.

THE LAW OF SELF-DISCLOSURE

Reciprocity is also linked with openness in communication. Individuals who disclose more personal information with other people are more likely to receive a similar level of personal information in return. This phenomenon is further enhanced if the people who are communicating have shared interests.

Self-disclosure promotes attraction. People feel a sense of closeness to others who reveal their vulnerabilities, innermost thoughts, and facts about themselves. The sense of closeness increases if the disclosures are emotional rather than factual. This is partly due to the intensity of such disclosures, which positively affects the likability of the person making them.

Disclosures that are too general reduce the sense of openness, thus reducing the feeling of closeness and likability. Disclosures that are too intimate often highlight character and personality flaws of the person, thus decreasing likability. People who make intimate disclosures too early in a relationship are often perceived as insecure, which further decreases likability. Thus, if you are meeting someone who you would like to have as a long-term friend or significant other, you should be careful about making your most intimate disclosures in the early stages of the relationship.

Self-disclosure is a two-step process. First, a person has to make a self-disclosure that is neither too general nor too intimate. Second, the self-disclosure must be received with empathy, caring, and respect. A negative response made to a genuine self-disclosure can instantly terminate a relationship.

Self-disclosures are often reciprocal. When one person makes self-disclosures, the listener is more likely to reciprocate by making similar ones. The exchange of personal information creates a sense of intimacy in relationships. A relationship in which one person makes personal self-disclosures while the other person continues to make superficial disclosures is not progressing and is likely to end.

WANT TO INCREASE THE LONGEVITY OF YOUR RELATIONSHIP?

Use the Hansel and Gretel approach. Hansel and Gretel, in the classic fairy tale, set off into the woods, and to ensure that they can find their way back, they leave a trail of bread crumbs along the way. I recommend you use the "bread crumb" approach to distributing information about yourself. Relationships tend to wane over time. To increase the longevity of these liaisons, release self-disclosures over an extended period of time.

Once somebody finds a person whom they can trust, they are often tempted to open the emotional floodgates—telling too much too quickly—overwhelming their partner in the process. Disclosures should be made over a long period of time to ensure that the relationship slowly increases in intensity and closeness. A steady trickle of information, like Hansel and Gretel's bread crumbs dropped one piece at a time, increases the longevity of the relationship because each partner continually feels the closeness that comes with a steady stream of self-disclosures.

Mutual self-disclosures create trust. People who make personal disclosures become vulnerable to the person to whom the disclosures are made. Mutual self-disclosures create a safety zone because each person has exposed their vulnerabilities and tends to protect all the disclosures to avoid mutual embarrassment resulting from a breach of trust.

Social network users tend to rely more on self-disclosures to create a sense of closeness because they do not receive verbal and nonverbal cues that would be otherwise exchanged in face-to-face communications. The veracity of information exchanged online is suspect, thus forcing individuals online to spend more time verifying information about each other. Once veracity has been established, the lack of a physical presence increases the probability of more intimate disclosures online, which in turn leads to the illusion of a closer relationship.

THE LAW OF PERSONAL ATTRACTIVENESS

Attractiveness is a tangible benefit for those who possess it. Even though it is said that "beauty is in the eye of the beholder," the reality is that every culture has widely accepted standards of what is "attractive." Although these standards might change over time, most members of the culture internalize the prevailing, current norm of what is considered beautiful or handsome.

Attractiveness is not "absolute." You can become more attractive if you are willing to put some effort into achieving such a goal. According to Gordon Wainwright, author of *Teach Yourself Body Language,* anyone can increase their attractiveness to others if they maintain good eye contact, act upbeat, dress well, add a dash of color to their wardrobe, and listen well. Wainwright also stresses the importance of posture and bearing and suggests that for one week you stand straight, tuck in your stomach, hold your head high, and smile at those you meet. From the results of many experiments, Wainwright predicts you will begin to be treated with more warmth and respect and start attracting more people to you.

Attractive people are seen as having more positive attributes. Good-looking men and women are generally judged to be more talented, kind, honest, and intelligent than their less attractive counterparts. Controlled studies show that people go out of their way to help attractive people, of the same or opposite sex, because they want to be liked and accepted by good-looking people.

Attractiveness can have financial implications. On a scale of less attractive to more attractive, less attractive people earn 5 to 10 percent less than individuals of average looks, who in turn earned 3 to 8 percent less than those deemed good-looking. Studies also show attractive students get more attention and higher evaluations from their teachers. Good-looking patients get more personalized care from their doctors, and attractive criminals receive lighter sentences than less attractive lawbreakers. One need look no further than Hollywood to see the impact beautiful movie stars have on our system of justice.

THE LAW OF HUMOR

Individuals who use humor in social encounters are perceived as more likable. In addition, both trust and attraction increase when a lighthearted approach is used during person-to-person interactions. Judicious use of humor can reduce anxiety and establish a relaxed mood that helps a relationship to develop more rapidly. A slightly risqué joke can help to escalate the level of intimacy in a flirtatious conversation. Of course, as is the case with any verbal communication, the speaker must be sure that the words, or, in this case, the humor used, is appropriate and will not be perceived as offensive by the listener.

The added benefit to using humor is that laughing causes a release of endorphins, which makes you feel good about yourself, and, according to the Golden Rule of Friendship, if you make people feel good about themselves, they will like you. A woman who likes a particular man will laugh at his jokes, no matter how lame, more often and with more gusto than she will laugh at jokes told by a man in whom she has little romantic interest. This phenomenon further supports the Golden Rule of Friendship.

THE LAW OF FAMILIARITY

The more we meet and interact with people, the more likely we are to become friends. Behavioral scientist Leon Festinger and two colleagues studied relationships in a small two-story apartment building. They found that neighbors were most likely to be friends. The residents who were least likely to be friends were on separate floors. Those residents near ground-floor staircases and mailboxes had friends on both floors.

The Law of Familiarity points to the importance of **proximity** (a component of the Friendship Formula) in affecting relationships. People who share the same physical space are more likely to be attracted to one another. Proximity predisposes one person to like another person, even before they are formally introduced. Classroom seating charts can be good predictors of which students will become attracted to one another. In my class, I've observed that students who sit in the vicinity of each other are more likely to become friends as opposed to students who sit on opposite sides of the classroom. Likewise, in professional settings, romances and friendships can be predicted based on who sits next to whom.

The old adage "Absence makes the heart grow fonder" is not necessarily true. The farther apart an engaged couple live from one another, the greater the probability their engagement will not survive.

THE LAW OF ASSOCIATION

When people associate in large groups, people on the outside of the group tend to assess individual members of the group based on their overall impression of the total group. So, when a less attractive individual wants to be seen as more attractive, he or she should associate with a group of attractive people. Conversely, an attractive person may be viewed as less attractive if he or she is in the company of unattractive people.

It seems that adult life doesn't change all that much from high school. If you want to be "popular," you still need to hang out with the popular people. In a business situation this means always try to "friend up," not down. Who you associate with matters. If you want to be seen as successful, you need to hang out with successful people.

The Law of Association works differently when, instead of looking at how one person's attractiveness is affected by being in a large group, the focus is on how people are compared and perceived when they are with just one or two others. In these circumstances, if a person wants to appear as more attractive, he or she should be seen in the company of a *less* attractive individual. This phenomenon helps explain the behavior of prospective buyers when they visit model homes. They leave their own homes, which are satisfactory in the morning. After spending all day looking at model homes, they return to what they now perceive as an unattractive home. Their house becomes less attractive because they compare it with the more elegant models they recently viewed.

THE LAW OF SELF-ESTEEM

People like to associate with individuals who display high levels of self-esteem. Thus, such individuals have an easier time attracting others and making friends. Individuals with high levels of self-esteem are also self-confident and comfortable with being the center of attention.

They are also comfortable with self-disclosure, which is a building block in creating close personal relationships.

To people with high self-esteem, rejection is part of life, not a reflection on their self-worth. Conversely, people with low self-esteem are reluctant to disclose personal information. Their inability to make self-disclosures serves as a defense mechanism to guard against criticism and rejection. Self-disclosure is the path to closer personal relationships; unfortunately, for a person with low self-esteem it is the "path less traveled." Ironically, it is the fear of self-disclosure that can lead to the rejection a person with low self-esteem is trying to avoid.

A fine line exists between self-esteem and arrogance. Arrogant people often feel superior and set themselves apart from others. For this reason, they are perceived as being "different." As a result, the probability of mutual attraction is significantly reduced, except with other arrogant individuals who share their attitudes and behavior.

In American society, men and women often define self-worth in different ways. In the most general terms men derive a sense of self-esteem and social status from their ability or potential ability to earn money, impress women, and own high-priced objects like nice cars and real estate. Conversely, though the American marketplace is experiencing a remarkable shift with more women graduating from college than men, it is still true that many women gain a sense of self-esteem and social status through displays of physical beauty, youthfulness, and relationships with others. These differences are evident when game show hosts ask contestants to briefly describe themselves. Male contestants usually describe themselves by their occupations ("I am an electrician"), whereas, women characterize themselves by their relationships ("I am a wife and mother of three children"). As more women work outside the home, they, too, may begin to identify with their professions instead of their relationships.

When it comes to establishing short- or long-term romantic relationships, high-status women (young and physically attractive) tend to couple with high-status men (high earning potential and disposable income). This pattern of mate selection parallels typical mating strategies. Men select young and physically attractive women to ensure procreation and women select high earners with disposable incomes to achieve the security necessary to raise children. Men with lower self-esteem tend to select women who are less physically attractive and women with lower self-esteem tend to select mates who are lower income earners and with less disposable income.

Sometimes lower-status individuals will try to "fake" higher status in an attempt to establish relationships with people "out of their league." For example, a man might pretend to be a high-income earner by lavishing a woman with expensive gifts, driving a car he cannot afford, and spending money he does not have. This strategy, although effective in the short run, usually ends catastrophically as time passes and the suitor, unable to afford his ruse, is unmasked and his true worth revealed.

DON'T BANK ON IT

One of my students told me of a common ruse that he and his friends often employ on nights out. On the way to a bar, they will stop by a large bank's ATM and pick through dropped receipts until they find ones that have especially large balances printed on them. These they pocket for later. Then, if the student or one of his friends meets a girl who is above his financial standing, he will casually write his phone number on the back of the purloined receipt—creating the illusion that he is a wealthy man.

THE LAW OF AVAILABILITY (SCARCITY)

People are attracted to individuals and things they cannot readily obtain. In the case with things, people are more attracted to a coveted object because it is out of their reach. When the object of desire is finally gained, the attraction for the object rapidly diminishes. Christmas presents provide a good example of this phenomenon. Toys children wanted all year long are discarded several days after they are retrieved from gift boxes under the tree. The Law of Availability also holds true for human interaction, particularly in the early stages of a developing relationship. The dating rule your mom swore by has scientific merit. An individual should not always make him or herself readily available to the person they are targeting for a longer-term relationship. A certain level of unavailability will make you more of a mystery and a challenge.

Remember Vladimir, the spy discussed in the Introduction? As you may recall, after days of reading the newspaper and sitting silently with Vladimir, he asked me why I kept coming back day after day. I folded the newspaper over, looked at him, and said, "Because I want to talk to you." Then I immediately returned the newspaper to the upright position and continued reading, ignoring him. This action further increased Vladimir's curiosity and created scarcity. Finally, Vladimir made up his mind to talk to me and I ignored him, increasing Vladimir's drive to talk to me.

INCREASED RESTRAINT INCREASES DRIVE

Parents are fully aware of this law! If you tell your children not to do something, they want to do it all the more. My own daughter went through a teenage phase of testing her mom and me. She once brought home a young man to meet us. He had four-inch-high gelled prongs that stood atop his head, tattoos covering most of his exposed skin, and a motorcycle in our driveway. I cordially greeted him without saying what I really felt about him or how disappointed I was with my daughter's choice of companion.

The next day, my daughter asked me what I thought of the young man. I wanted to command her never to see him again, but I knew that if I increased restraint, she would be that much more motivated to continue to date him. Instead, I chose the following strategy. I told my daughter that her mother and I raised her to make good judgments and that we trusted her decisions. If she felt the young man was a good person to have in her life, we would support her decision.

I never saw him again.

Fast-forward ten years. My daughter is now twenty-six years old. We sat in the kitchen reminiscing about her teen years. To my surprise, she brought up the young man. She admitted that she brought him home to make her mom and me mad for some now forgotten transgression we committed. She further admitted that when I told her that I trusted her judgment and knew she would make the right decision, her conscience panged. She knew he was wrong for her and that she was wrong to bring him home to spite us. She commented that it was ironic that she intended to make us mad but, in the end, she was the one who felt guilty. It took ten years to know if my strategy worked or not. I was relieved to know that it did.

THE LAW OF THE ROCKY ROAD

When two people meet and do not immediately like one another, especially in a romantic context, and then bond at a later time, they form a closer relationship than if they had hit it off immediately. This phenomenon is frequently highlighted in "romcom" (romantic comedy) movies. In the usual scenario, a man meets a woman. The man does not like the woman and the woman doesn't like the man. Before the film ends, they become romantically involved. A romantic rocky road often leads to a more intense romantic relationship.

A NEW STRATEGY TO BUTTERING UP THE BOSS: BUTTERING DOWN THE BOSS

I recall a time when I was assigned to a new supervisor. Instead of welcoming her with open arms, as did the rest of my squad mates, I purposefully remained distant and displayed neutral to slightly negative body language. Gradually, with each conversation we had, I began to display more positive nonverbal cues. I completed the turnaround several months later by telling her I thought she was a good supervisor and respected her strong managerial skills. From that day forward, we formed a closer relationship than if I had immediately accepted her. This closer relationship provided me with a distinct advantage when I asked for scarce investigative resources, time off, and other favors.

THE LAW OF PERSONALITY

There are literally hundreds of personality "types" or "characteristics" that have been identified in scientific and popular literature. They refer to consistent behavioral patterns exhibited by an individual in his or her everyday behavior. When somebody says, "that individual just isn't my type," they might be commenting on the person's physical appearance or strongly held beliefs (for example, religious or political). However, in many cases they are referring to the individual's personality, which is incongruent with their own.

Two pervasive personality types, extroversion and introversion, are of particular interest when it comes to personal interaction and the development of both short- and long-term relationships.

Extroverts, as compared to introverts, appear more attractive because they are seen as gregarious and self-confident. Prior to entering into any type of relationship, knowing whether the person you want to meet tends toward extroversion or introversion is useful information as it will give you an idea of what types of behavior you can expect to encounter.

If you are an extrovert and the person you want to meet is an introvert, expect to see some inherent differences in the way each of you perceives the world. Extroverts get their energy from being with other people and seek stimulation from their environments. Extroverts often speak spontaneously without thinking. They do not hesitate to use a trial-and-error method to arrive at a decision. Conversely, introverts expend energy when they engage socially and seek alone time to recharge their batteries. Introverts seek stimulation from within and seldom speak without thinking. They also carefully weigh options before making decisions.

Extroverts maintain a wide variety of relationships; however, those relationships tend to be relatively shallow. Introverts, on the other hand, have few relationships, but they are characterized by greater depth. Introverts who date extroverts typically seek a closer relationship to which extroverts are less willing to commit. This inability to reach a mutually satisfying level of commitment highlights dissimilarity, which ultimately reduces mutual attraction.

Extroverts use stream of consciousness to communicate. What they think, they say. This spontaneity often gets extroverts into trouble, particularly with introverts who think before they speak and are more easily embarrassed by what they consider to be personal information when it is blurted out by an extroverted companion. If you are an introvert who is thinking of becoming involved with an extrovert, be prepared for the unexpected when it comes to the words that come tumbling out of their mouth.

Generally, introverts and extroverts behave differently in social situations. Extroverts tend to be more outgoing when they don't know many people. Introverts, on the other hand, tend to feel uncomfortable in large groups of unfamiliar people. However, when introverts are in the company of friends or are comfortable with their surroundings, they can become as outgoing as extroverts (for a while, at least).

One method to determine if a person is an extrovert is to begin a sentence and deliberately pause for a few seconds. Extroverts will generally complete the sentence for you. Introverts will not. The same method can be used to determine if you have established rapport with an introvert. When introverts are comfortable with the people they are with, they will often complete sentences in the same manner in which extroverts do. The difference in the use of this method is that you can identify extroverts even if you don't know that the person you are speaking with is an introvert or an extrovert. To test rapport with an introvert, you must first determine that the person you are talking with is an introvert.

I recall a case I spent months investigating. Sufficient personal and biographical information was painstakingly gathered to determine what type of personality the suspect possessed. Based on that information, I custom-designed an investigative strategy to dovetail with the suspect's personality. The key to the success of the operation was our secretary. Her assignment was to make a telephone call to the suspect that would initiate the operation. I rehearsed with the secretary until she was comfortable with her role. She made the telephone call but the suspect did not immediately take the bait. I encouraged her to engage the suspect in casual conversation to reassure him. The conversation became very casual and the suspect relaxed, and unfortunately so did the secretary. The suspect asked the secretary where she worked. She blurted out, "I work for the FBI." Thus ended the undercover operation. In true extroverted fashion, the secretary spoke without thinking.

PERSONALITY AND PURCHASES

If you are a salesperson, you might want to consider if your customer is an extrovert or an introvert before making your pitch. Be sure to allow your introverted customers time to think about your sales proposal. Introverts take in information, mull it over, and then come to a decision. Pressing introverts to reach a quick decision may force them to say no because they are not comfortable making immediate decisions. Conversely, extroverts can be pressured to some degree to buy your product "right now" because they are more comfortable making impulsive decisions.

Rarely do people exhibit entirely extroverted or introverted characteristics. Personality traits fall somewhere along a continuum. Some people actually exhibit almost equal extroverted and introverted characteristics; however, most people do have a preference for one or the other, and behave accordingly.

Introverts can act like extroverts when required to do so. If, for example, an introvert has a job that requires them to be outgoing and gregarious, they can do it, although it is more taxing to behave in such a manner than it would be if they were natural extroverts. Moreover, when they are off the job, they return to being introverts. These contrasting lifestyles rarely conflict because a person's working world and private world normally don't overlap.

The same can't be said when it comes to personal relationships. If introverts act like extroverts when they first meet someone, the person they are seeing often receives a shock if the relationship continues and the introvert reverts to their "normal" behavior. Revealing your true personality when first meeting someone is far better than engaging in a Dr. Jekyll and Mr. Hyde approach when you want to develop healthy, strong relationships.

THE LAW OF COMPLEMENTARITY (GIVING COMPLIMENTS)

People like to be complimented. It makes them feel good about themselves and, according to the Golden Rule of Friendship, they are going to feel good about you. The result: a better chance to make a friend or strengthen an existing friendship.

Compliments, to be effective, should be sincere and deserved. Paying someone a compliment when you don't really believe what you're saying or when the recipient of the compliment hasn't earned the accolade is counterproductive to good relationship building and is lying (the antithesis of trust).

As author Steve Goodier notes: "Sincere compliments cost nothing and can accomplish so much. In ANY relationship, they are the applause that refreshes." Use compliments when you get the opportunity; they work and are an effective tool in your friendship toolbox.

5

SPEAKING THE LANGUAGE OF FRIENDSHIP

Ultimately the bond of all companionship, whether
in marriage or friendship, is conversation.
—OSCAR WILDE

In Chapter 2, you learned that you can use *nonverbal communication* to make friends. In a sense, these "friend signals" act like snowplows, clearing the way for you to approach your person of interest and make a positive first impression along the way. Used alone, however, these smiles and head tilts are insufficient to sustain a relationship. For that, verbal communication is required and, in fact, the words you say, and those said to you, will not only play a large role in making friends, they will also impact the length and strength of the friendships you acquire.

If there is only one thing you remember about how to make friends through verbal communication, let it be this: *The more you can encourage the other person to speak, the more you listen to what they say, display empathy, and respond positively when reacting to their comments, the greater the likelihood that person will feel good about themselves (Golden Rule of Friendship) and like you as a result.* This means that when I ("ME") desire YOU as a friend, I want to let you know I am interested in what you have to say, and, in addition, give you plenty of time to say it.

GREAT INVENTION, GOOD INTENTION, WRONGFUL MENTION, SHARP DISSENSION

Take the following scenario, which could easily play out any day in organizations around the world. It illustrates the power of verbal communication in determining relationship effectiveness. It also demonstrates how the words we use can make the difference between success and failure in making friends and achieving our objectives.

Stacey, a recent college graduate, secured a coveted position at a prestigious chemical company. She completed each assigned task with passion and skill. She kept up with new developments in the field and always sought new and more cost-effective techniques to shore up the company's bottom line.

One day, Stacey discovered an innovative method to reduce the cost of manufacturing a certain chemical. It was a major breakthrough and she went directly to her manager to report what she had found.

She could hardly contain her excitement when she entered her boss's office and didn't even sit down before she blurted out the good news: "You've been manufacturing this chemical all wrong. I found a new and cheaper way to do it!"

Much to her dismay, Stacey's manager dismissed her findings with a wave of his hand and admonished her to concentrate on her assigned work. Crushed, Stacey returned to her cubicle and vowed never to take the initiative again.

Sadly, Stacey never understood why her idea was rejected. In reality, her intentions were good, but the manner in which she communicated her idea was not well thought out or appropriate. Communication is much more than conveying ideas; it also encompasses how you convey the ideas in real-world situations. Stacey failed to consider some basic psychological tenets of successful communication. In Stacey's statement to her manager she made several communication errors that led to her manager's rejection of her idea.

1. **"If I'm Right, Then You're Wrong."** People rarely consider the push-pull qualities of declarations such as "I'm right" or "My way is better." If you are right, then the other person is automatically assumed to be wrong. If your way is better, then the other person's way is automatically assumed to be worse. The "I'm right and you're wrong" paradigm forces people to assume a defensive posture to protect their egos or reputations, or for myriad other reasons. A person who is forced into a defensive posture by such statements is less likely to consider new ideas, let alone adopt them.

2. **Us Against Them or I Against You.** Stacey used the pronouns *you* and *I*. The use of these pronouns creates an adversarial situation. The *you* and *I* paradigm pits one person against the other. In Stacey's case, she unintentionally created an adversarial relationship between herself and her boss. Adversarial settings create winners and losers. Winners conquer; losers are left to lick their wounds. Adversarial relationships invite competition along with negative feelings, which are not conducive to effective communication.

3. **Cognitive Dissonance.** Cognitive dissonance is triggered when a person holds two or more conflicting beliefs simultaneously. When people experience cognitive dissonance, it is not pleasant: They become frustrated, angry, and experience psychological disequilibrium. In Stacey's situation, she unintentionally created cognitive dissonance in her manager. If Stacey is right, then her manager is wrong. If Stacey is right, then she is smart and her manager is not so smart. People experiencing cognitive dissonance have several options to regain their equilibrium. In Stacey's circumstances, her manager could admit that she is right and he is wrong. Or he could try to convince Stacey that

his method is correct and her method is not viable. Finally, he could dismiss Stacey outright as an immature, well-meaning employee who needs to be put in her place. Stacey's manager chose the latter to resolve his dissonance. When someone experiences cognitive dissonance, it rarely produces a positive outcome.

4.   **Ego.** People are naturally egocentric; they think the world revolves around them. Stacey demonstrated her self-focus when she used the "I" word. She elevated herself above her boss, thus unintentionally attacking his ego. Faced with such a challenge, his thought process was predictable. "I've been a manager for twenty years. Who does this inexperienced, snot-nosed college graduate think she is? She needs to get some experience under her belt before prancing into my office and telling me I've been doing things wrong for two decades. She needs to go back to her cubicle and do as she is told." In this instance, the manager's ego trumped common sense and the company's all-important bottom line. Egos have hurt more people and torpedoed more good ideas than one would care to admit.

LEARNING TO KEEP YOUR EGO IN CHECK

Instead of saying, "You've been manufacturing this chemical all wrong. I found a new and cheaper way to do it," Stacey should have employed psychologically sound principles to shape her communication. A more appropriate way to inform the boss of her significant breakthrough would be:

"Sir, I would like your advice on something that would make our company more profitable."

Addressing her manager as "Sir" shows respect and demonstrates that Stacey sees her boss as a superior. The introductory phrase "I would like your advice on something . . ." accomplishes five objectives. First, Stacey creates an inclusionary environment. The manager feels as though he is included in the process. Second, cognitive dissonance is avoided, thus increasing the probability that the manager will be open to new ideas. Third, the manager's illusion of self-focus is bolstered. The manager will likely think, "Of course, Stacey is seeking my advice because I am intelligent and I have twenty years of experience behind me." Fourth, this introductory phrase could foster a mentor-mentee relationship. If this is achieved, then Stacey's success also becomes her manager's success. Fifth, showing the manager respect and acknowledging his expertise makes him feel good about himself. This brings the Golden Rule of Friendship into play. "If you make other people feel good about themselves, they will like you."

People who like you are probably going to be more open to your suggestions. The use of the words "our company" signals that Stacey has emotional equity in the organization and is a team player. Her statement "make our company more profitable" is very appealing, especially if the manager receives credit for an increased bottom line. When the manager gives his advice, he takes partial ownership of the idea or proposed project. When individuals feel as though they are part owners of a good idea or project, they enthusiastically advance it.

THE GLORY ENCHILADA

The downside for Stacey in using the statement with her boss that we recommend is that she must share the "glory enchilada" with him. At first glance, this might not seem fair or palatable since Stacey came up with the idea and feels she should (rightfully) get all the credit. The problem is people seldom take into account the benefit of sharing the glory: goodwill. Glory has a short expiration date; goodwill has a long shelf life. A good idea produces a large plate that can be divided into many pieces. Freely distributing the pieces increases likability, puts people in your debt, and gives you allies should you need their help in gaining successes down the road.

THE CAT, THE RAT, AND THE METRONOME

Listening to what another person is saying can be difficult to achieve, particularly for extroverts. They are so busy thinking about what they want to say, interrupting the speaker, or letting their mind wander that they literally don't hear what is being said. Obviously, a person can't respond effectively to another individual's message if he or she doesn't receive and process it. Is it really possible that we can "block" out a person's speech and not hear it? Yes. This was demonstrated in an experiment conducted more than a half century ago.

Psychologists conduct some pretty strange and morally suspect experiments with animals. In this particular investigation, electrodes were implanted in the auditory area of a cat's brain. Then they didn't feed the cat for a few days so it was good and hungry. Once the cat was wired and ravenous, it was placed in a room with a metronome, an instrument that makes a clicking sound on a regular basis. Also in the room was an oscilloscope, the kind that translates sounds into blips on a screen, similar to the way heartbeats are represented by spikes on a moving piece of paper.

What happened? Every time the metronome made a clicking sound, it was picked up by the electrode implanted in the cat and simultaneously a blip appeared on the oscilloscope screen. Translation: The cat heard the clicking sound. Not really a very dramatic experiment, you might be thinking; hardly worth depriving a cat of food and making it undergo an operation.

But there's more, and here is where the experiment gets interesting. A mouse was introduced into the room. The cat immediately turned its attention to the potential meal, watching the rodent's every move with intense interest. And here's the shocker: the oscilloscope screen went flat! The metronome was still clicking, the sound was still entering the cat's ear, but somehow the animal was able to block the sound at the brain level. The cat, basically, was no longer hearing the tick, tick, tick of the metronome. It was so focused on the mouse that it was able to block out the sounds it was "hearing."

As it was with the cat so, too, is it with humans. We are able to block out what a person is saying. The upshot of all this: Just because a person is speaking to someone does not guarantee that the listener is hearing what is being said.

The way to be sure you hear what someone is saying is to pay attention to their verbal pronouncements. This is referred to as *active listening* and is something you'll want to practice if you want to use verbal behavior as a tool to build new friendships.

When it comes to establishing and building friendships through verbal behavior, take your cue from **LOVE (Listen, Observe, Vocalize, and Empathize).** This acronym captures the four rules you'll want to follow if you want to maximize your chances for making friends through the use of communication.

RULE #1: *L*ISTEN: PAY ATTENTION WHEN PEOPLE SPEAK SO YOU ARE FULLY AWARE OF WHAT THEY ARE SAYING.

Listening is more than simply remaining silent while your person of interest is speaking. It involves total focus on what is being said. Because we can think at about four times the rate the normal person talks, there is a temptation to let our thoughts wander. Resist this temptation.

Speakers notice when a person isn't listening. The best way to focus on the listener's speech and, at the same time, transmit to the speaker nonverbally that you are paying attention to what is being said is to maintain eye contact. It is also a friend signal that helps build stronger relational bonds. You needn't stare at the speaker to accomplish this; however, maintain eye contact with the speaker about two-thirds to three-fourths of the time he or she is talking to establish the appropriate degree of connectivity and to indicate you are tuned into what is being said. Make a concerted effort *not* to interrupt speakers when they are talking. Extroverts must be particularly careful not to do this, as they have a tendency to begin talking before the speaker is finished speaking, and, in fact, finish what the person is saying to hurry the conversational turn-taking process.

People like individuals who let them talk, particularly when it is about themselves. As one unknown writer once observed, "Friends are those rare people who ask how you are and then wait to hear the answer." Wise counsel!

The empathic statement is the perfect tool to demonstrate that you are listening to the other person. In order to form a good empathic statement, you must listen to what the person is saying or take note of their emotional or physical disposition. Paraphrasing what the person said keeps the focus on that individual. For example, if you need help in a department store and you observe that the salesperson looks tired, you might not get the service you expect. To increase the probability of getting better service, you could use an empathic statement such as: "You look like you've had a busy day" or "It's been a long day. Looks like you're ready to go home." These empathic statements demonstrate to the salesperson that you took the time to notice their personal disposition, and more important, make them feel good about themselves. During casual conversations, people tend not to listen to the person speaking. Even a dull conversation can be enhanced using empathic statements. For example, your coworker is talking excitedly about his weekend trip to the lake. Unless you went to the lake with your coworker, the experience might not interest you. An empathic statement such as "Sounds like you really enjoyed your trip" will let the speaker know that you are listening and taking an interest in what he or she is saying. Empathic statements are the spice of conversations. If you make it a habit to use empathic statements, you will force yourself to listen more carefully to other people. As a consequence they will feel good about themselves and like you.

Remember, individuals enjoy talking about themselves and feel good when people listen as they verbalize their thoughts, which brings us back to the Golden Rule of Friendship. When you can make a person feel good about themselves, they are going to be more favorably disposed to liking you and accepting you as a friend.

BUILDING TRUST IN LESS THAN TEN MINUTES

This was the title of an article written by an anesthesiologist named Scott Finkelstein. In the article, he describes what it's like to face life-and-death problems on a daily basis and emphasizes the importance of doctor-patient communication in dealing with medical crises. "I give each patient my full attention," explains Dr. Finkelstein. "I maintain eye contact. I listen. I validate their feelings, . . . The fear melts away. And then they trust me. All in less than ten minutes."

Giving a person the opportunity to talk, listening to what they say without interruption, and giving nonverbal cues that what they say is of interest to you can make a huge difference, whether it be in gaining a patient's trust or a person's friendship.

RULE #2: *O*BSERVE: IN ANY VERBAL INTERACTION BE SURE TO OBSERVE THE OTHER PARTY BEFORE, DURING, AND AFTER RECEIVING AND TRANSMITTING INFORMATION.

Whenever you interact with another person, communication takes place on two levels: verbal and nonverbal. Before, during, and after verbal interaction it is important that you *observe* the other individual's nonverbal signals and body language, as they can serve as a barometer to assess if a conversation is appropriate, how an ongoing conversation is progressing, what impact the conversation had when finished, and, also, as a warning should something be said that a party to the verbal exchange finds objectionable. Backward leaning, crossing the arms over the chest, and lip compressions are good nonverbal indicators that the conversation is not being well received. People tend to distance themselves from things they don't want to see or hear. This is the opposite of the leaning-forward nonverbal cue discussed earlier. Crossing the arms over the chest is a blocking gesture, which could indicate the person wants to symbolically and physically block what they are seeing or hearing. Other signs of disengagement are looking around the room, when the person looks at their watch as if to say, "Time's up," or turning their feet, torso, or both toward the door or other parts of the room. When you see the other person beginning to disengage from the conversation, change the subject. You are probably spending too much time talking about yourself and not focusing on the other person.

It is important to observe nonverbal behavior even before any attempt at conversation is made. Of course, the importance of observation doesn't stop there. Should a person's nonverbals signal that beginning a conversation is appropriate, then let the talking commence. Just don't take that as the reason for ending your observation! Continual observation during an ongoing verbal interaction is critical for spotting any potential problems that might otherwise go unnoticed.

This is particularly true when it comes to "word mines."

Words mean different things to different people. When these words are used they can, like land mines, blow apart a developing relationship. When a party to the conversation is offended by one of these word mines, he or she doesn't normally say anything about their discomfort but simply begins the process of distancing and/or exiting the relationship. However, their nonverbal behavior often provides a clear indication that something troubling was said. They might wince, get a shocked or surprised look on their face, or take a step backward. A person who is processing information on the verbal *and* nonverbal levels will pick up these signals and can often save the day by asking if they said something offensive and, if so, assuring the listener that it certainly wasn't their intention to do so. A further examination of what the offending word means to both parties can usually put any bad feelings to rest and the conversation can restart on a positive note. The hazard of word mines is that people don't know what emotional meanings others attach to otherwise innocuous words.

IS IT SOMETHING I SAID?

A friend was lecturing about interviewing techniques to a group of seminar participants. At one point he said, "People need to listen more than they talk. The proof of this is the Lord gave you two ears and one mouth, so you should listen twice as much as you speak."

During the lunch break, the conference host walked into the banquet room and informed my friend that a charge had been filed against him by the Equal Employment Opportunity Commission. She had come to investigate exactly what happened. My friend was dumbfounded. He had no idea who would file such a complaint and why they would do it.

It turned out that one of the attendees had a son who was born with only one ear, and when my friend made the remark about "two ears and one mouth," this father thought my friend was making fun of his child.

Once my friend was told of the circumstances surrounding the complaint, he explained to the host that his comment was a truism that had been around for decades and when he said it, he in no way meant it as a slight against anyone.

The host wasn't moved. "If the father is offended," she said, "it's his perspective of what happened we need to address, whether you think it is offensive or not."

My friend thought the entire situation was ludicrous. He didn't see that he had done anything wrong and certainly didn't want to apologize to the father for what he saw as perfectly acceptable language.

The host would have none of it. "If you want to keep this consulting job, you need to apologize to the father."

Faced with that ultimatum, my friend decided discretion was the better part of valor and offered his apology to the distraught father.

WHEN EVERYTHING ISN'T BLACK-AND-WHITE

The classroom seems to provide a particularly conducive environment for word mines to rattle an unsuspecting lecturer. Two reasons for this is the diversity of today's student body and the larger number of enrollees in any particular course. When it comes to racial issues, teachers must tiptoe carefully through their lectures, being careful not to set off a word mine by using words or phrases that mean different things to different students. In one of my classes, I couldn't get my laptop to boot up. Every time I switched it on all I got was a black screen. So I asked my students, "Does anyone here know how to make this thing work?" One student nodded, walked over to the laptop, made a few adjustments to the machine, and handed it back to me. I said, "Well, the screen is white and white is better than black at least."

A black student in the class took immediate offense at my comment. "I heard you say 'white is better than black,' " he declared. "That's a racist remark."

I had no intention of making a racial slur. Race never crossed my mind. I was anxious to get my laptop functional so I could present my lecture. My comment referred to how my laptop was operating. A black screen indicated the laptop was not booting up. A white screen indicated that the laptop was booting up. In other words, a laptop that is booting up is better than a laptop that is not booting up. Yet, my student heard the comment from a different perspective and it triggered a deep emotional response. Such is the nature and danger of word mines.

Another teacher related another good example of this to me. She teaches a course in international management, which means a large number of students from other countries are in attendance. At the beginning of one class, about halfway through the semester, a male American student walked up to another male student and greeted him by saying, "How's it going, dawg?!" The recipient of this greeting almost punched the speaker in the mouth. It turns out that the angry student was from the Middle East, where it is considered a great insult to be referred to as a "dog."

Word mines. Watch for them and be ready to treat the injured relationship quickly and decisively so as to minimize any damage done. It's worth saying again: the hazard of word mines is that speakers do not know what emotional meanings others attach to otherwise innocuous words. Thus, they never know when a word mine can be "set off." If, as noted earlier, speakers are not watching the listener, they might not be aware that they insulted or offended them.

Even if they do become aware that they have set off a negative response in the listener, most speakers, rather than trying to defuse the situation, tend to respond defensively to the unexpected emotional outburst, which unfortunately only intensifies the initial response of that individual. A speaker who steps on a word mine and reacts defensively when confronted with an angry listener is often seen as insensitive and lacking compassion. The speaker, on the other hand, is often left confused, not knowing what to do or what to say in response to the listener's emotional explosion.

Empathic statements are the best way to respond to word mine explosions. They capture a person's feelings and reflect them back to the person, using parallel language. Empathic statements acknowledge the person's feelings without the need to go on the defensive.

As you'll recall from an earlier chapter, the basic formula for constructing empathic statements is "So you . . ." This basic approach keeps the focus on the other person and away from the individual who stepped on the word mine. People naturally tend to say something to the effect of "I understand how you feel." That leads the other person to automatically think, *No, you don't know how I feel because you are not me.*

Empathic statements allow individuals to vent their emotions. Once the pent-up emotions are vented, the conversation can usually return to a normal exchange of information. Avoiding a heated argument with an emotional person increases the probability that the relationship will have a chance to survive and grow.

Once you step on a word mine, learn from it. Be sure to affix a mental red flag to avoid detonations in the future. Unfortunately, the problem of word mines is unlikely to go away in the near future. In fact, the virtual world in which we live is strewn with dangerous word mines. You can never be sure when you will step on one. Personal relationships are more difficult to initiate and maintain when the verbal landscape is dotted with word mines, both discovered and hidden.

Communication mishaps are likely to increase in the coming years because people rely more and more on electronic media such as texting, emails, and Internet postings to communicate. Symbols such as brackets, periods, and commas that form happy, winking, or surprised faces often punctuate sentences to provide additional clues to the reader as to the true meaning of the communication. Emoticons are also used to clarify messages. When text messaging first became popular, I remember texting my daughter. She responded to one of my text messages with the letters "LOL." I wrote back, "I love you too." Her response was "Ha, ha. LOL means laugh out loud." I wrote back, "I thought it meant Lots of Love." Her final exchange was "I love you too, Dad." My communication faux pas with my daughter ended with a chuckle, but it demonstrates the danger of miscommunication when people don't have nonverbal cues to guide a conversation. When using electronic media to communicate, don't use sarcasm, understatements, or words that have double meanings if you want to avoid the possibility of miscommunication.

The best way to keep your verbal communication effective in a world filled with word mines is to:

1. Think about the words you are going to use before you say them. Scan ahead for possible word mines that you'll want to eliminate from your speech.
2. Observe your listeners for any unusual reaction while you are speaking. It might indicate that a word mine has been tripped.

3. Do not become defensive or angry if a listener becomes agitated over your use of a word mine (even if you didn't know it existed); and

4. Immediately take the time to find out if the listener's discomfort is the result of a word mine detonation. If it is, apologize for using the word or phrase, explain that you were unaware that it had a negative connotation to the listener, and assure him or her that you will not use it again. And then, be sure you don't.

THE LIP PURSE

No one can read minds, but they can come close by observing nonverbal displays. Some nonverbal cues are more obvious than others. The obvious cues are easier for observers to read and interpret. Likewise, obvious cues are easier for speakers to control, thus camouflaging their true thoughts. Subtle nonverbal cues are harder to control and reveal more intimate information. The lips are one area of the body that can reveal these subtle cues.

A lip purse display is a slight, almost imperceptible, puckering or rounding of the lips (see photos on page 135). This gesture signals dissension or disagreement. The more pronounced the lip purse, the more intense is the dissension or disagreement. Pursed lips mean the person has formed a thought in their mind that is in opposition to what is being said or done.

Knowing what a person thinks gives you an advantage. The trick is to change their mind before they have an opportunity to articulate their opposition. Once an opinion or decision is expressed out loud, changing a person's mind becomes more difficult due to the psychological principle of consistency. Decision-making causes tension to some degree. When a person makes a decision, tension dissipates. They are less likely to change their mind because to do so would mean admitting their first decision was a bad one, thus causing tension. Maintaining an articulated position causes less tension than going through the decision-making process again no matter how persuasive the arguments for change may be. In other words, when people say something, they tend to remain consistent with what they said.

Pursed Lips

Observing for lip purses is also useful when talking with your spouse, colleagues, and friends, as it is a universal nonverbal cue that tells us what people are thinking. However, a lip purse is *not* a foe signal; someone can be happy with you and still use it.

Again, remember why watching for and observing lip purses is so critical: Once a person is able to articulate a "No" response to your idea or suggestion, or voice a negative remark, the principle of "consistency" comes into play, meaning now it is very hard for the listener to go back on their verbal response and change their mind. The lip purse allows you to see a negative response coming and gives you a chance to counter it before it is spoken, giving you a better chance of getting your idea or project accepted.

You can use this nonverbal signal to help you increase your verbal effectiveness at home and at work. As an example, consider this statement you might make to your wife:

"Honey, I can show you how we can afford a bass boat [or substitute with any item you may wish to purchase] so I can go fishing."

Now, as you begin to present your financial argument you can see your wife's lips purse. She has formed a sentence in her mind, which is in opposition to what you are saying. (Her lip purse is telling you she doesn't want you to get into *her* purse!) You know now that you have to come up with an additional justification before she articulates her objection; otherwise her public proclamation will make it more difficult for you to end up with a boat or any other big-ticket item you wish to purchase. Ladies, this technique also applies to men.

WHEN THE BOSS GIVES YOU A LIP (PURSE)

At work, I was always trying to get money or manpower support for some operation I wanted to run. Both were in short supply and I had to compete for resources. I remember once explaining to my boss why I needed money for this particular project and I saw him purse his lips. Now I knew he thought up a statement in opposition to what I was saying and I needed to change his mind before he had a chance to say no. If he publicly rejected my proposal, getting his approval would be next to impossible.

In an attempt to forestall a verbal rejection, I used an empathic statement. "Boss, I'll bet you're thinking that this idea isn't going to work, but let me explain why it will." I knew exactly what point the boss had issues with, because his lips pursed when I made a specific statement. Now I knew what was troubling him and my statement bought me some time to respond to his concern and convince him my idea was worthy before he made any verbal declaration, which is hard to reverse once it is publicly stated.

The next time you present a project or proposition to your supervisor, watch for the lip purse display. If your supervisor purses his or her lips during your presentation, you know that he or she has already formed a thought in opposition to your proposal. Once you see a lip purse, you should attempt to change your supervisor's mind before he or she vocalizes opposition. Be ready with an empathic statement. Try: "So, you don't think what I am saying makes much sense. Let me go over a few things that will show you that what I am proposing is the best course of action." You acknowledge your supervisor's doubts and present counterarguments to change his or her mind before the negative thought is voiced.

Lip Bite

LIP BITE

Another technique to "read a person's mind" is to watch for a lip bite. A lip bite is the soft biting or tugging of the upper or lower lip with the teeth. This nonverbal gesture indicates that the person has something to say but is hesitant to say it, for myriad reasons. Hence the old adage

"Bite your lip," meaning keep your mouth shut and don't say anything has validity. I often see lip biting when I lecture. I'll take it as a signal to construct an empathic statement such as "It looks like you want to add something to the conversation," to encourage the students to express themselves. Most students are surprised that I can read their minds and they feel good about themselves because I'm paying attention to them.

LIP COMPRESSION

Lip compression has a similar meaning to the lip bite, but it has a more negative connotation. A lip compression occurs when the upper and lower lips are tightly pressed together. The lip compression indicates that the person you are talking to has something to say but is reluctant to do so. Right before suspects confess, I often saw a lip compression. The suspects wanted to say something but they pressed their lips together to prevent the words from coming out.

Lip Compression

LIP TOUCHING

Self-touching of the lips with hands, fingers, or objects such as pencils and other inanimate objects indicates the person is feeling uneasy about the topic that is being discussed. Stimulating the lips momentarily draws your attention away from the sensitive topic and thus reduces anxiety. Suspects would often unwittingly signal to me that the question I just asked exposed a sensitive topic or made them feel uncomfortable. Seeing this silent cue, I would construct an empathic statement such as "You seem a bit uncomfortable talking about this topic," to further explore the topic. The suspect would either confirm or deny that they were uncomfortable and, in most cases, provide reasons for feeling the way they did.

Lip touching demonstrates that the person
is feeling uneasy or uncomfortable.

This self-touching signal can be effectively used in business and social settings. For example, if you are in a one-to-one sales meeting presenting a new product and you see your client lightly rubbing his lips with his fingers, take note. Upon seeing this nonverbal cue, you should formulate an empathic statement such as "This may be a bit overwhelming because you have never used this product before" to allow the client to express any concerns or misgivings they might have about the product or service you are offering. Once you have identified your client's specific concerns you can adapt your sales presentation to more effectively sell your product or service.

In social settings, you can avoid embarrassing moments by observing the person you are talking to. If you introduce a sensitive topic and you see the other person pursing or compressing their lips, you are best advised to change the subject before more damage is done. You can safely return to the subject when sufficient rapport has been built between you and the other person.

RULE #3: VOCALIZE: THE *WAY* YOU VOCALIZE AND *WHAT* YOU VOCALIZE WILL IMPACT YOUR EFFECTIVENESS IN MAKING AND KEEPING FRIENDS

How you say something can sometimes be as important as the message itself. Of particular concern is your *tone of voice,* which transmits information to the listener irrespective of what is being said. Attraction and interest, for example, are communicated much more by the tone of voice than by the words being spoken.

HOW YOU SPEAK INFLUENCES HOW OTHERS PERCEIVE YOUR MESSAGE . . . AND YOU

Tone of voice can convey messages that words alone can't. A deep, low-pitched voice conveys romantic interest. A high-pitched voice conveys surprise or skepticism. A loud voice will give the impression that you are overbearing. The tone of voice you use can embrace others or dismiss them out of hand.

The speed of your voice also regulates conversations. Fast talking adds a sense of urgency to the conversation or can act as a prompt to end a boring exchange. Dragging out a word can signal interest. Actors in movies often drag out the greeting "Hello" to signal romantic interest. Conversely, a slow, soft-spoken monotone voice signals lack of interest in the listener or extreme shyness in the speaker. Conversely, a slow, soft-spoken voice with normal inflections conveys empathy. I often hear this type of communication at funerals or during tragedies.

Most parents learn to control their kids' behavior with tonal inflections. I often spoke to my kids in a deep, slow voice to express my displeasure. As with many parents, if I was extremely displeased, I would drag out my kid's first, middle, and last name with great effect. A short, clipped "Good" expresses approval.

Tone of voice delivers the emotional part of your message. I have a Chicago accent and I tend to clip my words. When I'm in Chicago, word clipping goes unnoticed because everybody clips their words. However, when I travel to other parts of the country, people perceive word clipping as being overbearing and dismissive. Sarcasm can also be misinterpreted without the accompanying tone of voice that lets the listener know that there is a hidden meaning to the message. This is the reason why sarcasm should be avoided in emails and text messages.

Voice intonation also plays a large part in conversational turn-taking. Lowering your voice at the end of a sentence signals that you are finished talking and it is now the other person's turn to talk. If the speaker lowers their voice at the end of a sentence and continues to talk, the listener will become frustrated because they think it's their turn to talk. Dominating a conversation violates the Golden Rule of Friendship by keeping the focus of attention on yourself instead of on the other person.

Conversely, taking your turn to speak when your person of interest has not given any vocal "turn-yielding cues," even if he or she has finished a sentence, can impede friendship development. Violating conversation etiquette can cause irritation and have a detrimental effect on friendship development.

Make it a habit to pause for a nanosecond or two before speaking, especially if you are an extrovert. This pause gives introverts a chance to gather their thoughts. Remember, introverts tend to think before they speak. If you interrupt their thought process, they tend to become frustrated and, consequently, like you less. The pause gives extroverts time to think about what they are about to say. This habit saved me from countless embarrassing moments.

WHAT YOU SAY INFLUENCES HOW OTHERS PERCEIVE YOUR MESSAGE . . . AND YOU

This seems like common sense and, to a degree, it is. But the focus here is on saying certain things or saying them in a certain way that you might not otherwise use to make and keep friends. Here are some verbal strategies you can use to make or keep friends in everyday situations, strategies you might otherwise ignore or downplay, to the detriment of your relationships.

Strategy #1: When you are right and someone else is wrong, give that individual a face-saving way to carry out your wishes with a minimum of embarrassment and/or humiliation. The person will like you a lot more for your efforts on their behalf.

Human beings have an inherent need to be right, but being right comes with some unintended consequences. One of those is the loss of friendship if the person who is right doesn't give the person who is wrong a face-saving way to extricate himself or herself from the situation in question.

I learned this the hard way while presenting a lecture on report writing to a group of parole and probation officers. Prior to the beginning of my lecture, I spoke with several of the participants about their current report writing practices. One participant identified his supervisor as the writing guru. The other participants agreed and made comments such as "He really knows his stuff," "He's a wordsmith," "He forces us to use a variety of words to say the same thing," and "I don't know what we would do without him."

I glanced over at the supervisor. His eyes were alight and he was smiling proudly. That conversation and the supervisor's reaction was a red flag I failed to recognize until it was too late. The supervisor's esteem was wrapped up in his identity as the group's grammar guru. His value to the agency also stemmed from his reputation as an outstanding writer.

During my lecture, I demonstrated a simple yet effective method to write reports patterned after the FBI model for producing such documents. Several participants commented they were going to start using this model because it was easier and reduced the possibility of their reports being successfully challenged in court.

I was taken aback when the supervisor protested. He argued that the method of writing I was teaching may work for the FBI, but it was not suitable for his agency. He declared that he was a college English major and believed that creative reports using synonyms were more interesting than reports using the same words over and over. I then made a fatal mistake by engaging the supervisor in spontaneous role playing to prove that I was right and, consequently, that he was wrong. I asked him what synonyms he would use for the verb *said*. He offered the following alternatives: *told, explained,* and *mentioned*. I stopped him there and told him to play the role of a witness in court and I would play the role of defense attorney. He agreed. The exchange went like this:

ME (DEFENSE ATTORNEY): Officer, please define the word *stated* as you used it in your report.

SUPERVISOR (OFFICER): Express a fact with certainty.

ME (DEFENSE ATTORNEY): Thank you officer. How would you define the word *explained* as you used the word in your report?

SUPERVISOR (OFFICER): To talk about.

ME (DEFENSE ATTORNEY): Thank you, Officer. So what you wrote is that what my client initially said he said with certainty and the second thing my client said he did not say with certainty.

SUPERVISOR (OFFICER): "No, that's not what I meant. The suspect said both things with certainty."

> **ME (DEFENSE ATTORNEY):** That's not what you wrote. By your
> own definitions of the words *said* and *explain,* you are saying that
> the first statement was said with certainty and that the second
> statement was not said with certainty. Is that correct?
> **SUPERVISOR (OFFICER):** No, both statements were said with
> certainty.
> **ME (DEFENSE ATTORNEY):** If both statements were said with
> certainty, then why didn't you use the word *said* in both
> sentences?
> **SUPERVISOR (OFFICER):** Uhhh. I don't know.

I won my point, but it was a Pyrrhic victory. My need to be right
caused everything to go wrong. From that point forward, the tension
in the room was obvious. I forced the participants to choose between
a more efficient method of writing and their supervisor's less efficient
method of writing. Of course, they sided with their supervisor.

The unintended consequences of being right occur every day in
offices and homes across the country. We unintentionally alienate our
bosses, colleagues, friends, and spouses and cause unnecessary strife
and tension.

There is a better way. You can be right without wronging someone.
Instead of asserting your right to be right, ask people for their advice.
That allows them to be part of the decision-making process. Additionally, they feel good about themselves because you came to them to seek
their advice, which elevates them to an honored position. The Golden
Rule of Friendship states that if you make people feel good about
themselves, they will like you.

Using this "ask for advice" strategy still allows you to be right, get
the results you want, and maintain (or increase) friendships with those
individuals who now have a face-saving way to maintain their dignity
and avoid being seen as "wrong."

The following exchange between a subordinate and her boss illustrates the technique of seeking advice. The subordinate found an error

in a newly formed controversial policy prepared by her boss. Rather than trumping her boss with the "right" card, she sought her supervisor's advice.

SUBORDINATE: Do you have a minute, Boss?

BOSS: Sure, what's up?

SUBORDINATE: I was reviewing your latest policy and noticed something. I'd like your advice on the matter.

BOSS: Sure. Let me take a look.

The subordinate can now point out the discrepancies in the policy and her supervisor has the opportunity to clarify his mistake without losing face.

Salespeople can use the same technique when they meet longtime customers or new customers. Textbook publisher representatives regularly visit my office pitching new books for use in my classes. Instead of personalizing their sales approach, they tell me how their book is better than the one I am currently using. The sales rep could be right, but there are unintended consequences of such an approach. The salesperson is implying that my judgment in picking textbooks is bad. This realization does not make me feel good about myself. I would be more likely to listen to the representatives if they introduced themselves and then said, "Professor, I would like to get your advice about this new book designed for use in your course."

THE FACE-SAVING TECHNIQUE THAT AVOIDED A MUG SHOT

As an FBI agent, I always dreaded the moment I would be flying somewhere on a long-awaited vacation and be called upon to deal with an unruly passenger or handle a crisis. Well, it happened on a 6 a.m. flight out of Los Angeles. I had boarded and was sitting quietly in my seat when a flight attendant came up and said there was a drunk passenger in the back of the plane whom the captain wanted offloaded. I looked around and, sure enough, there was a passenger staggering in the aisle while another flight attendant was yelling at him. "You get off this flight . . . you're an idiot." So much for trying to calm things down. The attendant standing over me said, "You're an FBI agent, take him off the plane."

I thought, "I might as well use a bit of my training." So I walked over to where the man was leaning against his seat. I told him I was an FBI agent, showed him my badge and credentials, and suggested we both sit down and talk. He wasn't so drunk that he failed to understand me. He sat down and I edged into the empty seat next to him.

"Look," I said, in a soft voice that would be difficult for other passengers to hear, "the endgame is you're getting off this plane. When the captain says you're getting off, you're getting off. Now, you have a choice. Either you can walk off and keep your dignity, voice your complaints once you're in the terminal, and complete your trip to Dallas on a later flight . . . or I'm going to arrest you, put you in handcuffs, and forcibly take you off the plane. Then you're going to go to jail, have to bail yourself out, and come back here for a trial, where you might be sentenced to prison. So," I whispered to him, "sir, the choice is yours. I'll allow you to make this decision. Take a few seconds to think about it. What do you want to do?"

It only took a moment for the passenger to say, "I think I'll just get off, make my complaint, and get on another plane."

I said, "I think that's a very intelligent decision. Here, I'll be glad to walk you off."

After I had accompanied the man to the terminal and returned to my seat, the flight attendant who had spoken to me earlier came up and wanted to know how I had managed to end such an ugly confrontation so peacefully. I told her I had given the passenger the opportunity to make a choice on his own.

I gave him the opportunity to feel he had some control in the situation, that he was free to choose his fate. And, most important, I provided him with a face-saving way to exit the aircraft with a minimum of embarrassment.

FOOD FOR THOUGHT

Giving someone the feeling they have some control over a situation can work wonders, even with children. In fact, parents can use this approach to help their kids make decisions, especially when they are younger. Children, like adults, want to feel as though they are in control of their lives. The illusion of control can be conveyed if parents give their kids an opportunity to choose their destiny. This can be accomplished without losing parental authority. For example, you are taking your son out to lunch. You have already made up your mind that you are either going to McDonald's or Burger King for a kid's meal. You don't want to let your child choose another restaurant, yet, you still want him to practice his decision-making skills. This can be accomplished by setting up an alternate response question such as "We are going to lunch. Do you want to go to McDonald's or Burger King for a kid's meal?" An alternate response question gives your child an illusion of control, but you are really in control because you limited the restaurant choice to McDonald's or Burger King and you limited the food choice to a kid's meal.

Salespeople use the alternate response question all the time. When you go to a car dealership, a good salesperson will not ask you if you want to buy a car. They will ask you if you like blue cars or red cars. If you answer, "Blue cars," the salesperson will show you blue cars. If you answer, "Red cars," the salesperson will show you red cars. If your answer is a color other than blue or red, then the salesperson will show you that color of car. Good salespeople give the customers the illusion that they are in control of the car buying experience, when in fact the salespeople are directing you through a well-choreographed presentation.

Strategy #2: Use the verbal technique of "status elevation" to make people feel better about themselves and see you as a friend. Status elevation is a technique that satisfies an individual's need for recognition. I discovered this approach one day when I was with my son, Bryan, at a bookstore. An author was signing books at a booth in the front of the store. Nobody was at the booth, so Bryan and I went over to talk with the author. While my son spoke with the woman, I looked through her book. I noticed that her style of writing reminded me of Jane Austen. I mentioned this to the author. Her eyes lit up and her cheeks took on a pinkish hue. She replied, "Really? I don't have much time to write. I have three kids. My husband is in the military and is gone a lot of the time. I want to go back to college to finish my degree. I left school to get married. That was a mistake I'll always regret." With one comment, this woman was telling me her life story like I was a long-lost friend.

I tried this technique several more times with the same results. Once, I met an aspiring candidate from the Republican Party. After we talked politics for several minutes, I remarked that his political style reminded me of Ronald Regan. The young man puffed up and told me about his family upbringing, where he went to college, and many other personal details that indicated he saw me as someone worthy of being liked. Status elevation can take the form of a simple compliment.

MOPPING UP A SCHOOL GRAFFITI PROBLEM

On one occasion, I interviewed a janitor at a high school regarding some racist graffiti that had appeared sometime during the previous night. At the outset of the interview, I attempted to build some rapport with him. I commented that he had a big job taking care of such a large building all by himself. He told me about how he designed a system that allowed him to accomplish multiple tasks at the same time by following the shortest routes through the building. I responded that most schools of the same size would require several janitors to accomplish the work he did using the system he designed (I was providing him with an opportunity to pat himself on the back).

As we talked, it was clear that I had developed a solid rapport with the janitor. He explained to me in great detail about how he designed his maintenance routine and went on to share stories about the teachers and administrative staff. The tales were interesting but of no use to my investigation. But I listened anyway, and gained a friend in the process. I gave him my business card and asked him to call me if he learned any new information about the graffiti incident.

Several weeks later, the janitor called me with a rumor he had heard from one of the students. The rumor turned out to be true and led to the apprehension of the parties responsible for the graffiti.

It is doubtful that the janitor would have taken the time to call me about the rumor he heard if I had not developed a good rapport with him during our only visit.

Strategy #3: If you want to get information from somebody without arousing their suspicion or putting them on the defensive, use the *elicitation* approach. You use elicitation devices in conversation to obtain information from a person without that individual becoming sensitive (aware) of your purpose.

People often hesitate to answer direct questions, especially when the inquiries focus on sensitive topics. If you want people to like you, use elicitation instead of questions to obtain sensitive information. Elicitation techniques encourage people to reveal sensitive information without the need for making inquiries.

Asking questions puts people on the defensive. Nobody likes nosy individuals, especially when you first meet them. Ironically, this is the time you need the most information about persons of interest. The more information you know about an individual, the better you will be able to develop strategies to cultivate successful personal and business relationships.

Elicitation is the ability to obtain sensitive information from people without them realizing they are providing you with this data. During my career in the intelligence community, I trained agents to obtain sensitive information from adversaries while at the same time maintaining good rapport with them. The characteristics of elicitation:

1. Few, if any questions are asked, thus preventing a defensive reaction from the person of interest;

2. the process is painless because your person of interest is not aware they are revealing sensitive personal information;

3.   people will like you because you are making them the focus of your undivided attention; and

4.   individuals will thank you for being so kind and will likely contact you in the future, which provides another opportunity to glean additional information from them.

Elicitation works because it is based on human needs.

The Human Need to Correct: Using Elicitation Through Presumptive Statements

People have a need to be right, but people have a stronger need to correct others. The need to be correct and/or to correct others is almost irresistible. Making *presumptive statements* is an elicitation technique that presents a fact that can be either right or wrong. If the presumptive is correct, people will affirm the fact and often provide additional information. If the presumptive is wrong, people will provide the correct answer, usually accompanied by a detailed explanation as to *why* it is correct.

Recently I was buying a piece of jewelry, but I was hoping to not pay retail. In order to negotiate the best price, I had to know the markup on the jewelry in the store where I was going to make the purchase and also the clerk's commission, if any. For obvious reasons, this information is closely held. I knew if I asked direct questions about prices, I would not get the answers I needed to negotiate the best deal, so I used elicitation to get the information I wanted.

CLERK: May I help you?
ME: Yes, I'm looking for a diamond pendant for my wife.
CLERK: We have lots of those. Let me show you what we have.

The clerk handed me a velvet case containing several pendants. I looked intently at one of them.

ME: How much is this one?

CLERK: One hundred and ninety dollars.

ME: Woooh, the markup must be at least 150 percent. (presumptive statement)

CLERK: No. It's only 50 percent.

ME: And then your 10 percent commission. (presumptive statement)

CLERK: Not that much. I only get 5 percent.

ME: I suppose you don't have the authority to discount. (presumptive statement)

CLERK: I am authorized to give a 10 percent discount. Anything after that, the manager has to approve.

At this point, I could either take the 10 percent discount or press further. Given the poor economic conditions when I visited this jewelry store, I suspected the manager would be willing to give me a further discount, if he still made a profit.

ME: Ask the manager if he will sell this piece at a 40 percent discount. (I waited patiently as the clerk went into the back room. She returned a few minutes later.)

CLERK: He said the best he can do is 30 percent if you pay cash.

ME: It's a present for my wife.

CLERK: No problem. I'll gift wrap it for you. (I not only saved $57, but got gift wrapping, too!)

In this case, using elicitation instead of direct questions yielded valuable information. I was able to ascertain the markup on the jewelry (50 percent) and the clerk's commission (5 percent), which allowed me to negotiate with confidence. If I did not want to negotiate, I could have taken the automatic 10 percent discount for a savings of $19. Had the clerk not divulged this information, I would have paid full price. Based on the clerk's behavior, she did not realize she had revealed closely held information.

EMPATHIC ELICITATION

The Empathic Statement is versatile because it can be combined with elicitation techniques. Two empathic elicitation techniques that are based on the human need to correct will be discussed, the *empathic presumptive* and the *empathic conditional*. Salespeople routinely use empathic elicitation. Customers are less likely to buy something from someone they don't like. Salespeople use empathic elicitation to accomplish two goals. First, empathic statements quickly build rapport, and second, empathic elicitation gleans information from customers that they would not normally reveal under direct questioning.

EMPATHIC PRESUMPTIVE

The empathic presumptive keeps the focus of the conversation on the customer and presents a fact as the truth. The presumptive can be either true or an assumed fact regardless of its veracity. If the presumptive is true, the customer will usually add new information to the conversation.

The salesperson could then construct another empathic statement based on the customer's response to prompt more information. If the presumptive is false, the customer will typically correct the presumptive. Just look at this example:

SALESPERSON: May I help you?

CUSTOMER: Yes, I have to buy a new washer and dryer.

SALESPERSON: So, your old washer and dryer are on their last legs? (empathic presumptive)

CUSTOMER: No, I'm moving to a small apartment.

SALESPERSON: Oh, so you'll need a compact washer and dryer. Let me show you a popular stacked unit that we sell.

CUSTOMER: Okay.

The salesperson listened to what the customer said, "I have to buy a new washer and dryer," which suggests the customer's current washer and dryer are not functioning well. The salesperson used the empathic presumptive to keep the focus on the customer and encourage the customer to affirm or deny the presumptive, "So, your old washer and dryer are on their last legs?" The customer corrected the salesperson by saying, "I'm moving to a small apartment." This added information identifies what type of unit the salesperson should direct the customer to. The words "have to buy" indicates that the customer is serious about buying a washing machine and dryer as opposed to just looking. The salesperson obtained important facts during the opening exchange of information. First, the customer is a serious buyer and the salesperson knows exactly what category of washer and dryer the customer is likely to purchase. This information saves the customer and the salesperson time. The customer goes home with the product he needs and the salesperson has more time to serve other customers.

EMPATHIC CONDITIONAL

The empathic conditional keeps the focus of the conversation on the customer and introduces a set of circumstances under which the customer would purchase a product or service.

> **SALESPERSON:** Can I help you?
>
> **CUSTOMER:** No, I'm just looking.
>
> **SALESPERSON:** So, you haven't decided which model you want to buy. (empathic statement)
>
> **CUSTOMER:** I need a new car, but I'm not sure I can afford one.
>
> **SALESPERSON:** So you'd buy a car, if it were priced right? (empathic conditional)
>
> **CUSTOMER:** Sure.
>
> **SALESPERSON:** Do you like red or blue cars?
>
> **CUSTOMER:** Blue.
>
> **SALESPERSON:** Let's take a look at some blue cars in your price range.

In response to the empathic elicitation, the customer identified the reason preventing him from buying a car. The salesperson then used the empathic conditional approach. The empathic conditional keeps the focus on the customer and, at the same time, sets up the if/then conditional "So you'd buy a car, if it were priced right?" The underlying presumption is that the customer is going to buy a car if certain conditions are met. In this case, the condition is price. The empathic conditional helped the salesperson to identify a buying objective. With this new information, the salesperson can direct the customer to lines of cars within his price range.

THE NEED TO RECIPROCATE USING THE PRINCIPLE OF QUID PRO QUO

When people receive something either physically or emotionally, they feel the need to reciprocate by giving back something of equal or greater value (Law of Reciprocity). Quid pro quo is an elicitation technique that encourages people to match information provided by others. For example, you meet a person for the first time and want to know where they work. Instead of directly asking them, "Where do you work?" tell them where you work first. People will tend to reciprocate by telling you where they work. This elicitation technique can be used to discover information about people without being intrusive and appearing nosy.

If you don't want people to know where you work but are still curious about where they are employed, you can get the needed information from the other person and short-circuit reciprocity by asking the question in a novel way. Say, "Where do you labor?" This question requires additional cognitive processing, which disrupts the need to reciprocate with the question, "Where do you work?"

I used the need to reciprocate when I interviewed suspects. I would always offer the suspect something to drink such as coffee, tea, water, or soda at the beginning of the interview (the television term is *interrogation*). I did this to invoke the need to reciprocate. In return for the drink, I hope to receive something in return such as intelligence information or a confession.

During your conversation, you should seek common ground (Law of Similarity) with the other person. You should also use empathic statements to keep the focus on that individual. In short, you want to make the other person feel good about themselves (Golden Rule of Friendship), and if you are successful, they will like you and seek future opportunities to share your company.

USING A THIRD-PARTY APPROACH TO DISCOVER THE WAY PEOPLE REALLY FEEL

In general, people are reluctant to talk about themselves and how they really feel about someone or something. However, people are less hesitant to talk about others, perhaps to avoid revealing too much information about themselves. You can use this human characteristic to learn some very closely held (intimate) information about a person of interest. This is achieved by using the elicitation technique known as *internal/external foci*.

Here's an example of how the technique works. Most couples in a monogamous relationship would like to know if their partner is predisposed to cheat on them. If you ask your significant other if they would, in fact, cheat on you, rarely will you hear, "Yeah, I don't have any problem with that." They may be *thinking* that, but would surely not say it out loud.

To find out what your loved one really thinks about cheating, you need to approach the topic from a *third-person perspective*. Instead of asking the direct question, "What do you think about cheating?" you want to say, "My friend Susan caught her husband cheating. What do you think about that?" When a person is confronted with a third-party observation, they tend to look inside themselves to find the answer and tell you what they really think.

Of course, the answer you want to hear is "Cheating is wrong. I would never do that to you." However, be prepared for answers such as "Everybody cheats nowadays," "If a wife can't take care of her husband's needs, what else is a man to do?" "If my wife treated me the same way she treated him, I'd cheat on her, too," and "It's no wonder, they haven't been getting along lately."

These answers tend to reflect what a person *really* thinks about cheating. The individual in this case tends to think that extramarital affairs are acceptable under certain conditions, and he or she is therefore predisposed to cheat when those conditions are met. These "third-person" responses are not 100 percent accurate, but they do provide insights into your loved one's predisposition to cheat and are much more reflective of his or her true feelings than any answer you might get through direct questions on the issue.

HE'S NOT WORTH THE WEIGHT

A student of mine, Linda, was in a serious relationship with a young man and contemplating marriage. She struggled with a weight problem and exercised regularly to keep in shape. However, she knew that she would eventually gain weight as she aged or if she were to become pregnant. She wanted to know how her boyfriend would feel if she put on extra pounds. She was concerned he might have problems with it.

One evening, Linda suggested to her boyfriend that they watch the TV show *The Biggest Loser*. The program highlights morbidly obese people who enter into a program that includes exercise, diet, and lifestyle changes to shed pounds. The person who loses the most weight by the end of the show wins a large prize. Halfway through the show, her boyfriend blurted out, "If my wife ever got like that, I'd kick her to the curb."

Linda's concerns appeared justified. Her boyfriend was commenting from a third-person perspective, so he revealed his true feelings. She tested him by asking the direct question, "If I ever became overweight, would you kick me to the curb?" Predictably, her boyfriend replied, "No, honey, I'd love you no matter how much you weighed."

But by using the internal/external foci elicitation technique, she found out how he really felt. She eventually broke up with him.

If you have children, you can use the internal/external elicitation technique to probe their feelings about sensitive issues. For instance, let's say you want to know if your kids are using drugs. If you asked them the direct question, "Are you using drugs?" they would frame their answer within social norms and answer, "No, of course not, drugs are bad."

The best way to find out how your children *really* feel about drugs is to ask them from a third-party perspective. For example, "My friend's son got caught in school with marijuana. What's your take on that?" You want to hear "Marijuana is bad and I would never use it." However, be prepared for "That's stupid. He should have never brought it to school," "It's only weed," or "No big deal. I know lots of kids who smoke marijuana." These responses indicate that your kid may be using marijuana or is predisposed to experimentation. Again, these responses are not foolproof evidence of drug use by your child, but they do provide insights into your child's predisposition.

RULE #4: *E*MPATHIZE: USE EMPATHIC STATEMENTS AND OTHER VERBAL OBSERVATIONS THAT MAKE YOUR LISTENER(S) AWARE THAT YOU KNOW HOW THEY FEEL.

People develop positive feelings toward those individuals who can "walk in their shoes" and understand what they are experiencing. Your empathic statements and/or statements of concern send a message to the listener that you comprehend their circumstances and realize what they have to say is meaningful. In doing so, you are fulfilling the other person's need to be recognized and appreciated. This makes them feel better about themselves and in turn makes them feel better about you, which encourages friendship development.

You'll be amazed at how often you will get the chance to use empathic statements to start conversations and jump-start getting people to like you. All it takes is a willingness to observe people for a few moments before you speak to them. What you will see, more often than you might expect, is the individual you are watching saying or doing something that reveals they are dissatisfied with the current situation they are in. This is especially true when you are dealing with individuals whom you might only confront once, or at infrequent intervals, during your life, such as salespeople, clerks, service personnel, and the like.

You can be almost certain, for example, that if you eat out at a restaurant during prime dinner hours, your server will be rushed. Simply saying, "Boy, you look busy!" will usually bring an affirmative response and, along with it, superior service. The individual you spoke with appreciates that you noticed them and recognized the work challenge they face. It makes them feel better about themselves and, based on the Golden Rule of Friendship, they are going to like you for what you did. If you want to be even more empathic, add a compliment to your original statement that allows them to flatter themselves. "Boy, you're really busy! *I don't know how you do it.*" Or: "Boy, you're busy! *There's no way I could keep up with all those orders.*"

There are times that you don't need to witness a person of interest's discomfort or complaints to make effective empathic comments. This happens when you can *infer* that a person might be experiencing difficulties and would appreciate recognition of their plight. To illustrate: If it is late in the day and you see a woman clerk in high heels working the floor in a department store, you might comment, "Wow, your feet must get tired with you having to stand up at work all day." Chances are you're going to be right and the salesperson will respond positively to your empathetic behavior.

Parents can effectively use empathic statements when they want to encourage their children to talk to them, especially when they are teenagers. Most teenagers are reluctant to openly share information and experiences with their parents, for a wide variety of reasons. Demanding, threatening, or cajoling a response typically ends in a shields-up reaction, causing the teen to become more resolute in their determination not to talk with you.

To avoid this nonproductive response, use an empathic statement such as "You look like you are thinking about something pretty serious," "You look as though something is really bothering you," or "You're worried about something." Your teen might respond in several ways. First, they could agree with you and disclose what is on his or her mind. Second, they could provide a partial response. In this event, construct another empathic statement to tease out a few more details. Most teens want to tell their parents what's bothering them. They just need a little encouragement and the belief that talking to you is their choice. The third response is a curt reply and silence. In this instance, the applicable empathic statement could be something to the effect of "Something's bothering you and you don't want to talk about it right now. When you feel the time is right, let me know and we can talk."

Showing empathy toward another person, whether it is done through empathic statements or other forms of verbal commentary, is a powerful way to make another person feel better about themselves and make them your friend at the same time. In your friendship toolbox, the empathy tool will be one of your most often used and effective techniques for shaping successful relationships. What you say and how you listen will go a long way in establishing or destroying friendships.

AVOIDING CONVERSATION PITFALLS

Getting people to like you, as we have seen, can be facilitated by encouraging them to talk about themselves while you listen to what they say and using that information to choose and use your various friendship tools to cement the relationship. For this reason, the last thing you want to do is *discourage* (usually unintentionally) the two-way flow of communication between yourself and the person who you hope will perceive you as a friend. To keep the communication flowing smoothly, be sure to steer clear of common conversation pitfalls that impede verbal exchanges between individuals.

1. Avoid talking about topics that engender negative feelings in your listener. Negative feelings make people feel bad about themselves and, consequently, they will like you less.

2. Don't constantly complain about your problems, your family's problems, or the problems of the world. People have enough problems of their own without hearing about yours . . . or anyone else's for that matter.

3. Avoid talking excessively about yourself. Talking about yourself too much bores other people. Keep the focus on the other person in your conversation.

4. Do not engage in meaningless chatter; it turns people (and the Like Switch) off.

5. Avoid expressing too little or too much emotion. Extreme displays of emotion may put you in a bad light.

PUTTING IT ALL TOGETHER

Verbal behavior is a vital component in activating the Like Switch and keeping it lit. What you say, how you listen, and how you respond to what you hear plays a huge role in determining how successful you will be in making friends and learning information without appearing intrusive. Using the tools in this chapter will help you achieve success in speaking the language of friendship. You have my word on that!

6

BUILDING CLOSENESS

The loftiest edifices need the deepest foundations.
—GEORGE SANTAYANA

Making friends requires a particular bonding agent to hold the relationship together: rapport. When you "connect" with another person you have rapport. It is the ground from which the relationships grows. As noted writer and speaker Kevin Hogan observed, "Building rapport begins with you." If you want to make friends, it is your responsibility to establish rapport and then, if you want to continue beyond a brief encounter, to strengthen that rapport to expand the relationship into a cohesive, long-lasting bond.

This chapter has all the tools you need to establish and build rapport, but first let's return for a moment to the friend-foe continuum.

FRIEND–STRANGER–FOE

The friend-foe continuum makes no distinction in the *levels* of friendship that are possible between not knowing anyone at all (stranger) and the friend end of the continuum. Obviously, such differences exist and these differences in turn dictate how rapport should be developed in our personal encounters. These different levels of friendship are depicted in the following:

STRANGER–CASUAL ENCOUNTER–ACQUAINTANCE– FRIEND–SIGNIFICANT OTHER

Looking at this "friendship continuum," you can see that the level of contacts increases in significance, moving from a brief, infrequent interaction to a potentially lifelong relationship. Building rapport becomes more important as we evolve along the continuum from the "casual encounter" to the "significant other." This is because the interaction becomes more intense and meaningful as people who were once strangers become an increasingly integral part of each other's lives.

This chapter is designed to help you understand how and whether you are effectively building closeness with persons of interest.

BUILDING RAPPORT

People are communal beings. We naturally seek to connect to other people. Rapport builds a psychological bridge between people and paves the way for various levels of friendship to develop. If I can build rapport with you I can be relatively certain you will like me. It's that simple.

When I interviewed witnesses and suspects, my first task was to build a psychological connection between myself and the person I was interviewing. People, especially suspects, rarely open up to people they don't like. In the case with suspects, I am asking that person to reveal secrets that would put him or her in prison for a long time. On one occasion, I interviewed a repeat sexual assault suspect. We connected on the topic of sports. Once the rapport bridge was established, I was able to delve deeper into his personal life. Eventually, the suspect confessed his crimes. The suspect voluntarily maintained his connection with me long after his trial, conviction, and sentencing through a series of unanswered letters he sent me. In the letters he thanked me for being his friend and treating him with respect. Treating the suspect with respect is possible; being his friend was an illusion; nonetheless, his letters provide a testament of the power of connecting with other people.

TESTING FOR RAPPORT

Testing for rapport is important in any personal interaction because it lets us know "how we are doing" and "where we stand" in developing a relationship with any given individual. Even in a onetime encounter with someone, particularly if we want something from them, testing for rapport is important to determine when and if we have reached a point in the relationship where we can attempt to achieve our relationship objectives. That being said, testing for rapport reaches its most significant level of importance when we are interested in developing closer, more enduring relationships over time.

Sometimes there is an overlap between the behaviors we use to build rapport and the behaviors we use to test for rapport. In these cases, the degree and intensity of the behaviors vary as personal relationships strengthen or weaken and provide us with an objective measure of a deepening or dying relationship. For example, eye gaze is a way to build rapport. The length of that gaze is used to test for rapport, providing a measure of how far the relationship has developed or deteriorated. What follows are some of the important behaviors that can be used to test for the foundation of friendships between individuals.

TOUCHING

Touching represents a reliable gauge to measure the intensity of a relationship. When strangers meet, they typically touch one another on the arms below the shoulders or on the hands, as was discussed earlier in the book. Any touching that occurs outside this public touch zone suggests a more intense relationship.

Women who feel comfortable with the person they are talking to will often reach out and give the other person a light touch on the forearm or knee if they are both seated. This light touch indicates that rapport has been established.

Men often mistake a light touch to the forearm or knee as an invitation to have sex. This is rarely the case. Men, more so than women, tend to interpret nonverbal gestures signaling good rapport as a sexual offer. When a woman gives a man a light touch, the only safe assumption he can make is that she likes him, and nothing more. This male tendency to assume a woman's touch is a sexual invitation often damages budding relationships, often beyond repair.

The most intimate (nonsexual) place a man can touch a woman in public is the small of her back. This place is reserved for men who have earned the right to make an intimate public display of affection. Touching the small of a woman's back can also serve as a relationship indicator. If, for example, you see a woman you'd like to meet speaking with another man, you can test the strength of their relationship by observing the actions of the man as you approach. If the man extends his arm and hovers over the small of the woman's back, he is staking his claim, but he has not yet earned the right to invade the woman's personal space. This gesture means that you still have a chance to gain her affection without interfering with an ongoing, committed relationship.

If a man attempts to prematurely touch the small of a woman's back, she will often flinch and show nonverbal signs of discomfort, or a combination thereof. On the other hand, if, as you approach, the man firmly touches the small of the woman's lower back or hip region, you should assume that the relationship has progressed well beyond the introductory stage and you should look elsewhere for companionship.

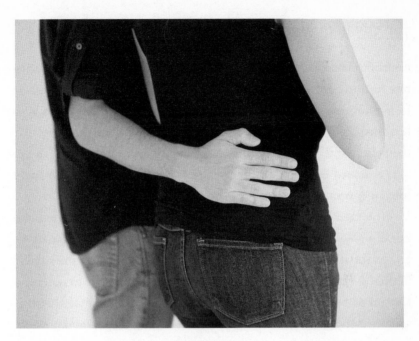

An intimate touch.

Staking a claim, but not a sexual touch.

THE SPY WHO WAS TAKEN ABACK

Touching the small of the back provided a critical clue in an espionage case against an FBI agent who, it turned out, provided classified information to a foreign government for over twenty years. This agent recruited a source from a country hostile to the United States. Over the period of their relationship, the source convinced the agent to provide classified information that was eventually passed on to the hostile foreign government.

The members of the Behavioral Analysis Program obtained a series of videotapes depicting the agent interacting with his source. On one of the tapes, he was observed touching his source on the small of her back. Based on this gesture, the BAP team was able to determine that on or before that date the FBI agent had engaged in sex with his source. A possible motive was detected for the agent to knowingly provide classified information to a hostile government. This led to an investigation that uncovered his complicity in the illegal transmission of classified documents to a foreign government.

PREENING ("GROOMING") BEHAVIORS

Preening gestures such as picking lint off a partner's clothes or straightening his tie or coat are also signs of good rapport. Self-preening, on the other hand, particularly when it is done to avoid looking at the other person or carried on over an extended period of time, is often a foe signal indicating lack of interest in the relationship.

Researchers identified a list of grooming behaviors that can be used to assess the intensity of romantic relationships. The more grooming behaviors that are present, the more intense the relationship. This checklist is a good way to assess your romantic relationships. Holly Nelson and Glen Geher developed the following partial list of positive grooming activities.

1. Do you run your fingers through your significant other's hair?

2. Do you wash your significant other's hair or body while showering/bathing?

3. Do you shave your significant other's legs/face?

4. Do you wipe away your significant other's tears when he or she cries?

5. Do you brush or play with your significant other's hair?

6. Do you wipe away or dry liquid spills off your significant other?

7. Do you clean and/or trim your significant other's fingernails or toenails?

8. Do you brush dirt, leaves, lint, bugs, etc. off your significant other?

9. Do you scratch your significant other's back or other body parts?

10. Do you wipe food and/or crumbs off your significant other's face or body?

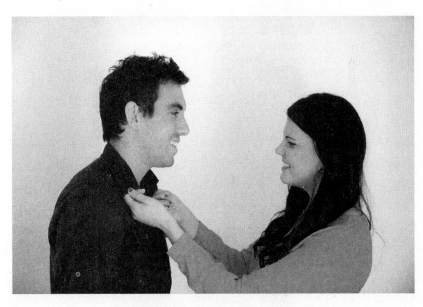

Getting "groomed" is a sign of good rapport.

ISOPRAXISM (MIRRORING THE BEHAVIOR OF ANOTHER PERSON)

We discussed isopraxism/mirroring to build rapport in Chapter 2. So, how do you test for it? By checking for its presence over time through what is referred to as the "lead and follow" approach.

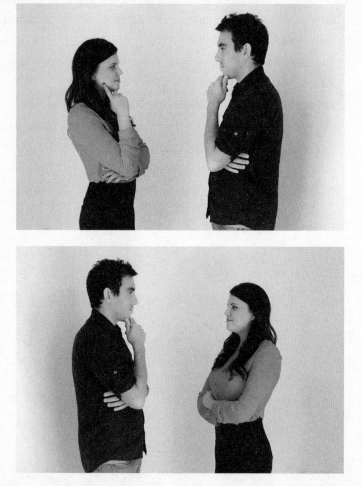

Examples of good rapport (top photo, mirroring clearly visible) and poor rapport (bottom photo, asynchronous posture and no mirroring in evidence).

People who are psychologically connected mirror one another's body gestures. Intentionally mirroring another individual's body language promotes rapport. When you first meet someone, you'll want to mirror his or her gestures to establish rapport. At some point during the conversation, you can test your rapport with the other person by using the lead-and-follow technique. Heretofore, you have been mirroring the other person. Now you want to see if they mirror your gestures, signaling rapport. Change your body position. If you have established rapport, the other person should mirror you within twenty to thirty seconds.

In the lead-and-follow approach to testing for rapport, you are changing your body position by crossing or uncrossing your arms and legs or making some other obvious change in your posture. If the other person mirrors the same gesture, rapport has been established. However, if the other person does not respond in like kind, then you have the option of continuing to build rapport, followed by a new lead-and-follow test to see if rapport has been established after your additional efforts have been expended.

HAIR FLIP

A head toss accompanied by a momentary flip of the hair with the hand is an indicator of rapport.

The key nonverbal display during a hair flip is mutual gaze, which is a strong positive sign that rapport has been established. The three pictures that follow show a "hair flip" in sequence, as it would actually appear in real time.

Observe the hair flip carefully when testing for rapport. This is because a hair flip, without mutual gaze, that is, a hair flip accompanied by broken eye contact, is a strong negative signal indicating a lack of rapport. This gesture is commonly referred to as a "bitch flip."

A hair flip

The bitch flip

The hair flip sequence

POSTURAL POSITIONING

A good way to test for rapport is to note the posture of the two individuals who are interacting. Two behaviors are of particular value.

INWARD LEANING

Individuals lean toward people or things they like and distance themselves from those they don't. People who are in good rapport lean toward one another. During predeployment training for interrogators going to Iraq, I noticed that the majority of the soldiers were leaning backward during the first hour of my presentation. Just prior to the break, using an empathic statement, I told them I didn't feel as though I was making a connection with them. The soldiers nodded in unison. They told me they had been to Iraq on two previous deployments and the material I was teaching them was too basic. I told them to take a fifteen-minute break and I would go to my office to retrieve the advanced training manual. Had I not noticed the lack of rapport between myself and the class during the first hour, the entire training session would have been wasted.

OPEN POSTURE

People who are in good rapport assume an open body posture. An open posture signals attraction and openness to communication. It consists of gestures that include uncrossed legs and arms, a high rate of hand movements during speech, palms-up displays, a slight forward lean, and the display of friend signals. This communicates warmth, trust, and friendliness. To add to the impact of open posture, one can use head nodding, head tilts, and verbal encouragers such as "I see," "Uh-huh," or "Go on."

A person experiencing good rapport does not feel threatened by the person with whom they are interacting and therefore is comfortable assuming an open posture. An individual who feels threatened in the same situation tends to assume a closed body posture to protect himself from a threat or perceived threat. A closed posture can also indicate a lack of interest.

Closed posture displays are typically the opposite of open posture displays. These include tightly crossed arms, a low rate of hand movements, and few friend signals. If the person you are talking with is looking at you but their torso and feet are pointing in another direction, he or she is not fully engaged. A person's feet will often point in another direction to subconsciously telegraph a desire to leave. Other signs of disinterest are backward leaning of the body or head, supporting the head with the hands, or negative grooming behaviors such as picking at teeth or nails.

TORSO REPOSITIONING

People who share rapport will orient themselves toward each other. Leaning in or away from someone is one form of torso shift indicating good or poor rapport. Another type of torso shift is illustrated in the two photographs on the following page. This type of nonverbal body movement involves shifting the torso so it faces the person of interest more directly. Such a body shift is a good indication of increasing rapport between the individuals involved.

In testing for rapport using torso movements, the basic rule to remember is that people who share rapport will orient their bodies toward each other. This is the typical sequence for achieving such an orientation: First, the other person's head will turn toward you. Second, the other person's shoulders will turn toward you. Finally, the other person will reposition his or her torso so that it directly faces you. When this occurs, you can be confident that rapport has been established.

Torso repositioning sequence

BARRIERS

A good way to test for rapport is to look for barriers that individuals place and/or remove between themselves and other people. People who do not feel comfortable with other individuals will erect barriers or leave ones already there in place. On the other hand, individuals who feel at ease with the person with whom they are interacting will keep an open space between them, even if it involves removing barriers that are already between them.

Attempts to block the body or chest are a foe signal. You can send this nonverbal message at the dinner table by placing or leaving a centerpiece between yourself and the individual sitting across from you.

Barriers can be formed by the positioning of hands and feet or placing an inanimate object between individuals. Some of the nonverbal behaviors and inanimate objects that create barriers are listed below. When you see these kinds of barriers, you can assume that good rapport has *not* been established between the individuals involved.

Arm crossing provides a barrier.
(The backward lean demonstrates a lack of rapport.)

ARM CROSSING

Arm crossing serves as a psychological barrier to protect individuals from topics that cause them psychological anxiety. People who are in good rapport do not feel threatened, nor do they feel anxious. If the person you are talking to suddenly crosses his or her arms, then rapport has not yet been established or it signals weakening rapport. People who feel uncomfortable with the person they are talking to or the topic being discussed tend to cross their arms over their chest.

BUILDING BARRIERS WITH INANIMATE OBJECTS

The placement of soft drink cans, pillows, purses, and other movable objects between you and another person signals discomfort and a lack of rapport. A woman who does not have good rapport with the person she is talking with will often use her purse to create a barrier. This usually involves picking up her purse from the floor and bringing it to her lap. This signals that rapport has not yet been established or that the rapport is deteriorating.

PILLOW TALK

I explained the function of barriers to a new agent I was training. He was a little skeptical about the effectiveness of the technique until he interviewed a particular witness. We interviewed the witness at her home. She sat on the couch and we sat in two wing-backed chairs across from her. The new agent asked the witness to provide a description of the suspect. The witness hesitated, reached for a couch pillow, and placed it on her lap. The new agent gave me a sideward glance to let me know that he had picked up on the nonverbal tell that the witness was uncomfortable describing the suspect. The new agent constructed an empathic statement. "Ma'am, you seem to be uncomfortable about identifying the suspect." "I sure am," she admitted. "I don't want that guy coming back and hurting me." The agent constructed a follow-up empathic statement: "So, you're worried about retribution." "Yeah," she sighed. A change in the witness's nonverbal language signaled a change in her psychological disposition. Watching for subtle changes in people's nonverbal language often communicates more information than anything the person might say.

The agent took the time to discuss the woman's fear and gave her reasons that her fear was unfounded. Once he was able to eliminate the witness's fear of retaliation, not surprisingly, she returned the couch pillow to the corner of the couch. The connection between the new agent and the witness had been reestablished.

PROLONGED EYE CLOSURE

Anxious people will signify their uneasiness by prolonged eye closure. Their eyelids serve as a barrier to prevent them from seeing the person or thing that makes them anxious or uncomfortable. On several occasions when I entered my boss's office I saw him close his eyelids for one to two seconds. This display let me know that he was busy and did not want to talk to me at that time. My boss and I generally shared good rapport, but on those days when he displayed prolonged eye closure, I quickly excused myself. My boss would not welcome my requests, comments, or suggestions when his nonverbal behavior indicated he wanted to be left alone.

EYE-BLINK RATE

When people experience anxiety, they tend to increase their eye-blink rate. The normal rate for most people is fifteen blinks per minute. As people become more anxious, their rate increases or decreases from their normal baseline rate. Each person has a slightly different "normal" eye blink rate and thus their personal rate must be calibrated at the beginning of your interaction with them.

CUP POSITIONING

As you may recall, 70 percent of all information is transferred between individuals over food and drink. People who eat or drink together are predisposed to talk. Watching where a person places his or her cup can signal if rapport has been established. If the person across from you places his or her cup between the two of you, the cup forms a barrier, which signals that rapport has not yet been established. If the person places it to either side, leaving open the space between the two of you, this signals that rapport has been established. The three pictures that follow show a couple developing good rapport.

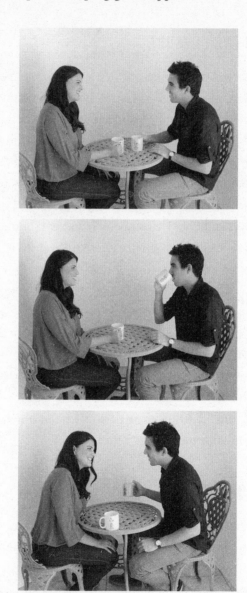

Cup movement helps you determine if rapport has been established.

Note in the first photo how the two cups form a barrier between the couple at the table. In the second photo, the young lady is about to take a drink, while the young man has already sipped from his cup. In the third snapshot, the woman has finished her drink and placed it to one side, leaving an open space between herself and the young man, who is still holding his cup but is clearly about to place it on the other side of the table to clear the space between them of any barriers.

Barrier-removing behaviors between you and the person you are talking to signal good rapport. You can monitor rapport during conversations by watching where people place their cups or other objects on the table. If the person you are talking to unexpectedly places their cup in front of you, then this gesture could signal weakening rapport. In other words, cup or object positioning can serve as a barometer of rapport to signal whether it is dissipating or increasing. This is seen in the series of photos that follows on page 180.

In the first photo, we see a couple seated at a table with a vase of flowers between them. In the next two photos, we see the young man removing the barrier (flowers) between himself and the young lady by picking up the vase and placing it on the side. The fourth photo shows increasing rapport with no barrier, and the young couple leaning in toward each other, displaying head tilts and smiling. The fifth picture displays still stronger rapport, as the male and female are now holding hands. The sixth picture captures the strongest rapport of all, as the young man is whispering to his companion, whispering being another strong sign of good rapport.

The buildup of good rapport over time

BEHAVIORS THAT INDICATE THE PRESENCE OR ABSENCE OF RAPPORT

Here are some of the "tells" you will want to watch for in determining where you are in the rapport-building process.

Friend Signals Signifying Rapport	Foe Signals Signifying a Lack of Rapport
Eyebrow flashes	Furrowed eyebrows
Head tilt	Eye rolls
Frequent smiles	Cold stares
Mutual gaze	Prolonged eye closure and/or gaze aversion
Intimate touching	No (or very limited) touching
Isopraxism (mirroring behavior)	Asynchronous posture
Inward lean (toward another person)	Leaning away (from another person)
Whispering	Hair twirling (unless a "habit")
Expressive gestures	Aggressive stance and/or attack posture
Open body posture	Closed body posture
Removal of barriers/obstacles	Creation or use of barriers/obstacles
Wide-open eyes	Eye squints
Puckering or licking of lips (women)	Fake yawns
Frequent nods	Negative head shakes
Sharing food ("food forking")	Scrunched nose
Preening ("grooming") your partner	Self-preening
Hair flip	Bitch flip

WHAT DO YOU SEE? TIME TO TAKE A TEST ON WHAT YOU'VE LEARNED!

On the following pages are a series of photographs, each one accompanied by a question. Using the information you have learned in this book, answer the question to the best of your ability. Then check your responses against our answers found in the Appendix.

Identify the friend or foe signal depicted in the photograph.

Identify three friend signals depicted in the photograph.

(Difficult question): Identify (name) an additional
friend signal not found in picture #2.

How good is the rapport between the individuals in this photograph?
Using nonverbal behavioral cues, justify your answer.

How would you describe the way these individuals feel about each other? Use nonverbal cues to support your answer.

How would you describe the way these individuals feel about each other? Use nonverbal cues to support your answer.

Can you identify the friend signal not seen in any of the other photos that indicates good rapport between the two individuals?

How would you describe the way these individuals feel about each other? Use nonverbal cues to support your answer.

How would you describe the level of rapport between the two individuals in the photo? Use nonverbal cues to justify your answer.

(Difficult question): Who has the upper hand here, the guy or the gal? Use nonverbal cues to explain and justify your answer.

7

NURTURING AND SUSTAINING LONG-TERM RELATIONSHIPS

People don't care about how much you know
until they first know how much you care.
—ZIG ZIGLAR

All long-term relationships start out as short-term relationships and develop the same way as all friendships do, through an understanding and utilization of all the tools for building and sustaining rapport. As time passes, some of our relationships grow from friendship to romantic. When a relationship has matured to being a loving interaction, a new behavioral focus is required to keep the passion and the partnership intact and intense.

This behavior, simple to understand but challenging to sustain, is *caring*. Think for a moment of every person you have known on more than a casual basis, such as family, friends, colleagues, and mentors. Then ask yourself: "Which of these individuals would I hold in highest esteem and carry out their wishes most willingly?" Chances are that person is someone who *you believe* cares about you. You sense this in their actions and in their general demeanor.

Trying to define caring is a bit like defining the term *pornography*. When a Supreme Court justice was asked to define that term he answered, "I can't define it, but I can recognize it when I see it." So, too, with caring. To try to use words to capture the essence of caring leaves us struggling to recognize the emotional, deeply passionate component of what caring is all about, even though we can readily recognize it when we experience it. Caring is about the *heart* rather than the *head*. It is about a relationship that goes beyond robotic, intellectual, surface interactions and taps into the very essence of who we are at our innermost level of feeling.

Caring allows us to reach the higher elevations of relationship growth, and the letters that spell out the word also tell us what we need to do to care *effectively.*

C = Compassion/concern
A = Active listening
R = Reinforcement
E = Empathy

Let's examine each of these words in turn to help define what must be done to keep long-term relationships with significant others healthy and happy.

COMPASSION/CONCERN

People who are caring individuals show an honest *concern* for others. Not a passing comment or a flippant response to someone who is hurting, but rather a genuine sense of compassion for what that person is experiencing and a commitment to help make things better. In long-term relationships there will be many times when one or both partners are facing crises. It is here where the true level of concern, or lack of it, becomes evident. It is relatively easy to maintain a long-term relationship when things are going well; it is in the crucible of a crisis that the true character of an individual is revealed and found to be wonderful or wanting.

In a sense, there is little one can imagine that is more beautiful than two people who have come to depend on each other to be there as a caring partner when the need arises, as it most certainly will. Perhaps the most enduring form of caring comes when one person becomes a caregiver for a sick or injured partner. To witness this kind of selfless sacrifice, day after day, sometimes year after year, is to see the embodiment of caring in its purest form.

Hopefully, you will never be called upon to care for a significant other in sickness (rather than in health). Fortunately, on a daily basis you can do little things that let your partner know you care about them. Sharing the workload, doing something extra special for no reason, taking the time to give a compliment to your "special person," offering reassurance when they falter, being there when they need you, offering a kind word and a helping hand: These are all acts of caring that a compassionate individual undertakes. This kind of caring is "loving someone from the inside," and when you give it from your heart it will be received with heartfelt gratitude.

I was sitting in a crowded Washington, D.C., shopping mall food court having lunch and as I was walking to the trash receptacle, I thought I heard my name being called. I scanned the crowd and didn't notice anyone trying to get my attention so I continued walking. I then heard my full name being called. I turned and saw a young lady approaching. She stopped and introduced herself, but I didn't recognize her. She told me that she wanted to thank me for saving her life. I gave her a quizzical look. She continued, "I was one of the girls who was kidnapped about ten years ago." Instantly, I flashed back to the day she and her friend were rescued by two police officers in a hail of gunfire. I reminded her that the two police officers were the ones who saved her life. She acknowledged that the officers rescued her from her kidnapper, but I was the one who saved her life. "How so?" I asked.

"I was an emotional wreck," she said. "Your kindness and compassion got me started on the healing process." I recalled being assigned to the case. My supervisor tasked me to interview her after she was freed. It took about a month to get her calmed down enough to tell me what happened without breaking down. I spent about an hour each day just letting her talk things out. Empathic statements were crucial. We rarely discussed the actual kidnapping event but, eventually, I was able to conduct a detailed interview of the then-fourteen-year-old victim. I completed the interview and never saw her again, nor did I give her another thought, but she remembered. "You may have forgotten me," she said, "but I will always remember your acts of kindness. I don't think I would have recovered without your help." I thanked her and told her that I was just doing my job. I put my tray on the service counter and we parted. I realized then that words spoken, which are often long forgotten by the speaker, can continue to have a profound impact on the listener.

ACTIVE LISTENING

Active listening means you are using verbal and nonverbal cues along with empathic statements when the other person is speaking. Some of the earlier suggestions in Chapter 5 involving active listening take on added significance in long-term relationships, where years of interactive communication with the same individual can give us a better understanding of how to strengthen or weaken personal bonds.

In long-term relationships, communication is a key element in sustaining or draining the feelings we have toward one another. Open, honest interchanges between long-term partners build trust, demonstrate a caring attitude, and provide vital information about the ongoing health of the relationship.

If, from the start of any relationship, you have been a proponent and practitioner of active listening, you will have a great advantage the longer the relationship lasts. This is because you will have a far better understanding of your partner's particular needs, personal "quirks," interests, personality, desires, fears, and which conversational topics are to be explored or avoided.

Without *active* listening, it is possible for some couples who have been together for decades to have literally no idea how their partner really feels or what they want. This is because they haven't paid attention to what their partner was saying! As hard as it might be to believe this could happen, it does; sadly, more often than most people would care to admit. Active listening allows open, two-way communication, where the give-and-take of information is facilitated by active speaking and listening.

One of the greatest benefits of active listening in a long-term relationship is the ability to make finer discriminations concerning how to best care for your partner. Whereas in a new or early-stage relationship the chance of saying "the wrong thing" is a distinct possibility, these conversational errors should drop off dramatically (even disappear altogether) as the relationship matures and the parties to the interaction get to know each other better through active listening.

Any individual who has actively listened to his or her long-term significant other knows full well what word mines to avoid and the hot-button issues that shouldn't be pressed. A caring person uses this information to strengthen the relationship. On the other hand, this knowledge can be used to weaken and even destroy relationships. This occurs most frequently during fights when one party to the argument purposely "pushes" the other person's hot button, effectively escalating the conflict and inflicting mental pain at the same time. This is a very bad strategy to employ, even if a person is mad or it helps win an argument. The problem is that long after the argument is over and the reason it started is forgotten, the emotional aftermath of being hurt by a person's words will linger.

Even though it might be tempting to use information you have learned from previous discussions to win an argument or "get in your licks" during a fight, don't do it if your partner considers such information "off-limits." Resist the temptation to lash out with your tongue!

Over time, if a person persists in deliberately tripping word mines, pushing hot-button issues, or bringing up topics that are considered off-limits in arguments, the relationship might very well collapse as a result.

KEEP YOUR VOICE AWAY FROM THE HOT BUTTON!

Be an effective active listener. Not only will you be seen as more caring; you will also achieve a greater understanding of your partner and strengthen your relationship in the process. Here are a few additional hints to make your active listening more effective:

- Let your partner finish what they are saying before you begin talking.
- Important discussions deserve an appropriate setting where you can easily hear what your partner is saying (don't talk about finances or life-changing events in a noisy, crowded restaurant!).
- Don't be thinking of what you'll be saying while your partner is talking; focus on their words, not your thoughts.
- If your partner is introverted and finds it uncomfortable to speak, encourage them with head nods and verbal nudges (see Chapter 5).
- Observe your partner while they speak. Communication is nonverbal as well as verbal. Also, by paying attention to your partner they are most likely to see you as sincerely interested in what they have to say.
- Be prepared to compliment your partner when they make a good point or suggestion.
- When you hear something you don't like or agree with, don't automatically dismiss the comment or go on the offensive. Give the observation some thought and see if there might be some truth in what was said or, at least, some room for reaching a compromise that is satisfactory to both partners.

- If your partner is clearly wrong in a given situation, try to help them find a face-saving way to gracefully own up to their error.
- You can even suggest a "time-out" if you feel the conversation is becoming confrontational.

REINFORCEMENT

Reinforcement is the use of reward and punishment meted out by one individual to another in a relationship. Here are some errors you don't want to make in dealing with your significant other:

1. Being Unaware That Your Style of Interaction Leads to the Inappropriate Administration of Rewards and/or Punishments to Others on a Day-to-Day Basis.

Some people, when involved in a long-term relationship, exhibit consistent patterns of reinforcement with their partner that are not conducive to maximizing relationship satisfaction. There are three kinds of individuals who use reinforcement inappropriately.

The Negativistic Partner

Their motto: "Emphasize the negative; ignore the positive."
Their credo: "What credit do you deserve for doing something right? That's your job!"
Their behavioral approach to a partner: negativity and punishment.

Negativistic partners seem to have mastered the "See, I told you so" routine when you're wrong and the "I don't see you" routine when you're right. The person living with a negativistic partner usually utters this oft-heard lament: "The only time I hear from my partner is when I do something wrong." Is it any wonder such behavior creates bitterness and a sense of frustration? Nobody likes to feel that when they do something good, it is ignored, while any mistakes receive maximum attention. As one wife so aptly told her husband, "At least if you're going to criticize my mistakes, give equal time to my successes." Negativistic partners need to recognize that it is appropriate to criticize their significant other if they do something wrong that needs correcting; however, it is also appropriate to praise that individual when they do something well.

The Perfectionistic Partner

Their motto: "There's always room for improvement."

Their credo: "If it isn't perfect; it isn't worth it."

Their behavioral approach to a partner: sets unreasonable standards.

The perfectionistic partner demands high levels of effort to achieve perfection when competency will suffice with far less effort expended. Perfectionistic individuals aren't unwilling to praise their partners for a task or chore well done, as long as it is done *perfectly*. And therein lies the problem. Because the perfectionistic partner sets standards so high, hardly anybody can reach the level of performance necessary to trigger a kind word. Thus the perfectionistic partner does the negativistic partner one better, requiring such high levels of performance it is literally impossible to satisfy them in the first place! The most successful way perfectionistic partners can modify their over-the-top demands in a relationship is to temper their standards to a reasonable level, one that values competency and doesn't demand behavioral performance that is largely beyond reach. Perfectionistic partners should come to understand that the amount of time and effort needed to turn competent performance into perfect performance is seldom worth it.

The Sadistic Partner

Their motto: "One mistake wipes out all good performance."
Their credo: "To err is human; to pay for it, divine."
Their behavioral approach: a total imbalance between the rewarding
    of good performance versus the punishment of errors or mistakes.

Sadistic partners earn their title because they remind us of naughty children who pick the wings off butterflies. On the surface, they seem kind enough. They give praise and recognition to their partners on a regular basis. But, wait! These individuals have a unique, and unrealistic, way of balancing their compliments and criticism when it comes to dealing with their partners. Here's how they operate: Their partners can accumulate as many compliments as their behaviors warrant, but if they do something wrong along the way, that *one* mistake "wipes out" all or most of the praise earned along the way. To the sadistic partner who wants to change for the better, you must recognize a level of "equity" between the weighing of good versus not-so-good behavior on the part of your significant other, and a recognition that accumulated incidents of positive behavior should not be rendered worthless because of one negative incident.

2.   Not Paying Enough "Positive Attention" to Your Partner.

One of the unfortunate realities of long-term relationships is the natural tendency for partners to lose some of the passion that drove them to shower each other with attention, compliments, and "little acts of affection" during the early stages of their interaction. This is unfortunate, because human beings never outgrow the need for positive attention. The sense that someone close to them appreciates them and is willing to show it by performing small acts of kindness and offering compliments on a regular basis is critical to the health and robustness of long-term relationships.

Here are some ways you can give your partner that special feeling of being appreciated:

- Praise your partner when they do something well. It could be a problem they solved at work. Possibly, it could involve some civic or social honor they achieved. It might even be nothing more than they took the time to get you your special dessert at the bakery on the way home. Let your partner know you appreciate them by praising them. The praise should never be offered to "get something" from the person being praised. It should be given only when it is deserved and you can give it honestly. The good news is praise doesn't cost money. All it takes is a willingness to observe your partner so you can spot the praiseworthy behavior when it occurs and then the effort required to actually voice your positive attention.

- Don't forget a partner's significant milestones such as birthdays, anniversaries, special events, and so forth. It is remarkable what a store-bought card with a personal message included can do to make a partner feel really good about themselves and, based on the Golden Rule of Friendship, feel good about you as well.

- Encourage your partner to participate in decision making, particularly major decisions that affect both of you. That means including your partner in financial planning, large purchase decisions, occupational changes or moves, and health issues. People are more willing to go along with whatever decision is reached in a matter if they feel they have had some say in what is decided. This is because they feel included and have "ownership" of the idea. Not only will they be more likely to concur and go along with a decision when they have been consulted, but also they will do so in a more *motivated, enthusiastic* manner.

- When appropriate, give "public recognition" to your partner by letting others know what special accomplishment he or she has achieved. Although your partner might "act" embarrassed or downplay what they have accomplished when you point this out to others when they are present, this shouldn't deter you in most cases. Even introverts will be amenable to public recognition as long as it is done tastefully and not in too flamboyant a style.

3. Not Rewarding Your Partner Correctly Because What You Think They Want and What They *Actually* Want Do Not Coincide

Remember back to a holiday or birthday when, as a child, you received a gift you really didn't want. It was even worse if the gift came from the one relative or friend that had the most money to spend and you were depending on them for that new bike or wad of cash, and instead wound up with a suit or a set of encyclopedias.

Don't make this kind of mistake with your partner. Even if you are well-intentioned and spend a lot of thought and effort getting your special person that special gift, it will not be appreciated if it is not something he or she wanted in the first place. One would think that after ten, twenty, or thirty years or more, partners would have a good idea of what each other wants. Amazingly, this is not always the case. The husband who buys his wife a vacuum cleaner for Valentine's Day is not just the stuff of advertisements and urban legends; it actually does happen.

What's the best way to make sure that what you get someone is what he or she wants? Ask! Or, even better, listen to what they say and you will probably be able to detect what it is they want. Be observant. An open catalogue on the kitchen table with an item circled in red ink might provide a clue.

One of the problems with asking a person what they want is you give them what they desire, but it isn't a "surprise." One way around this, particularly when it comes to giving gifts for holidays, is to have your partner put suggested pictures of items they would enjoy receiving in a special box. For instance, it could be an ad for a vacation, or a desired household item or possibly a menu from a special restaurant. That way, the partner can choose one of the items from the box and purchase it, and the person receiving the gift won't know which one to expect. The element of surprise, although not total, does add more excitement to gift exchanges.

EMPATHY

Empathy is the final component of CARE and a critical component of any successful long-term relationship. Being able to sense how your partner feels, and *caring* about it, is essential to maintaining a good relationship. People who have been together for a long time have a natural advantage when it comes to empathizing with their partner. They have had years to learn even the most subtle nuances of that individual's moods, unique needs, and behavioral idiosyncrasies.

It is amazing what a kind word will do when you sense your partner is feeling down. Using empathic statements such as "You must really be hurting" when learning your loved one has suffered a setback sends a powerful message that you were caring enough to pick up on the problem and willing to take the time to express your concern. "Being there" for a partner who is physically or psychologically hurting provides great comfort, and such compassion is remembered and cherished.

Empathy is such an important part of relationships it has been recognized and extolled for decades as a critical tool in shaping relationships of all kinds: short term, long term, personal, and business. No less a luminary than Henry Ford summed it up nicely when he observed: "If there is any one secret of success it lies in the ability to get the other person's point of view and see things from that person's angle as well as from your own."

Concern/compassion, Active listening, Reinforcement, and Empathy are the components of CARE that turn short-term friendships into long-term relationships, and long-term relationships into all they are capable of becoming.

HOW TO DEAL WITH ANGRY PEOPLE (INCLUDING YOURSELF): PRACTICING ANGER MANAGEMENT

The tools you have been provided to carve out satisfying short and long-term relationships are designed to work with almost anyone (no, psychopaths are not included!). This doesn't mean that any given relationship will be totally satisfying and devoid of conflict. Even the best of friends and significant others can have disagreements, even *angry* disagreements, when in bad moods or on opposite sides of an issue. Learning to deal with anger, which is inevitable in any relationship, is an important skill you'll want to develop for getting over the rough spots in any interpersonal interaction.

HOW TO SUCCESSFULLY HANDLE ANGER IN PERSON-TO-PERSON INTERACTION

Angry friends, coworkers, or family members create stress. They can make your work and home life most unpleasant. Developing effective anger management strategies forms the cornerstone for goodwill and a distinctly more pleasant environment, at home and in the office.

An effective anger management strategy involves keeping the focus of the conversation on the angry party, allowing him or her to vent, and in addition provides a directed course of action to deal with the problem that caused the anger in the first place. This breaks the anger cycle and allows for the resolution of crisis situations without damaging personal relationships. People will like you more as a result of your handling of a crisis situation because in the end you will make the angry party feel good about themselves by reducing their stress and, equally important, yours as well. Here are some guidelines for handling anger in the best way possible.

Do Not Engage Angry People Because They Are Not Thinking Logically

Anger triggers the fight or flight response, which mentally and physically prepares the body for survival. During the fight or flight response, the body automatically responds to a threat without conscious thought. As the threat increases, a person's ability to reason diminishes. Angry people experience the same phenomenon because anger is a reaction to a real or perceived threat. Angry people talk and act without thinking. The level of their cognitive impairment depends on the intensity of their anger. The more angry people become, the less likely they are to logically process information. Angry individuals are not open to solutions when they are mad, because their ability to think logically is impaired.

The body takes about twenty minutes to return to normal after a full fight or flight response. In other words, angry people need time to calm down before they can think clearly again. Angry people will not completely comprehend any explanations, solutions, or problem-solving options until they can think logically again. Allowing for this refractory period is a critical part of any anger management strategy. The first strategy for breaking the anger cycle is "Never try to rationally engage angry people." Anger must be vented before offering problem solving solutions.

It is imperative when confronting an angry individual to take "time off to cool off." One writer suggests that when dealing with an angry friend, colleague, or partner you should "go to the balcony." This is another way of indicating that you need to step back from the fire and let things cool off a bit before returning to the flames.

In many instances, providing a simple explanation can assuage anger. People want to feel like they are in control. Angry people seek order in a world that no longer makes sense to them. The inability to make sense of a disordered world causes frustration. This frustration is expressed as anger. Providing an explanation for a given behavior or problem will often reorder a disordered world and soothe the angered person's feelings in the process. The following exchange between a supervisor and a subordinate demonstrates the use of this technique:

> **SUPERVISOR:** I expected you to have your report done by this
>   morning. Your behavior is unacceptable. (anger)
> **EMPLOYEE:** I couldn't complete the report because I didn't receive
>   the data from the sales department. They said they would send it
>   within the hour. (provide an explanation)
> **SUPERVISOR:** All right. Get the report finished as soon as possible.
>   (anger resolution)

If angry people do not accept the simple explanation for a problem, the potential for verbal escalation increases significantly. Anger needs fuel. The increased anger provokes you to give a more intense response, which provides additional fuel to an angry supervisor. If this anger cycle continues, at some point your fight or flight threshold is crossed, causing a reduction in your ability to think logically. Problem solving becomes impossible when both you and the other person get caught up in the anger cycle.

Try the "Big Three" Approach to Breaking the Anger Cycle: Empathic Statements, Venting, and Presumptive Statements

Empathic statements capture a person's verbal message, physical status, or emotions, and using parallel language, reflect them back to the speaker. Venting reduces frustration. Once angry people are provided a chance to vent their frustrations, they become more open to solutions because they think more clearly when they are not angry. Presumptive statements direct angry people to take a course of action that leads toward the resolution of the conflict that aroused their ire in the first place. Presumptive statements are constructed in such a fashion that angry individuals have difficulty not following the directed (recommended) course of action. The following dialogue demonstrates the big-three approach to breaking the anger cycle.

> **SUPERVISOR:** I expected you to have your report done by this morning. Your behavior is unacceptable. (anger)
>
> **EMPLOYEE:** I couldn't complete the report because I didn't receive the data from the sales department. They said they would send it within the hour. (provide an explanation)
>
> **SUPERVISOR:** That's no excuse. You should have gone to the sales department to get the report. You knew how important it was to get the report done by this morning. I have a meeting with the client this afternoon. I'm not sure what I'm going to do. (rejecting the explanation)
>
> **EMPLOYEE:** You're upset because the client is expecting the report this afternoon. (empathic statement)
>
> **SUPERVISOR:** Yeah. You're making me look bad. (venting)
>
> **EMPLOYEE:** You're disappointed because you expected me to have the report finished this morning. (empathic statement)
>
> **SUPERVISOR:** Exactly. That's an understatement. (shoulders droop accompanied by a deep exhale; venting completed)
>
> **EMPLOYEE:** I'll go get the sales report now and get you the report before your meeting this afternoon. (presumptive statement)
>
> **SUPERVISOR:** Okay. See what you can do. (anger resolution)

A CLOSER LOOK AT HOW THE "BIG THREE" WORK TO "BREAK THE ANGER CYCLE"

Empathic Statements

In breaking the anger cycle, empathic statements are invaluable. When an angry person first hears an empathic statement it can be surprising and confusing. When not expected, it can initially cause suspicion, but when sustained it is difficult not to appreciate the concern it represents. Empathy thus quickly leads to trust.

The more you can empathize, the more you can get immediate feedback on what a person is thinking about what you are saying to them. As a consequence, you can modify what you are saying and doing if you see your initial approach is not working.

The question is: How do you do this? How do you empathize effectively? How do you find out what other people are feeling? All you have to go on is observing: 1) what they say, 2) how they say it, and 3) what they do.

If you want to move an angry person toward a resolution, detecting their emotional state is the first step. When you can sense their emotion, you can then use this to move them in the direction you want them to take.

The trick to spotting a person's feelings is to pay close attention to verbal and nonverbal changes in that individual in response to external events. If you say, "How are you?" and the corners of the person's mouth turn down and their voice tone goes flat, then you might detect that all is not well.

The better you are at spotting changes in verbal and nonverbal cues, the greater your potential ability at empathizing. Watch for small changes on the face. Listen for tension in the voice and emphasis on specific words. Listen for emotional words.

To avoid getting swamped by another person's emotions, learn to dip in and out of the association that makes you feel what they do. Go in, test the temperature, and then get out to a place where you can think more rationally.

Unless you are sure, it can be a good idea to reflect back on the other person what you are sensing of their feelings, to check that you have it right. After all, the only individual who can confirm empathy is the person whose emotions are being sensed. Reflecting back has an effect, typically leading the other person to appreciate that you really care about them and hence increasing their trust in you.

To people who are *not* angry, empathic statements might seem patronizing, but this is not the case for angry people, for two reasons.

First, the fight or flight response is engaged, and angry people cannot logically process information; in this case, empathic statements fall within the human baseline and if properly constructed, will not be detected by the angry person. Second, people naturally think that others should listen to them and be sympathetic, particularly when they are angry.

The key to constructing effective empathic statements is to identify the underlying reason for the anger. Simply saying, "So you're angry" is an empathic statement, but it is stating the obvious and could sound patronizing, which would add more fuel to an already angry person. I remember a time early in my FBI career when I was required to travel extensively. We had three children at the time, a baby and two toddlers. On one particular trip, I was gone for two weeks. When I opened the front door and announced that I was home, I expected a warm hug and a kiss from my wife. That didn't happen. Instead she greeted me with "It's about time you got home. I'm going crazy because you haven't been here to help me with the kids." I could have used the simple empathic statement "So, you're angry," but that would not have gone over well. Instead, I used a sophisticated empathic statement that addressed the root cause of her anger. I said, "You feel overwhelmed because I haven't been home to help you with the kids." I struck a sensitive cord. She vented. "I usually go out every Wednesday night with my friends to take a break from the kids and talk to some adults for a change." I could have used a simple empathic statement such as "You miss going out with your friends," but, again, this would not have played out well. Instead, I used a sophisticated empathic statement that addressed the root cause of her anger. I said, "You value the time you spend with your friends because it gives you a chance to take a break from the kids."

Anger is just a symptom of an underlying problem. Empathic statements should target the underlying problem. Exposing the real cause of the anger will promote venting, which can be controlled by constructing effective empathic statements.

Venting

Venting is a critical component of breaking the anger cycle because it reduces frustration. Empathic statements portray the target of the anger as nonthreatening, which reduces the impact of the angry person's fight or flight response. Once angry people vent their frustrations, they become more open to solutions because they think more clearly when they are less angry.

Venting is not a singular event, but rather a series of events. The initial venting is typically the strongest. This allows angry people to "burn off" most of their anger at the onset of the exchange. Subsequent venting becomes increasingly less intense, unless fuel is added to reignite the anger.

A natural pause occurs after each venting event. During this pause, you should construct an empathic statement. Since empathic statements encourage venting, the angry person will likely continue venting, although with less intensity. After the next natural pause, you should construct another empathic statement. You should continue constructing empathic statements until the other person's anger is spent. Sighs, long exhales, slumping shoulders, and downward glances signal spent anger. At this juncture, you should introduce the presumptive statement.

Presumptive Statements

Presumptive statements direct angry people to take a course of action that leads toward conflict resolution. Presumptive statements are constructed in such a fashion that angry people have difficulty *not* following the directed course of action. Constructing presumptive statements requires practiced critical listening skills. The presumptive statement turns the force of the anger toward a resolution that is acceptable for both parties.

Let's return to my awkward homecoming discussed previously. After a series of empathic statements, my wife's anger burned off. She let out a great sigh and her shoulders slumped. Her anger was spent. Now was the time to present a presumptive statement to direct her to take a course of action that would bring a resolution. I constructed the following presumptive statement: "Why don't I gather the kids up and take them to my mom's house and we'll go out to a nice restaurant? You deserve it." My wife would have had a difficult time not following the course of action I presented. If she rejected my suggested course of action, she would have to admit that she didn't deserve to go to a nice restaurant, that she didn't feel overwhelmed, and that she didn't need a break from the kids, which are the very things she expressed as she vented her anger. Using this technique, I effectively resolved a situation that could have easily escalated into a major domestic dispute, which would have left us both angry and frustrated.

If an angry person rejects the presumptive statement, you should begin the breaking of the anger cycle again with a new empathic statement. If my wife had rejected my suggested course of action, our conversation might have gone something like this:

> **ME:** Why don't I gather the kids up and take them to my mom's house and we'll go out to a nice restaurant? You deserve it. (presumptive statement)
>
> **MY WIFE:** You're not getting off that easy, Mister. (rejection of the presumptive statement)
>
> **ME:** So you think one night out is not enough to make up for the work you did while I was gone. (empathic statement; reentering breaking the anger cycle)

Rejection of the presumptive statement typically indicates that the person has not completely vented his or her anger. Reentering breaking the anger cycle allows the person to vent any residual anger. Some people have deep-seated anger issues that may never be resolved. In these cases, the best course of action you could offer is to agree to disagree or you could both agree not to bring the sensitive topic up again. These possible resolutions set boundaries for your relationships, not abruptly end them.

The anger cycle can be used in virtually all situations when you are confronted by angry people. The following exchange between a customs officer and a foreign visitor illustrates the use of the anger cycle to resolve a dispute.

CUSTOMS OFFICER: Ma'am, you can't bring dirt into this country.

VISITOR: It is sacred dirt from a holy place. I will not give it up!

CUSTOMS OFFICER: So, you don't want to give up the dirt because it is special to you. (empathic statement)

VISITOR: Of course, it's special. It's blessed ground. It keeps evil spirits away. It protects me from illness. I will not give it up and you can't make me! (venting)

CUSTOMS OFFICER: This dirt fends off evil spirits and keeps you healthy. (empathic statement)

VISITOR: I haven't been sick even once since I got the dirt. I really need it. (venting)

CUSTOMERS OFFICER: Staying healthy means a lot to you. (empathic statement)

VISITOR: Yes, it does. (a sigh accompanied by a shoulder drop)

CUSTOMS OFFICER: Let's work together to come up with a solution to this problem. (presumptive statement) Would you like that?" (The visitor cannot say "No" without appearing unreasonable.)

VISITOR: Of course.

CUSTOMS OFFICER: The regulation states that you cannot bring dirt into the country because the microbes in the dirt could infest crops. (provides an explanation) I'm sure you don't want to be responsible for making millions of people sick, do you? (presumptive statement) (The visitor cannot say "Yes" without appearing unreasonable.)

CUSTOMS OFFICER: Give me the dirt and you will be able to begin your visit to the United States.

VISITOR: If I have to, okay. (voluntary compliance)

REENTERING THE ANGER CYCLE

In the event the visitor remained angry and did not voluntarily give up the dirt, the customs officer would reenter the anger cycle in an attempt to break it. The following exchange demonstrates reentry into the cycle.

CUSTOMS OFFICER: Give me the dirt and you will be able to begin your visit to the United States.

VISITOR: No, my dirt isn't contaminated. I have to keep it.

CUSTOMS OFFICER: You are pretty passionate about keeping your dirt. (empathic statement)

VISITOR: I want my dirt! Can I, at least, keep a teaspoonful? (movement toward voluntary compliance)

CUSTOMS OFFICER: You are trying to figure out a way to get at least some of your dirt into the country. (empathic statement)

VISITOR: Yes, of course. Can I keep at least a teaspoon? That surely won't hurt anything. (movement toward voluntary compliance)

CUSTOMS OFFICER: The smallest amount of dirt can do great harm to the crops. (provides an explanation) Give me the dirt and you will be able to begin your visit to the United States. (presumptive statement)

VISITOR: All right. If I have to, I'll give it to you. I really don't want to do this. (voluntary compliance)

In the event that reentering the anger cycle does not produce voluntary compliance, the customs officer should develop two options and then allow the angry person to choose one of the options. Giving angry people two options to choose from creates the illusion that they're in control. The following exchange illustrates the "You choose" technique.

> **VISITOR:** I refuse to give up my dirt.
>
> **CUSTOMS OFFICER:** You seem pretty adamant about keeping your dirt. (empathic statement) The regulation states that you can't bring dirt into the country. You're going to have to make a decision. The first option is to give up your dirt and enter the country. The second option is to keep your dirt and not be allowed to enter the country. (presents two options) It's your decision. What happens from this point forward is up to you. Choose the option you prefer. (creating the illusion that the visitor is in control)
>
> **VISITOR:** I have no real choice because I want to enter the country. You can have the dirt. (voluntary compliance)
>
> **CUSTOMS OFFICER:** You made the right decision. Welcome to America.

In each of these scenarios, the officer maintained the illusion that the visitor was in control of the situation, but in reality the officer directed the visitor one step at a time toward voluntary compliance.

Some people feel they relinquish their authority when they use compliance techniques that subtly influence rather than intimidate. Gaining voluntary compliance through breaking the anger cycle not only enhances your authority but also reduces the probability that the contact will go awry and the angry person will just get madder and less compliant. By your breaking the anger cycle, there is a good chance the angry person will go along with the decision you wanted them to make and, at the same time, feel you treated them with respect. One couldn't hope for a better outcome to an angry confrontation.

WHEN RELATIONSHIPS "GO SOUTH" EVEN AFTER YOU'VE TRIED TO SAVE THEM

If you utilize the tools described in this book to establish and maintain healthy, happy relationships, you will almost always be successful. But what if, even after your best efforts, a short- or long-term relationship goes bad? What then? Particularly with long-term interactions, where a significant amount of time and commitment has already been invested in the relationship, one would hope relationships would not be casually discarded at the first signs of distress. And, in fact, they usually aren't. Most individuals enter into marriages and other forms of long-term relationships with the intention of staying in them.

Yet there are times when even well-intentioned and responsible individuals find it difficult, if not impossible, to remain in a long-term relationship. Why? There are many reasons, but some of the most common include:

- **A divergence of interests.** Individuals who might have shared the same outlook and career paths in their twenties may have different perspectives thirty years later. A new career or life focus can weigh heavily on a long-term relationship if both parties are not seeing eye to eye on the change(s) involved.
- **The "empty nest" syndrome.** When children leave the nest, one or both of the parents sometimes choose the same option.
- **The need for more freedom.** Couples who have been together for a long time, particularly if they married young, sometimes feel "trapped" and yearn for the freedom they see their single friends enjoying. This is a classic case of "the grass is greener" syndrome. Married people yearn for the freedom that single people have and single people yearn for the commitment that married people enjoy.
- **The need for change.** Ever wonder why people in their late sixties and seventies opt to end long-term relationships? Some-

times it is simply the recognition that one doesn't live forever and that if one desires the chance to experience a different lifestyle, the window of opportunity is closing fast.

- **Changes in personality in one or both partners.** Our personalities are not static or set in stone by the time we are adolescents. We change over time and if these changes drive people apart, they usually end up parting.

- **Third-party disruptions.** Behavioral scientists have long debated the issue of whether humans are "naturally" monogamous. While they continue to argue, long-term relationships continue to crumble due to infidelity and partner replacement with a new love interest.

- **Boredom.** Too much of the same thing can create boredom, an accelerant for relationship breakdowns, which can make once-exciting interactions seem mundane and unsatisfying.

- **Emerging incompatibilities.** As relationships develop, so do the persons in the relationship. This can lead to problems, should one party to the relationship develop behaviors unacceptable to the other. For example, one partner in a relationship might start drinking or gambling too much, or show less interest in sex, or become more reclusive, even start snoring (to the dismay of their light-sleeping mate).

The good news is that many, if not all, of these problems can be overcome through mutual effort or counseling if the people involved are *committed* to staying together and are willing to do what it takes to repair the relationship and make it whole.

Even the best of friends can have the worst of arguments!

Good relationships, short or long term, take effort to bloom. Like the gardener who wants his plants and trees to fully blossom, you must nurture relationships with care, patience, and loving understanding if you want them to flower. Relationships can't be left to die at the first sign of blight. You need to be convinced that you've done as much as you can to save a relationship before you consider ending it.

IN CASE OF DIVORCE . . . BREAK GLASS

I was once given a wonderful piece of advice that I pass on to young couples whenever I can: When relationships are still new, vibrant, and full of love, write letters to each other. Pour your hearts out and go into great detail about what you like and admire about the other person. But don't share the letters. Instead, place them in separate sealed envelopes with your partner's name on the front. Then place the letters in a box, which you'll want to store in a safe place.

In the event the relationship goes sour, you can give each other the letters and read them. This emotional reminder may be enough to recharge the feelings of love and jump-start a new era of togetherness. The letters can also be used as an emotional icebreaker to motivate you to resolve any major issues where you are at an impasse and need "something" to get you and your partner back on track toward solving your problem(s).

One man I mentioned this idea to actually made a wooden container with a glass front similar to a fire alarm box found in many buildings. He then affixed a little metal hammer to the box with a metal chain. The sign on the box read, "In case of divorce, break glass." The letters in the box served as a constant reminder to the couple of the reasons they liked and admired each other when they first fell in love. In the middle of a fight or escalating disagreement, either one of them could comment, "Is it time to break the glass?" This not-so-subtle reminder quickly deescalated the fight or disagreement and helped the couple resolve their conflict successfully.

8

THE PERILS AND PROMISE OF RELATIONSHIPS IN A DIGITAL WORLD

Online everyone can be who they want to be. It only
gets tricky when you meet them in the real world.

—TOKII.COM

This is a true story. A love story of sorts, one that could only happen in our digital age. It involves a then-sixty-eight-year-old professor and a Czech bikini model. This particular academician was not lacking in brainpower: He worked as a theoretical particle physicist at the University of North Carolina, Chapel Hill, where he had been employed for three decades.

The professor, still lonely after his recent divorce, visited some online dating sites, where he connected with the Czech beauty. After a flurry of emails, chat room sessions, and instant messages, it became obvious to the professor that the stunning model wanted to give up her career and marry him. It never seemed to cross his mind that the woman on the Internet might have been an imposter or why a young, attractive model would choose him as a husband.

Sadly, he found out why, the hard way. After many unsuccessful attempts by the professor to speak with the young woman on the phone, she agreed to go from virtual reality to real life. All the professor had to do was fly down to Bolivia, where she was currently working, and meet her. This he readily agreed to do. The rest of the story is almost too painful to relate.

Upon arriving late in Bolivia due to a ticketing problem, the professor discovered that his "girlfriend" had already left. However, she told him not to worry, she would send him a ticket to Brussels, Belgium, where he could join her while she did a photo shoot. Her only request was to bring along a bag that she had left behind in Bolivia. At the Buenos Aires airport, the bag was searched. Hidden inside were 1,980 grams of cocaine. He did end up being charged for drug smuggling, but fortunately for him he received a very light sentence.

And what was the *real* Czech bikini model's reaction to all this? Fear, over her name being associated with drug smuggling and "sympathy" for her academic suitor, who, of course, she had never met on the Internet or anywhere else. According to Maxine Swann, a reporter who did an elaborate story on the incident for the *New York Times*, the professor "reported that he was a month into his prison stay before his fellow prisoners managed to convince him that the woman he thought he'd been in touch with all this time had probably been a man impersonating her."

Based on this story, you might think I recommend abstaining from using the digital world to meet people and make friends. However, nothing could be further from the truth. As long as you know how to tell the friends from the frauds (which this chapter will show you), the online landscape offers some distinct advantages.

THE INTERNET IS INTROVERT-FRIENDLY

Introverts disclose more information on social networks than they do in face-to-face encounters. This is because the Internet format allows introverts sufficient time to formulate meaningful responses. Introverts also experience difficulty initiating conversations, especially with strangers. Social networks eliminate this added social pressure. Social networks also allow introverts to express themselves without constantly being interrupted by extroverts. Finally, introverts are more willing to say what they really believe, not having to worry about the direct exposure to negative feedback that can occur in face-to-face communication.

Ease of Finding "Common Ground"

If ever there was a chance for the Law of Similarity (Chapter 4) to operate, it would be on the Internet. When it comes to finding common ground with individuals possessing similar interests, the digital world provides the perfect environment for matchups. Want to find fellow stamp collectors? There's an Internet group for that. Interested in people who exhibit antique automobiles? There's an Internet group for that. Looking for that special group of sports fanatics who also volunteer at animal shelters and eat organic apples from the state of Washington? There's an Internet group for that. Well, maybe.

The point is that with millions of people on the Internet and thousands of chat rooms and special interest groups devoted to almost any activity, real or imaginable, the chance to develop friendships with people sharing similar interests is never more than a click away.

Numbers

If you're looking for a friend with specific qualifications and interests, where would you rather look: in a bar or other public place that might hold a hundred people, or on the Internet, where tens of millions of people await to be clicked on? The sheer number of people that go online increases your chances of finding persons of interest who best fit your particular needs.

Less Chance of Being Embarrassed

Anonymity and the ability to start and end relationships with a click of a mouse make the online user much less likely to face the humiliation and embarrassment that comes with face-to-face disapproval or outright rejection. Of course, should an online user post information and pictures of a questionable nature, the chance of embarrassment definitely is increased (as has been the case with numerous high-profile politicians and celebrities over the years).

The Ability to Prequalify Potential Friends

Particularly on dating sites, individuals looking for partners have the opportunity to describe what they want in a potential respondent. Of course, not all people reading the qualifications abide by them. Many individuals will contact you on the Internet even when they do not possess the qualifications you are looking for. Still, screening mechanisms on certain online sites can be beneficial in limiting the number of people who contact you.

The Opportunity to "Check People Out"

The Internet is information-rich. It provides a wealth of information for those people who know how to get it or are interested in learning more about something or somebody. The Internet should be seen as a tool to learn more about the people you are considering to develop relationships with, whether that person is someone you meet face-to-face or online. Obviously, this information search is more important for potential online friends, because you don't have the advantage of information-gathering through verbal and nonverbal cues available in real-life interactions.

There is simply no denying that the advent of person-to-person online communication has dramatically altered the landscape of seeking friends and building relationships. As this form of digital inter-action continues to grow in popularity, it will have an even greater impact on the way people develop relationships in the years to come.

What does all this mean for you? To paraphrase Charles Dickens: "It can be the best of times; it can be the worst of times." When em-ployed correctly and with appropriate safeguards, establishing friend-ships in the digital world can be a rewarding and fruitful experience; however, plunging headlong into Internet relationships without proper attention to the potential risks involved is a surefire recipe for disaster. Before you fire up your laptop or reach for your smartphone, here are some important things to keep in mind.

CAUTION: IMMORTALITY AHEAD

Facebook. Twitter. Instagram. Chat rooms. Special interest groups. Email. Blogs. Internet search engines. Dating sites. A literal cornu-copia of opportunities to search for and meet people who could end up being friends or even lifelong partners.

But be afraid, or to paraphrase the famous *Jaws* trailer, *be very afraid* of the potential price you pay whenever you go on the Internet. Anything you say, anywhere you visit, any pictures you post, even your emails and instant messages can gain instant Internet immortal-ity, leaving you with a cyberfootprint, which, unlike a footprint in the sand, is not easily washed away!

Increasingly, prospective employers, potential lovers, would-be stalkers, businesses, and even government agencies are using your cyberactivities to learn more about you and make decisions about how they will treat you, even if the information they use is decades old!

Please keep in mind that what you post is who you are . . . forever. Whenever you sit down at the computer and sign onto the Internet, always keep this sentence in mind: "Would I be embarrassed if what I am about to do would suddenly appear on the front page of my local newspaper tomorrow, in a month, or in ten years?" If the answer is "yes" or "maybe," stop and think before you hit the send button or enter key . . . it just might save you heartache and disappointment tomorrow and down the road.

LEARN AND USE PROPER DIGITAL ETIQUETTE WHEN VISITING CYBERSPACE

Technology is evolving so quickly that social norms for using things like computers and smartphones don't always keep pace. Nevertheless, there are some general guidelines that, if followed, should make online experiences safer and more enjoyable for you and those around you. It will also increase your chances for making friends, rather than enemies, both online and in the immediate vicinity where you are texting, talking, or searching.

Smartphones

In a Florida movie theater a man was shot to death for using his smartphone after the house lights were dimmed. Chances are you won't experience a similar fate should you choose to text or talk in an inappropriate manner or place; however, there are simple guidelines you'll want to follow to protect yourself and your information from harm.

1. All mobile communication devices should be silenced in any public or private location where a ringtone would be distracting and/or inappropriate.

2. All mobile communication device *users* should refrain from speaking on their phones in any public or private location where vocalizations would be distracting and/or inappropriate. (Example: I didn't go out for a relaxing meal at a nice restaurant to hear your long-winded discourse about problems at home or work.)

3. Smartphones *can* be hacked. Pictures and other information you would not want to see reprinted in your local newspaper would best be removed from the device.

4. Most cell phone bills provide a detailed history of calls to and from your device. If you would prefer that others not know who you called and who called you, it might be wise to keep this in mind.

5. Recording yourself doing things which, for lack of a better word, might be deemed inappropriate by others is probably not a good idea. Case in point: A woman from the United Kingdom picked up her boyfriend's smartphone and found images of him having sex with a dog. To make matters worse, it was her dog! How the woman reacted to this chain of events was not reported.

6. "Sexting"—particularly when pictures are included—is just not a good idea, even between husband and wife. These photos have a nasty way of suddenly appearing on social media websites, particularly if the husband and wife get divorced and one or both of them are vindictive.

7. Don't Let V/R (Virtual Reality) trump R/W (Real World) relationships. Individuals vary in their tolerance of cell phone conversations (and constantly checking social media) undertaken by someone they are with. Even if your companion (date, friend, or business associate) is more tech-savvy and tolerant than most, it is still considered inappropriate for you to be taking calls, checking messages, and frequently glancing over at your cell during your time together. In an earlier chapter on verbal communication, I pointed out how important it was to listen in a focused manner to the person you are talking with. It shows interest and respect, fostering a superior environment for making people like you and keeping friends. If you insist on seeing your phone as an umbilical cord in the presence of others, don't expect the birth of a good relationship.

8. Because cell phones retain their initial area code (regardless of where they are used) and, further, because transmission of cell phone conversations is not always clear, it is important when you leave your number for a callback that you start with the area code and repeat the entire number twice. That way, you increase your chances that the recipient of your message will have the information necessary to get back to you.

Electronic Messages (Email)

1. Emails fall somewhere between text messages and letters when it comes to how formal or informal your communication can be. Obviously, emails to prospective employers or important business contacts should be more reflective of a traditional letter, well thought out, and grammatically sound. That being said, it is advisable to keep *all* emails free of the type of abbreviations normally used in texting, and check for spelling mistakes before transmitting your messages.

2. Carefully consider your screen name when using email communications. A screen name that might be acceptable for communications between friends could be wildly inappropriate if used when contacting prospective employers or your kid's school official. One of my colleagues who teaches human resource management in a business school showed me her "Inappropriate Screen Name Hall of Fame" list, which included names actually used by her students in applying for jobs. Number one on the list was "Lickmered."

3. Don't write email text in capital letters (LIKE THIS). It is considered to be the equivalent of shouting at someone in verbal interactions and is viewed as rude.

4. Never write an email when you are extremely angry or distraught. In an earlier chapter, I emphasized that people who are agitated in such a manner have difficulty thinking rationally.

An email written during these times often reflects this damaged thought process. If you must write such a message, *don't send it;* not immediately, anyway. Put it aside for several hours and then reread it when you have calmed down and you can think more rationally. Only then should you consider sending it . . . probably with significant revisions. Another good reason not to immediately send out an angry email is its potential to further escalate the situation. The problem might be resolved (or go away) within a few hours if "left alone." A hasty, angry response effectively eliminates this possibility.

5. When you are ready to send an email be sure to check to whom it is being sent. Many embarrassing incidents could have been avoided if the email sender had made sure his or her message was being sent to a specific person and not "reply all."

6. An email can be "forever" (or at least linger in cyberspace for months, even years). Once an email is "out there" it can take on a life of its own: reproduced, forwarded, archived. Each time you write an email you should ask yourself: "What if this email went public and stayed public for a significant period of time: would I still send it?"

7. Deleted emails can still be recovered for months after you have "erased" them. This is because many Internet servers "save" deleted emails on their computers. The recovery of supposedly "deleted" emails has revealed sensitive information about (or from) individuals they thought was safely destroyed. Often-times, these persons discovered this unsettling news in open court.

8. Never open an email attachment unless you are sure you know who sent it and that they, in fact, were the senders. (Email ad-dresses are sometimes illegally accessed from a person's computer and then used to send messages containing viruses to everyone on that person's contact list. It appears that the message is le-gitimate because it is sent from the compromised person's com-

puter.) In general, it is best not to open *any* email attachments unless absolutely necessary. Protecting your computer with security programs that screen attachments (for example, Norton or McAfee) is advised; otherwise, opening attachments on your computer is akin to having unprotected sex.

Social Sites (Facebook, Twitter, Tumblr, etc.)

1. Social sites vary in their filtering mechanisms: who can and cannot see your postings. Be sure you are familiar with these filters and use them appropriately.

2. Assume that *anything* you post on a social site can be accessed and reproduced for others to see. Further, keep in mind that those college parties where you were photographed drinking and having a "good old time" might someday be accessed by a prospective employer, potential (or actual) spouse, or even your parents and in-laws!

3. As a general rule, it is wise to limit your digital footprint online. Excessive use of social sites enlarges that footprint and might cause problems down the road.

4. Be careful who you friend!

DIGITAL DETECTIVES

As you know by now, I am a frequent flyer. This time, I approached the gate at the Nashville airport to see if I could fly standby on an earlier flight, but this story is not about me getting an upgrade. The gate clerks, a man and a woman, were intently examining a very expensive digital camera. I heard them comment to each other, "There's no name on the camera or any other unique identifying information. We have to find out who this camera belongs to and give it back to them." I asked them what they were doing." In unison they said, "We're the FBI agents of American Airlines." I told them I was a real FBI agent, although I was retired. I asked them how they could find the owner of the camera without any clues. The man explained that they would turn the camera on and look for clues in the pictures the owner took. I was intrigued as I saw them go through the process of solving the digital puzzle. As they shuffled through the date-stamped pictures, they gathered digital clues. The owner was a male of Hispanic descent. It appeared that he had spent three days in Las Vegas, probably on business, because there were no family pictures. He stayed at the Bellagio Hotel. They continued to scroll through the pictures. The woman high-fived the man and shrieked, "I found it!" She showed me the picture on the camera that was taken the previous week. The photo depicted a newer, wood-frame house with blue siding. I saw the picture, but I didn't see what triggered their excitement. She pointed to the house and said, "Those kinds of houses are typically built on the East Coast in mid-Atlantic states." "Okay," I thought, "so what?" She then directed me to the barely visible "For Sale" sign in the front yard. "Okay," I said, not sure of the significance of the sign. She used the camera's zoom feature to make the address and telephone number of the real estate agency clearly visible. The real estate office was in Columbia, South Carolina. I finally got it. I blurted out loud, "The owner of the camera was probably from Columbia, South Carolina, because people typically don't take pictures of houses for sale unless they are considering a purchase." The woman added, "An earlier flight we boarded was headed to Columbia, South Carolina." She pulled up the passenger list and, fortunately, there were only a few Hispanic names listed. I had to board my flight, but I was confident that the FBI agents of American Airlines would locate the owner and return the camera. I was amazed by how easy it was to track the movements of the owner of the lost camera using a few abstract digital clues. I was even more amazed that they went the extra mile to return the lost camera. They said they returned many lost or forgotten electronic devices using similar methods. The point of the story is that in a digital world, it's hard to remain anonymous. Keep this in mind the next time you post something on the Internet or do something as benign as taking a digital photograph.

CATPHISH OR CAVIAR: WHAT YOU NEED TO KNOW BEFORE DEVELOPING ONLINE RELATIONSHIPS

The Internet provides a fertile environment for growing friendships and even lifelong liaisons between individuals. This has led to the development of websites that facilitate the online "dating" process and make it easier for individuals interested in finding significant others to "hook up." The people who own these websites claim great success in getting "soul mates" together: providing the mechanism through which people meet online and, eventually, establish long-term commitments in the real world.

Using the Internet to find "Mr." or "Ms. Right" can be a rewarding experience. It can also be a living hell. How *your* experience turns out depends on many factors, most of which will be discussed here. Although no one can guarantee that your Internet-generated relationships will be successful and trouble-free, there are some things you can do to increase your chances of experiencing positive outcomes—and reducing negative ones—when it comes to choosing friends and potential partners online.

LOVE AT FIRST BYTE

The young man was a star Notre Dame football player who fell in love with a woman he met online. Then tragedy struck: his sweetheart died of leukemia. To make matters worse, she died on the same day the football player's grandmother passed away.

The star player's twin tragedies became a national news item. But that story was soon eclipsed by an even bigger story: it turned out that the woman he loved didn't die after all, because she never lived in the first place! It turned out she was a person created in cyberspace by someone with a very sick sense of humor.

And then there's the saga of Sana and Adnan Klaric. It seems the couple's married life was not going well and so, unbeknownst to each other, each Klaric assumed a fake screen name, Sweetie and Prince of Joy respectively, and hit the online chat rooms complaining about their dismal marriage and searching for a new "Mr." and "Mrs." Right.

It took some time and a lot of keystrokes but at last the two estranged partners found online individuals who seemed to resonate with their problems and provide the kind words so missing in their marriage.

Sana and Adnan knew they had found the real loves of their lives. They agreed to meet their new partners at a prearranged time and place. On the big day, Sana and Adnan made excuses to each other about having to leave for appointments, each making sure their indiscretion would not be detected. Then they set off to meet their online paramours, the perfect replacements for what they had back home.

When they arrived at their rendezvous point, Sana and Adnan met their online lovers for the first time. It was *not* love at first sight. It turned out that Sana and Adnan had unknowingly been carrying on their online affair with each other!

One might best leave it to ethicists and lawyers to decide if Sana and Adnan were being unfaithful, as it is difficult to imagine committing adultery with your own spouse; however, "Sweetie" and "Prince of Joy" were not pleased and, at last report, were accusing each other of being unfaithful and filing for divorce.

What do all these stories demonstrate?

1. Relationships developed over the Internet can be as powerful as those developed in face-to-face interactions, sometimes more so.
2. On the Internet, things are not always as they appear.
3. If a world-class physicist can be duped over the Internet, you probably can be, too.
4. There are creepy, mean, sick people populating the Internet just as they do in the real world.
5. Scams involving relationships on the Internet are more common than most of us imagine. They have become so widespread, in

fact, that a documentary film, MTV reality series, and feature film have been based on the problem. A word has even been coined, *catfish,* which, as Internet attorney Parry Aftab says, refers to "anybody who pretends to be someone who they're not on social media. It's done all the time." I've taken that expression one step further with "catphish" to also include the hackers who wish to steal your identity.

6. Because of the "cloak of secrecy" provided by the Internet, people will say things in cyberspace they would never say in a personal interaction.

7. On the Internet, as in real life, if it's too good to be true, it probably is! Social networks can be hazardous. No communication posted to the Internet can be guaranteed to remain private. You must assume that your posts are permanent and public.

8. As in face-to-face communications, pretending to be someone you are not often leads to unpleasant outcomes.

9. There are things you can do to navigate the Internet more safely and effectively. Some suggestions are provided in the following pages. These suggestions are not only relevant for individuals seeking love on the Internet; they will be helpful for anyone looking for friends in cyberspace.

TESTING FOR VERACITY ONLINE AND OFFLINE

Letting our teenagers roam freely on the Internet, especially my daughter, was a scary proposition for my wife and me. So I taught them some techniques I used on suspects to determine their veracity. I did this to help protect them from both online and real-world predators. I offer these techniques to you for the same reason, to help you guard against deceptive on- and offline communications. The results of these seeming innocuous veracity tests are not absolute proof of deception but they do provide you with strong indicators that someone might be lying or, at least, stretching the truth beyond acceptable limits.

THE WELL . . . TECHNIQUE

When you ask someone a direct yes-or-no question and they begin their answer with the "Well," there is a high probability of deception. It indicates that the person answering the question is about to give you an answer that they know you are not expecting. The following exchanges will clarify the "Well" technique.

> **DAD:** Did you finish your homework?
> **DAUGHTER:** Well . . .
> **DAD:** Go to your room and finish your homework.
> **DAUGHTER:** How did you know I didn't do my homework?
> **DAD:** I'm a dad. I know these things.

The dad didn't need to wait for his daughter to finish her answer because he knew by her use of "Well" in response to his direct question that she was about to give him an answer she knew he was not expecting. The daughter knew her dad was expecting a yes answer to the question "Did you do your homework?"

In another example, I interviewed a person who I thought witnessed a murder. The person was in proximity to the crime scene, but he denied seeing the shooting. After giving me some evasive answers, I decided to test his veracity by asking him a direct yes-or-no question.

> **ME:** Did you see what happened?
> **WITNESS:** Well . . . from where I was it was hard to see much of anything. It was dark and it all happened so fast.

I asked the witness a direct question to which he knew I expected a yes answer. Since he began his response with "Well," I knew he was about to give me an answer other than yes. I let the witness finish his response so as not to alert him to the technique.

The "Well" technique only works with direct yes-or-no questions.

Beginning a response with "Well" in answer to an open-ended question such as "Who will win the Super Bowl next year?" indicates the person is evaluating how to answer the question. You should allow others to finish their answers before responding so as not to alert them to this technique. Be advised that if the person you are talking to is aware of this technique, he or she will deliberately avoid using "Well."

Get into the habit of asking people a direct yes-or-no question and listening for their response. Answering such a question with "Well" or not directly answering the question is a strong indicator of deception, requiring additional probing.

THE LAND OF IS

When people choose not to answer yes or no, they go to the *Land of Is*. The Land of Is occupies the space between truth and deception. This murky area contains a labyrinth of half-truths, excuses, and suppositions. President Clinton's now famous statement to the grand jury inspired the concept of the Land of Is. To paraphrase what Clinton stated, "It depends upon what the meaning of the word *is* is. If *is* means is, and never has been, that's one thing, if it means there is none, that was a completely true statement." Clinton cleverly took the prosecutor to the Land of Is to avoid directly answering the prosecutor's direct yes-or-no question.

The following exchange between a mother and daughter demonstrates the Land of Is technique.

MOM: Your teacher called this afternoon and told me that she suspected you of cheating on an exam. Did you cheat on your exam?

DAUGHTER: I spend two hours a night studying. I study more than anybody I know. People who don't study are the people who have to cheat on exams. I study all the time. Don't accuse me of cheating!

MOM: I'm not accusing you of cheating.

DAUGHTER: Yes, you are!

The mom asked her daughter a direct yes-or-no question. Her daughter chose not to respond with a simple yes-or-no answer but, instead, took her mother to the Land of Is to avoid directly answering it. The daughter ended her response with an accusation, which put Mom on the defensive. The topic was no longer about cheating but about Mom making unwarranted accusations.

Mom could have prevented her daughter from going to the Land of Is by first recognizing that the technique was being used and then redirecting the conversation back to the initial topic of inquiry. For example:

MOM: Your teacher called this afternoon and told me that she suspected you of cheating on an exam. Did you cheat on your exam?

DAUGHTER: I spend two hours a night studying. I study more than anybody I know. People who don't study are the people who have to cheat on exams. I study all the time. Don't accuse me of cheating!

MOM: I know you study hard and get good grades. That's not what I asked you. I asked you whether or not you cheated on your exam. Did you cheat on your exam?

Redirecting the conversation back to the initial question forced her daughter to answer the question, "Did you cheat on your exam?" Her daughter must answer yes or no or take her mother back to the Land of Is. Failure to answer a yes-or-no question with a yes-or-no answer is not conclusive proof of deception, but the probability of deception does increase significantly. If her daughter did not cheat on her exam, answering no would not be difficult. The truth is simple. The truth is direct. The truth is not complicated.

WHY SHOULD I BELIEVE YOU?

When someone provides you with an answer to a question, simply ask them "Why should I believe you?" Honest people typically answer, "Because I am telling the truth" or some derivation thereof. Truthful people simply convey information. They focus on accurately presenting facts. Conversely, liars try to convince people that what is being said is true. Their focus is not on accurately presenting facts, but rather, on convincing listeners that the facts presented represent the truth. Since liars cannot rely on facts to establish their credibility, they tend to bolster their credibility to make their version of the facts appear believable.

When people answer with other than "Because I'm telling the truth" or some derivation thereof, tell them that their response did not answer the question and repeat the question, "Why should I believe you?" If they again do not respond with "Because I'm telling the truth" or some derivation thereof, the probability of deception increases. The following exchange between a dad and his son demonstrates the Why Should I Believe You technique.

> DAD: There was ten dollars on my dresser this morning. It's no longer there. Did you take money from my dresser for any reason?
>
> SON: No.
>
> DAD: Son, I want to believe you. But I'm having a hard time. Tell me. Why should I believe you?
>
> SON: I'm not a thief.
>
> DAD: I didn't ask you if you were a thief or not. I asked you why I should believe you. Why should I believe you?
>
> SON: Because I didn't steal the money. I'm telling you the truth.
>
> DAD: I know you are and I believe you.

In this exchange, the son responded that he was not a thief. This response did not answer the question "Why should I believe you?"

Dad gave his son a second chance by telling him that the question was not whether he was a thief but rather "Why should I believe you?" This time the son answered, "Because I didn't steal the money. I'm telling you the truth," which indicates the son was probably telling the truth. The fact that the son correctly answered the question "Why should I believe you" does not mean he told the truth, but it does decrease the likelihood of deception.

When you communicate with people, especially on the Internet by instant messaging or by texting on a smartphone, use these simple, noninvasive techniques to test the person's veracity. These techniques are so subtle that the people you are communicating with will not even recognize that they are being tested for veracity. Although these techniques are only indicators of deception, not proof of deception, they do provide you with a strong line of defense against online predators.

DETECTING DECEPTION IN ONLINE PROFILES

Most people do not accurately describe themselves in online profiles, especially dating profiles. Researchers Toma, Hancock, and Ellison surveyed eighty people who submitted online profiles to various dating websites. An astounding 81 percent of the online daters lied about one or more of their physical attributes, which included height, weight, and age. Women tended to lie about their weight and men tended to lie about their height. Women whose weight scored further from the mean lied more about their degree of obesity. Likewise, men whose height scored further from the mean lied more about how tall they were. The survey respondents reported that they were more likely to lie about their photographs than in relationship information such as marital status and the number of children they have.

In a follow-up study by Hancock and Toma, they found that about one-third of the online photographs examined were not accurate. Women's photographs were judged as less accurate than men's photographs. Women were more likely to be older than they were portrayed in their photographs. Their photographs were more likely to be Photoshopped or taken by professional photographers. Additionally, less attractive people were more likely to enhance their profile. The most interesting finding was that although people frequently lied in their online profiles, they attempted to keep their alterations within believable parameters in the event they met their correspondents in subsequent face-to-face meetings.

The magnitude of deception in online profiles should not come as a big surprise. An online profile is the equivalent of a first date. Anyone who has been on a first date will remember putting his or her best foot forward. (Just as in a first job interview, we wear our "interview" suit.) Women dressed with great contemplation and took extra minutes to put on their makeup. Men ensured their clothes were color-coordinated and wrinkle-free. Conversations were rehearsed before any words were exchanged. Personality flaws and behavioral quirks were carefully camouflaged with polite talk and impeccable manners. The extra steps were taken to make the right first impression.

Putting your best foot forward when meeting someone is not construed as deception because the foot put forward still is recognizably yours, albeit an enhanced version. People who present themselves on the Internet should try to put a positive face on their profile, but remain within the bounds of truth when including a photograph and a description of who they are. Likewise, people who use the Internet to search for potential relationships should learn to take online profiles with a grain of salt, recognizing that the person they are scrutinizing is never going to appear more attractive or qualified than the picture and résumé they post.

Men and women feel the need to meet standards of beauty that society establishes, and which are reinforced by the media. People lie to bring themselves closer to the standard image in the hope of attracting a friend or a mate. People who believe they do not meet those standards feel less attractive and are less confident that they can attract and keep a partner without lying about who they really are and how they really look. This pattern will not change in the foreseeable future; to the contrary, it will most likely intensify as online dating and Internet chat rooms become more popular and proliferate.

Anyone who seeks relationships on the Internet should be aware of the line that separates a "best impression" profile from a deceptive one. A deceptive online profile may attract a suitor or friend, but once the deception is discovered, trust, disappointment, and betrayal becomes the centerpiece of the relationship instead of excitement, hopes, and dreams. If you want to try Internet relationship building, be honest in your online profile and be patient. The right relationship is worth the wait.

HOW TO REDUCE YOUR CHANCES OF BEING HOOKED BY A CATPHISH

The flit of an eye, the turn of the head, or a slight change in voice pitch provides clues to a person's personality, sincerity, and veracity. As cited earlier in the book, our brains constantly monitor verbal and non-verbal cues to assess others to see if they pose a potential threat. If the cues are friend signals, then the brain tends to ignore the behaviors. If the cues are foe signals, the brain initiates the fight or flight response and we go shields up to protect ourselves against the threat or potential threat.

Nonverbal and verbal cues can undergo dramatic changes from second to second and from one word to the next. Monitoring these changes can mean the difference between relationship happiness and relationship hell. People are comfortable using verbal and nonverbal cues to assess others and rely heavily on this method to protect them-selves against initiating or continuing bad relationships.

Internet relationships lack the cues necessary for people to make similar judgments. Emoticons help decode written communications, but they are not enough. Decoding an unseen person's personality, sincerity, and veracity requires additional skills when communicating on the Internet. People are poor judges of their Internet partners because the cues they rely on in face-to-face exchanges are missing. The most reliable method people have to assess others is no longer available to them. They must rely on unpracticed techniques that have not yet been tested for reliability. The brain has not built up enough data to discriminate between friend and foe signals embedded in Internet communications. Building Internet detection skills takes time. Here are some of the potential problems you might encounter in determining the veracity and value of a potential online relationship.

TRUTH BIAS

People tend to believe others. This phenomenon, referred to as the *truth bias,* allows society and commerce to run smoothly and efficiently. Absent the truth bias, people would spend an inordinate amount of time checking data collected from others. The truth bias also serves as a social default. Relationships with friends and business colleagues would become strained if their veracity were constantly questioned. Consequently, people typically believe others until evidence to the contrary surfaces.

The truth bias provides liars with an advantage because people want to believe what they hear, see, or read. The truth bias diminishes when people become aware of the possibility of deception. The truth bias predisposes people to believe what others write in emails and texts. Absent verbal and nonverbal cues, the veracity of written communications is not as easily called into question.

Another characteristic of the truth bias is that when people do see a few loose ends or minor contradictions in a person's story, they tend to excuse the discrepancy because to do otherwise would call the person's words or behaviors into question. It's easier to excuse away minor differences than to confront the person. The best defense against the truth bias online is judicious skepticism and use of the "competing hypotheses" technique (see the following page).

THE PRIMACY EFFECT

Truth bias creates the primacy effect. The primacy effect, as you will recall from Chapter 3, creates a filter through which we view communication and events. The primacy effect does not change reality but alters people's perception of it. Truth bias creates a primacy filter. Anything a person writes tends to be evaluated as truthful unless there is something to cause you to doubt what is written. Absent verbal and nonverbal cues, individuals are at a disadvantage when judging written correspondence on the Internet.

COMPETING HYPOTHESES

Developing competing hypotheses prevents the truth bias and the primacy effect from unduly undermining your ability to judge the character and veracity of the person who is writing to you. Hypotheses are nothing more than educated guesses. A competing hypothesis is an educated guess that supposes a different outcome based on the same or similar set of circumstances.

For example, say one hypothesis posits that the person who is writing to you is genuine and telling the truth. A competing hypothesis posits that the person who is writing to you is an imposter and a liar. During the course of your written exchanges with another person on the Internet (for example, in an instant message session) you should seek evidence to support your initial hypothesis (the writer is genuine and truthful) or your competing hypothesis (the writer is an imposter and a liar).

Rarely does all the evidence support the initial hypothesis or the competing hypothesis, because honest people often say and do things that make them look dishonest and, conversely, dishonest people often say and do things that make them look honest. In the end, however, the weight of the evidence should support one hypothesis over the other. Countering the effects of truth bias and the primacy effect reduces your vulnerability to being deceived on the Internet . . . catphished, so to say.

LAWS OF ATTRACTION

As discussed in Chapter 4, attractive people receive preferential treatment and garner more attention than do unattractive (or less attractive) individuals. The effect of physical beauty is reduced in Internet communications, unless a picture accompanies an Internet profile. Keep in mind that people often lie in their Internet profiles to enhance their ability to attract partners. Since people do not have face-to-face interaction with the person writing to them, they have no point of reference against which to judge their written communication.

Contrast plays an important role in attraction. When two people stand side by side, people tend to contrast one against the other. In the absence of a second person for comparison purposes, an individual will tend to compare the single person against their "idealized" person. Since the person writing to you on the Internet is singular, you will have a tendency to compare that person against your idealized person. Over time, people tend to attribute the characteristic of their idealized person to the person writing them. This misattribution leads to the increased probability of being the victim of a catphish.

RAPPORT BUILDING

Building rapport on the Internet relies solely on written text, assuming no use of Skype or other photographic transmission. This limits the techniques people normally have available to establish rapport in face-to-face communications. As mentioned earlier in the book, finding common ground is a powerful technique to establish rapport. In order to find common ground on the Internet, you must disclose personal information to the person to whom you are writing. Disclosing this kind of information is another powerful technique to develop rapport. Since Internet communications are anonymous, people tend to disclose more information, and do it more quickly, than they would face-to-face. One reason for this is that the sender does not have verbal and nonverbal cues to gain feedback about the acceptance or rejection of his or her information by the receiver of the written information.

When people receive rejection cues in face-to-face communications, they tend to stop disclosing. This is not the case online. In fact, people tend to increase the disclosure of sensitive personal information. The result of an increase in self-disclosure propels the relationship to a higher level than if the relationship were a face-to-face encounter. As a result, a vital step in the relationship developing process is skipped. During this vital step in face-to-face communication, prospective partners have the opportunity to slowly disclose information using verbal and nonverbal cues to pace the development of the relationship and the rate of information release. If things go awry during this initial step, the two people can go their separate ways without having disclosed too much sensitive information to create personal vulnerabilities. Because of the absence of this vital step in written Internet communication, where no face-to-face interaction occurs, the chances for catphishing increase.

Recruiting people to spy for the United States follows a similar relationship pathway. Spies need to be groomed. The steps required to develop close friendships or romantic relationships are the same ones required to convince a person to become a spy. In several cases, I tried to rush the relationship due to operational demands. These recruitments always failed because I skipped the initial step in relationship development. The first step is critical. Revealing too much information too soon will dampen the relationship. The recruitment target will disengage. As mentioned earlier, a partner is seen as too "fast" or too "slow" if the expectation milestones for relationship development are hurried or lagging. Internet relationships often violate relationship expectations because partners are propelled to a higher level of relationship intensity before they are psychologically prepared to do so. This creates vulnerabilities for both partners to the interaction.

EMOTIONAL INVESTMENT

The longer the Internet relationship continues, the more likely people are to remain in the relationship because of their deep emotional investment. This doesn't mean they are actually a good couple, but because they've spent too much time in the interaction, they don't feel they can just quit, and besides, the relationship has developed to a point where the volume of sensitive information released creates personal vulnerabilities so significant that giving up is not an option.

AN EXAMPLE OF HOW EMOTIONAL INVESTMENT WORKS IN THE REAL WORLD

To illustrate how *emotional investment* affects a person's behavior, let me illustrate how you can use it to your advantage in certain situations, particularly when buying big-ticket items. Let's assume you want to purchase a new car. In this case, you would first find the vehicle you want and then tell the salesperson that you will buy it today if you can get it for the right price. Then take out your checkbook and write the date and name of the dealership on a check. Explain to the salesperson all that's required to wrap up the deal is the amount of the down payment and your signature. This partially completed check sends a message to the salesperson that you are serious about buying a car. State the price you want to pay and be ready to wait the salesperson out.

In one instance that I tried this, I negotiated eight hours for a vehicle! At the end of the salesperson's shift, she relented. She reasoned that she spent eight hours negotiating with me and to not sell me the car would be a waste of her time, time she could have spent selling cars to other people. The *emotional investment* she put into the negotiations psychologically pressured her into taking my ridiculously low offer; otherwise she would have had to face the prospect of failure.

COGNITIVE DISSONANCE

Cognitive dissonance occurs when people hold two or more conflicting ideas or beliefs simultaneously. People continue in Internet relationships when they know the relationship should stop to avoid cognitive dissonance. They do not want to believe that the person they are communicating with is not who they say they are, because that creates cognitive dissonance.

Take yourself as an example. You view yourself as a knowledgeable, discerning person. You also love the person you have met and are communicating with online. If you admit that you are the victim of catphishing, then you are naïve and gullible; therefore, you refuse to believe that the person you are writing to is a fraud, to avoid the bad feeling that comes with cognitive dissonance.

Manti Te'o, the Notre Dame football player who fell victim to an online predator, expressed the conflict caused by cognitive dissonance in this comment about his catphishing experience: "This is incredibly embarrassing to talk about, but over an extended period of time, I developed an emotional relationship with a woman I met online. We maintained what I thought to be an authentic relationship by communicating frequently online and on the phone, and I grew to care deeply about her. To realize that I was the victim of what was apparently someone's sick joke and constant lies was, and is, painful and humiliating. . . . In retrospect, I obviously should have been much more cautious. If anything good comes of this, I hope it is that others will be far more guarded when they engage with people online than I was."

EXPOSING CATPHISH

To prevent yourself from being hooked by a catphish, force him or her into the visual world, where you can use your well-honed knowledge of nonverbal signals to verify if the person matches up with their online persona and if the relationship looks as good "in the light of day" as it did on a computer screen. During the early stages of an Internet relationship, you must realize that the lack of nonverbal cues puts you at a disadvantage. Establish competing hypotheses to prevent the relationship from developing too fast.

Always assume that you are the victim of a catphish until visual evidence proves otherwise. Insist on a face-to-face meeting as soon as possible. This meeting should take place in a well-populated, public area to reduce the possibility of personal danger. Also, to make the meeting more comfortable for both Internet users, a casual, relatively short first face-to-face meeting is recommended; a coffee shop rendezvous or lunch date might be best.

In the event a face-to-face meeting is not practical, insist on a visual meeting on Skype or similar service. An Internet partner who makes excuses to avoid a face-to-face meeting, or constantly makes excuses as to why a visual meeting on the Internet is not possible, is sending a strong signal that something is amiss. At this point, you should immediately break off your Internet relationship. To do otherwise puts you in peril, possibly significant peril.

Demanding a visual meeting early in the relationship is a simple yet effective technique to avoid being hooked by a catphish. Visual meetings allow you to evaluate nonverbal cues to assess the veracity of your Internet partner. Visual contact also prevents the development of idealized characteristics to an unknown person. Developing competing hypotheses reduces the effect of truth bias. The need to reveal sensitive, personal information is reduced in face-to-face encounters, thus preventing the relationships from developing too quickly. Slowing the development of the relationship reduces your emotional investment, thus minimizing the emotional cost of breaking off the relationship.

In genuine relationships, people are eager to communicate visually, especially early in a relationship. People feel more comfortable in visual relationships because they can use the social skills they have come to rely on to evaluate others more accurately. Visual meetings expose cat-phish and level the Internet relationship playing field.

A NEW GENERATION: TURN ON, TUNE IN, AND TAKE PRECAUTIONS

There is simply no denying that the advent of person-to-person on-line communication has dramatically altered the landscape of seeking friends and building relationships. As online interaction continues to grow in popularity it will have an even greater impact on the way people form relationships in the years to come.

By being aware of the Internet dangers mentioned above, and using the techniques I recommend to minimize them, meaningful Internet relationships are possible. In fact, for reasons listed at the beginning of this chapter, they might be the preferred method for con-necting with people in the *initial* stage of relationship building.

Used with appropriate caution and common sense, the Internet is another tool in your friendship toolbox for finding and developing friendships for a moment or a lifetime. Conversely, if you use the tool carelessly, with a disregard for what is inputted and downloaded, it can lead to disappointment and potential personal disasters. In the final analysis, how *you* use the digital universe will determine its ultimate value, good or bad, in shaping the quality of your life and your rela-tionships.

EPILOGUE

The Friendship Formula in Practice

And as every spy knows, common enemies
are how allies always begin.
—ALLY CARTER,
DON'T JUDGE A GIRL BY HER COVER

Here is one final spy story. This one didn't involve my time at the FBI;
in fact, it is more than a hundred years old.* The story begins at the
turn of the last century, when a German prince had a romantic rendezvous with a woman of royalty from England. The sexual nature of
the rendezvous was not that disturbing to the German government;
however, they were extremely unhappy when they discovered the
prince had written his paramour love letters filled with state secrets.
They turned to "Dr. Graves," a talented German spy, and gave him his
marching orders: "Get those letters back!"

And so he did. He traveled to England to meet this woman and
reclaim the prince's love letters for his homeland. Printed on the following pages are excerpts from Dr. Graves's diary explaining how he
accomplished his mission. As you read the material, see if you can

*A. K. Graves, *The Secrets of the German War Office* (New York: McBride, Nast, 1914).

identify the *Like Switch* strategies Dr. Graves utilized to successfully retrieve the letters.

I quartered myself at first at the Russell Square Hotel, in a few days transferring to the patrician Langham. I began by making tentative inquiries. I purchased all society papers which I read from cover to cover, and then carefully feeling my way put further questions that would locate the set in which my lady was a central figure. From acquaintances I made around the hotel, from the society reporters of newspapers, I began to get little scraps of information. Fortunately, it was the season in London and everybody was coming into town. I soon knew who the Lady's intimates were and their favorite rendezvous. The next step was to become familiar with the personality of the lady and to gain some idea as to her habits and her likes and dislikes. I heard that the lady was in the habit of going horseback riding in Hyde Park. Every day I made it my business to take a two hour canter along the bridle path. My patience was rewarded on the fifth morning for I saw her galloping by with a party of friends.

The next morning I was on the bridle path at the same hour. Finally, she came galloping along with the same group, and after they had almost gone from sight, I galloped after them. I found out where they kept their horses and after they had dismounted, I sauntered up to the stable and made inquiries. I learned that they always went out at the same time of day. Thereafter, I made it my business to pass the lady on the bridle path day after day. I pride myself on few things, but my horsemanship is one of them. Many a hard tussle and bleeding nose I got riding Brumbies (wild horses) across the wild tracks of Australia. I also learned a trick or two among my Tuareg friends, which I exhibited for the lady's benefit on various occasions. I did not hope to gain an introduction, but only to attract attention and familiarize her party with my appearance, applying one of the test points of human psychology. I employed the theory of the subconscious attraction of an oft seen though unknown face.

I soon ascertained that my lady and her friends followed all the whims of London society. One in particular interested me. They were in the habit of frequenting Carlton Terrace between three and four every afternoon and eating strawberries. I also went to eat strawberries.

Carlton Terrace during the strawberry season is an exquisitely colored fashion plate of life's butterflies and drones. This throng of fashion and beauty, marked with its air of distinction carelessly abandoned to pleasure, ever murmuring pleasant nothings and tossing light persiflage from table to table, is truly an interesting study of the lighter sides of life. One sits on a magnificent marquee-covered glass enclosed terrace overlooking the Thames with its ever changing scenes of fussy tugs and squat barges.

At Carlton Terrace one pays well for the subtleties of eating. By courteous consideration of the waitresses, I managed to secure a much coveted outside corner table near to the one reserved for the lady and her party. I always made it a point to withhold my entrance until the lady was in the terrace; then I would stroll in alone, take a seat alone, and show a desire to be alone. They have a very clever way of serving strawberries at the Carlton. A vine growing from ten to twelve large luscious berries is brought on in a silver pot. It is the acme of luxury. You pick the fresh berries from the vine on your table, the Terrace supplies quantities of cream, and you pay half a sovereign—$2.50— for a dish of strawberries. One dish is enough for the average customer. Every afternoon I ordered five.

Day after day, I consumed in strawberries two sovereigns and a half—$12.50—of the Grand Duke of Mecklenburg-Schwerein's money. Always tipping the girl a half sovereign which made my daily strawberry bill come up to three sovereigns ($15). For about ten days, I did this always at the same time; always being careful to make my entrance after the lady's party was seated, always ordering the same number of portions, always giving the girl the same tip. It wasn't long before I began to be observed. I soon saw that not only the attendants but also the patrons of the Terrace were becoming interested in my foible. One day as I passed, I heard someone say, "Here comes the strawberry fiend."

I was satisfied. I knew it would be easy now to effect an entrance to the lady's set. I had been marked as something out of the usual in the restaurant that from three to four in the afternoon at that time of the year is the most fashionable in London. Now, a woman like my lady does not flirt. If you glance at her under favorable conditions such as my strawberry "stunt" had created for me she will return the glance. You both half smile and do not look at each other again that afternoon. That is not flirting. Splitting hairs, we shall call it psychic interest.

I continued my strawberry festival and one day a manager of Carlton Terrace told me that people were making inquiries about me. Several men had wanted to know who I was. Under questioning, he told me that one of the men was a member of the lady's set. It was easy to put together two and two. Obviously, the inquiry had been inspired by her.

Meanwhile I had sent several communications to the Grand Duke, insisting that pressure be brought to bear upon his nephew and to keep him away from London; not even permitting him under penalty of stopping his allowance, to write the lady in the case until the Grand Duke gave his permission. By now, London had gradually filled and the season was at its height. I went the rounds of the theaters from Drury Lane to the Empire and I visited the clubs. I found here men whom I had met previously and presently I rounded up two or three fellows with whom I had been fairly intimate at one time or another on hunting expeditions and at continental watering places. I made them introduce me to different sets. Dexterous maneuvering obtained me invitations to afternoon teas and at-homes in the same circle frequented by my lady.

I was introduced to her at an afternoon reception. She was a typical outdoor Englishwoman. Not particularly handsome, but possessing to the full the clearness of skin and eyes and strong virile health, that is the hereditary lien of Albion's daughters. Tall, willowy, and strong, of free and independent manners and habits, she was the direct antithesis of the usual German woman. I reasoned that this was probably the reason of the young Duke's infatuation.

"How do you do you wild Colonial boy. Still as fond of strawberries as ever?"

We both burst out laughing.

"So your ladyship observed and classified my little maneuvers."

"Of course," she said with a toss of her head.

Unforced and pleasant chatting followed. I could more and more understand the Grand Duke's infatuation; in fact, considered him quite a "deuced, lucky beggar."

From that day on, I made it a point to be present whenever she attended public places, such as the theater, concerts, or restaurants. Gradually and imperceptibly by little services here and there I won her confidence. There was an after-theater supper in the Indian room of the Windsor, and I was invited. By this time, people had come to know something about me. I was a globe-trotter, a man of leisure, interested as a hobby in research work in medicine. I discovered that her affair with the young Grand Duke was a fairly open secret in her set; also, that she was expecting him in London almost daily. Gradually I hinted that I knew the young Grand Duke. As I gained her confidence further, I invented amorous affairs for him and hinted to her about them. In this way, I finally managed to induce her to talk. Subtly I instilled a vague resentment against him, which was accentuated by his non-appearance in London society up to now. His Highness having been kept away by his Serene Uncle, the serene one having been cautioned to do so by me.

Two months passed before I was invited to the lady's home in Mayfair and by that time partly because I pretended to know the young Grand Duke, I was on a more intimate footing. I had learned that she had met him at a hunting party at the Earl of Crewes' shooting box in Shropshire. Later, she intimated that this was but their official meeting and that their acquaintance actually dated from a mountain trip she had taken to Switzerland, the universal playground of royalty traveling *incog*. I learned too that her heavy bridge gambling had cost her a lot of money.

The information that the lady was in debt did not come easily. To obtain it, I had to work on her maid. Whenever the occasion arose, I made it my business to tip the maid liberally. I contrived to do a number of little things for her. Knowing the lady to be out, I called at the house one day and while pretending to be waiting for my hostess, I put some leading questions to the maid. I learned that her mistress was pressed for money. That was an opening worth working on.

Thereafter, I contrived to be present whenever there was a bridge party at the lady's. They are pretty high gamblers, those English society women, and I came to see that the lady was generally a heavy loser. It was my good fortune for her to lose to me one night. Now, it is the custom at these gatherings not to hand over cash; instead, the unlucky one pays with what corresponds to an "on demand note." I took her note that night and with others—the whereabouts of which I learned from the maid and which I indirectly purchased from the holders—I took all these to a notorious money-lender and made a deal with him. He was to take the notes and press the lady for payment, of course keeping my name out of it. It is obvious that, trying, as I was to win her confidence, I could not go myself and hold these obligations over her head. That same day the money-lender paid the lady a call. He paid her a good many other calls, harassing her, threatening legal action and driving her until she was almost to a state of nervous collapse. Well-placed sympathies soon made her talk and she burst out pettishly that she was in debt and that most of her acquaintances were in debt—nothing unusual in that set.

This was an opportune chance to be of material benefit to the lady. Seriously, we talked over her affairs. I found them pretty well entangled. We discussed the young Grand Duke. I gradually persuaded her that there was no hope of a legitimate marriage with the house of Mecklenburg-Schwerein, but because of her association with the young Grand Duke and the fact that she had been betrothed to him, it was only right that the Duchy provide her with some means of assistance. The ice was perilously thin, for the lady is a high-spirited woman of ideals and I had to be careful to word my language so that it would not appear as though she were blackmailing. In justice to her, I believe that if she had taken that view of it she would have dropped the entire matter and retired from society for the season rather than go through with my plan. Finally, I said, "Have you any means by which you could compel the ducal house to make adequate acknowledgments and redresses to you?"

After a long hesitation, she jumped up, swept from the room, and returned presently with a handful of letters. I saw on some of them the Grand Duke's coat of arms. The young fool had been careless enough for that! She shook the letters in a temper and cried, "I wonder what Franz's uncle would say to these? Why I could compel him to marry me."

Here was the chance. The iron—in this case my lady's temper—was hot. I suggested that we sit down and talk it over. As an introductory attack, to create the impression that I knew what I was talking about, I hinted that I was connected with a leading family in Germany and that I was in London *incog*. I approached the situation from the viewpoint that I was her friend, not a friend of the house of Mecklenburg-Schwerein, but that, by knowing them and their ways, I could be of great assistance to her.

"It is regrettable," I consoled; "but you have no chance for a legitimate, even a morganatic alliance with the young Grand Duke. I consider their entire attitude toward you utterly unfair. In view of your understanding with him, you are most certainly entitled to adequate recompense from his house. If you went into court you could obtain this on grounds of breach of promise, but I can understand your feelings. Such a step would only cast odium upon an old and noble family such as yours."

That seemed to her liking.

"But what can I do?" she said.

"In view of my friendship for you," I told her, "I would consider it an honor if you would permit me to act on your behalf. I think I can negotiate with the young Grand Duke's uncle and I promise that he will regard the matter in a fair light. I appreciate the extreme delicacy of the situation and you must observe the necessity of a man handling this affair."

She shook her head and tapped the letters nervously.

"No. It is intolerable," she said. "Not to be thought of."

I saw that I had to make it stronger. I thereupon invented the most ingenious lie it has ever been given me to tell. In about five minutes I had painted the young Grand Duke in such colors that the adventures of Don Juan were saintly compared to the escapades of his ducal highness.

"Why consider it yourself," I said. "He was to be over here with you during the season. He has not come. You told me yourself that he has not even answered your letters. Well that's all there is to it. Your ladyship, he and his house deserve any punishment that you can visit upon them."

The idea of punishment appealed where the other had failed. The outraged pride of a woman, especially an Englishwoman, is a terrible thing. Soon after that I made haste to take my leave. At my quarters I wrote two letters to myself and signed the Grand Duke's name to them. In these I offered to pay her ladyship's debts. They were addressed to me and after allowing a reasonable time to elapse, I again went out to Mayfair and read them to her. She was now cold and hard and gave me full permission to go ahead and make any arrangements I deemed advisable. I thereupon went to the Grand Duke's bank in London and notified them that I must have 15,000 pounds ($75,000). In four days I had the money. The rest of the transaction was commonplace. She handed over all the letters and documents and I gave her the 15,000 pounds. I know today that her ladyship travels extensively in a very comfortable manner on the yearly appanage allowed her by the old Grand Duke. I do not know whether she still goes to Carlton Terrace to eat strawberries, but I flatter myself that her present good fortune is partially due to the fact that she once went there.

HOW DR. GRAVES ACCOMPLISHED HIS MISSION

It is truly remarkable, when reading Dr. Graves's diary, to realize this man was a full century ahead of his time in using behavioral analysis and psychological techniques to achieve his objective. If you take the time to reread the portion of Chapter 1 detailing how the Friendship Formula was used to entice "Seagull" to betray his country and become a spy for the United States, you will be amazed at the parallels between the strategies employed by the FBI and Dr. Graves in their work. Consider them:

1. In both cases, recruiting their targets was a well-choreographed plan that was executed over an extended period of time. Both agents used the techniques presented in this book to predispose their targets to like them prior to their first meetings.

2. Dr. Graves, like the FBI agent Charles, used the Friendship Formula to establish a relationship with the English lady. First they established proximity with their targets followed by an increase in frequency and duration, and gradually introduced intensity, curiosity hooks, and increasingly more intense nonverbal cues.

3. In both cases, the principle of **proximity** was used to establish nonthreatening contact between the agent and the target (Chapter 1). In Seagull's case, the FBI agent took pains to place himself in public places where Seagull walked and would be aware of his presence. In Dr. Graves's case, he did the same by establishing proximity with his target on the riding trails and

seating himself at a table close to the one where his target routinely sat in the restaurant.

4. In both cases, the principles of **frequency** and **duration** were also utilized. With Seagull that involved the FBI agent positioning himself on Seagull's shopping route in a manner that increased the number of instances (frequency), where the foreign diplomat saw him and adding duration by following Seagull into the grocery store, extending the contact time between the two men. With the English Lady, Dr. Graves increased frequency by the number of times he passed the woman on the riding trails and saw her in the restaurant. Dr. Graves even pointed out the power of frequency when he wrote, "I employed the theory of the subconscious attraction of an oft seen though unknown face." To achieve duration, he extended contact time by being around the woman at additional public places, like the theater and concerts. The more time (duration) you spend with people, the more you are able to influence their decision-making process and thought patterns.

5. In both cases **intensity** was achieved through the use of non-verbal cues and a "curiosity hook." The constant presence of a stranger being around Seagull and the English lady aroused their curiosity. In the case of Dr. Graves, the "Strawberry Stunt" served as a curiosity hook. What type of man eats five servings of strawberries in one sitting and gives the waitstaff such a large a tip? Who was this person? What did he want? This curiosity motivated both Seagull and the English lady to make an effort to discover who Charles (the FBI agent) and Graves (the German spy) were and what they wanted. Dr. Graves noted, "If you glance at her under favorable conditions such as my strawberry 'stunt' had created for me [increased intensity], she will return the glance. You both half smile and do not look at each other again that afternoon." When Dr. Graves first met the lady, she

displayed a "hair flip" (the toss of her head), which is a friend signal indicating that Dr. Graves established some degree of rapport before their first words were spoken. Both Charles and Graves had confidence in the psychological principles they employed and allowed time for them to work. They did not rush the development of the relationship. Instead, they let the relationships develop naturally over time, as "normal" relationships would.

6. In both cases, Dr. Graves and the Special Agent used friend signals to present themselves as nonthreatening (see Chapter 1), thus preventing their targets from going shields up when the first meetings took place. The Special Agent did not approach Seagull until he was comfortable with the agent's presence. Dr. Graves sat alone in the restaurant and showed no desire to meet anyone, giving the illusion that he was not a threat. Dr. Graves also ensured that he was noticed by walking in after the lady and her friends were already seated.

7. In both cases, information was gathered about their targets from various sources. In the Seagull case, the agent received information from FBI analysts. In the case of Dr. Graves, he read local newspapers, society pages, spoke with reporters, and later the groomsmen at the stables to obtain information about his target. In both cases, vital information was gathered surreptitiously to discover the things that motivate the targets to act as they do, to assess their personalities, and to learn about the things that could be used to establish common ground. Dr. Graves used elicitation techniques (see Chapter 6) to obtain sensitive information about his target without alerting the elicitation sources to the fact that they were providing sensitive information.

8. Dr. Graves went to the Carlton Terrace not only to be close to his target but also to establish common ground by eating strawberries every day like his target did.

9. Dr. Graves took advantage of the psychological principle of misattribution (see Chapter 4) to predispose the lady to like him. Horseback riding, like other exercises, triggers an endorphin release, which makes people feel good about themselves. If there is no apparent reason for that good feeling, people tend to attribute their good feeling to the people nearest to them. According the Golden Rule of Friendship, if you want people to like you, make them feel good about themselves. Dr. Graves was fostering rapport before he even said a word to his target.

10. In the end, Dr. Graves made it appear that it was the lady's idea to exchange the letters for her accrued debt, not Dr. Graves's idea. In Seagull's case, he watered and fertilized the seed of treason planted by the FBI agent. This is the true sign of a successful operation.

The two spy stories, separated by a century, remind us that human nature is a constant and that friends can be made if you are willing to use the tools presented in this book to flip the Like Switch and turn people on to you.

APPENDIX

Answers to "What Do You See" Quiz (page 181)

Picture 1: The foe signal depicted in the photo is the young lady yawning. However, this signal might not indicate that the young lady is bored with the young man. You should use an empathic statement to discover the source of her yawn.

Picture 2: The three friend signals depicted in the photo are (a) full smile; (b) head tilt; (c) mutual gaze. Also appropriate: (d) Open body posture.

Picture 3: The additional friend signal not found in picture #2 is the "palms up" displays in both the young man and woman.

Picture 4: The asynchronous posture between the two individuals signals poor rapport.

Picture 5: The young lady is leaning in and smiling, indicating interest; however, the young man, with his armed crossed and leaning backward, signals he is not interested in her.

Picture 6: The young man, smiling and leaning forward, indicates interest in the young lady, who, by her closed body posture (arms crossed) and skeptical eye signal, does not share his interest.

Picture 7: The friend signal indicating good rapport is "preening" (grooming your partner). In this case, it is the young lady straightening the collar of the young man's shirt.

Picture 8: The young man is interested in the young lady based on his full smile and leaning-in, open posture. Unfortunately, based on the young lady's torso position, she probably doesn't share the young man's feelings, although in this case one would want to see a bit more of the girl's nonverbal behaviors before ruling out any possible interest.

Picture 9: The rapport between the two individuals is very good. This can be seen in the (a) shared enthusiasm; (b) torso positioning: inward lean and open; (c) expressive gestures (including "thumbs-up" sign); (d) prolonged eye contact; and (e) smiles.

Picture 10: At first glance, it looks like the young man is in charge because he is pointing his finger. However, note that he is leaning backward. (Pointing a finger at someone while leaning backward is counterintuitive, you don't stick your finger in someone's face and lean away if you feel you're in charge.) The young lady is displaying "arms akimbo" (an aggressive nonverbal signal) in an attempt to make up for the young man's height advantage. The young lady has her head tilted, with the carotid artery exposed, signaling that she is not afraid of the young man. Diagnosis: The young man is on the losing end of this interaction based on his backward lean and the young lady's nonverbal posturing, which indicates a lack of fear based on her aggressive stance.

BIBLIOGRAPHY

Ajzen, I. (1977). Information processing approaches to interpersonal attraction. In S. W. Duck (ed.), *Theory and practice in interpersonal attraction* (pp. 51–77). San Diego, CA: Academic Press.

Antheunis, M. L., Valkenburg, P. M., & Peter, J. (2007). Computer-mediated communication and interpersonal attraction: An experimental test of two explanatory hypotheses. *Cyberpsychology and Behavior, 10,* 831–835.

Aristotle (1999). *Rhetoric* (W. R. Roberts, trans.). In *Library of the Future,* 4th ed. [CD-ROM]. Irvine, CA: World Library.

Aronson, E. (1969). The theory of cognitive dissonance: A current perspective. In L. Berkowitz (ed.), *Advances in experimental psychology,* vol. 4. New York: Academic Press.

Asch, S. E. (1946). Forming impressions of personality. *Journal of Abnormal and Social Psychology, 41,* 303–314.

Aubuchon, N. (1997). *The anatomy of persuasion.* New York: American Management Association.

Balderston, N. L., Schultz, D. H., & Helmstetter, F. J. (2013). The effect of threat on novelty-evoked amygdala response. *PloS ONE, 8,* 1–10.

Ballenson, J. N., Blascovich, J., Beall, A. C., & Loomis, J. M. (2001). Equilibrium theory revisited: Mutual gaze and personal space in virtual environments. *Presence, 10,* 583–598.

Barrick, J., Distin, S. L., Giluk, T. L., Stewart, G. L., Shaffer, J. A., & Swider, B. W. (2012). Candidate characteristics driving initial impressions during rapport building: Implications for employment interview validity. *Journal of Occupational and Organizational Psychology, 85,* 330–352.

Brady, E., & George, R. (2013). Manti Te'o's "Catfish" story is a common one. *USA Today,* January 18.

Branham, M. (2005). How and why do fireflies light up? *Scientific American,* September 5.

Buffardi, L., & Campbell, W. K. (2008). Narcissism and social networking web sites. *Personality and Social Psychology Bulletin, 34,* 1303–1314.

Byrne, D. (1969). *Attitudes and attraction.* In L. Berkowitz (ed.), *Advances in Experimental Psychology,* vol. 4. New York: Academic Press.

Carlzon, J. (1989). *Moments of truth.* New York: Harper Business.

Carnegie, D. (2011). *How to win friends and influence people.* New York: Simon & Schuster.

Carter, R. (1998). *Mapping the mind.* Berkeley: University of California Press.

Chaplin, W. F., Phillips, J. B., Brown, J. D., Claton, N. R., & Stein, J. L. (2000). Handshaking, gender personality and first impressions. *Journal of Personality and Social Psychology, 79,* 110–117.

Chen, F. F., & Kenrick, D. T. (2002). Repulsion or attraction? Group membership and assumed attitude similarity. *Journal of Personality and Social Psychology, 83*, 111–125.

Cialdini, R. B. (1993). *Influence: The psychology of persuasion.* New York: William Morrow.

Clark, M. S., Mills, J. R., & Corcoran, D. M. (1989). Keeping track of needs and inputs of friends and strangers. *Personality and Social Psychology Bulletin, 15*, 533–542.

Clore, G., Wiggens, N. H., & Itkin, S. (1975). Gain and loss in attraction: Attributions from nonverbal behavior. *Journal of Personality and Social Psychology, 31*, 706–712.

Collins, N. L., & Miller, L. C. (1994). Self-disclosure and liking: A meta-analytic review. *Psychological Bulletin, 116*, 457–475.

Craig, E., & Wright, K. B. (2012). Computer-mediated relational development and maintenance on Facebook. *Communication Research Reports, 29* (2), 118–129.

Curtis, R. C., & Miller, K. (1986). Believing another likes or dislikes you: Behavior making the beliefs come true. *Journal of Personality and Social Psychology, 51*, 284–290.

Dalto, C. A., Ajzen, I., & Kaplan, K. J. (1979). Self-disclosure and attraction: Effects of intimacy and desirability of beliefs and attitudes. *Journal of Research in Personality, 13*, 127–138.

Davis, J. D., & Sloan, M. L. (1974). The basis of interviewee matching and interviewer self-disclosure. *British Journal of Social and Clinical Psychology, 13*, 359–367.

DePaulo, B. M. (1992). Nonverbal behavior and self-presentation. *Psychological Bulletin, 111*, 203–243.

DeMaris, A. (2009). Distal and proximal influences of the risk of extramarital sex: A prospective study of longer duration marriages. *Journal of Sex Research, 44*, 597–607.

Dimitrius, J., & Mazzarella, M. (1999). *Reading people: How to understand people and predict their behavior—anytime, anyplace.* New York: Ballantine.

Egan, G. (1975). *The skilled helper.* Monterey, CA: Brooks/Cole.

Ekman, P., Friesen, W. V., & Ancoli, S. (1980). Facial signs of emotional experience. *Journal of Personality and Social Psychology, 39*, 1125–1134.

Festinger, L. (1957). *A theory of cognitive dissonance.* Oxford, UK: Peterson Row.

Finkelstein, S. (2013). Building trust in less than 10 minutes. *Huffington Post,* July 18.

Frank, M. G., Ekman, P., & Friesen, W. V. (1993). Behavioral markers and recognizability of the smile of enjoyment. *Journal of Personality and Social Psychology, 64*, 83–93.

Franklin, B. (1916). *The autobiography of Benjamin Franklin* (J. Bigelow, ed.). New York: G. P. Putnam's Sons.

Gagne, F., Khan, A. Lydon, J., & To, M. (2008). When flattery gets you nowhere: Discounting positive feedback as a relationship maintenance strategy. *Canadian Journal of Behavioral Science, 40*, 59–68.

Givens, D. G. (2014). *The nonverbal dictionary of gestures, signs and body language cues.* Spokane, WA: Center for Nonverbal Studies. Online at http://www.center-for-nonverbal-studies.org/6101.html.

Gold, J. A., Ryckman, R. M., & Mosley, N. R. (1984). Romantic mood induction and attraction to a dissimilar other: Is love blind? *Personality and Social Psychology Bulletin, 10*, 358–368.

Grammar, K, J., Schmitt, A., & Massano, A. H. (1999). Fuzziness of nonverbal courtship communication unblurred by motion energy detection. *Journal of Personality and Social Psychology, 77*, 487–508.

Grant, M. K., Fabrigar, L. R., & Lim, H. (2010). Exploring the efficacy of compliments as a tactic for securing compliance. *Basic and Applied Social Psychology, 32*, 226–233.

Greville, H. (1886). *Cleopatra.* Boston: Ticknor.

Griffeth, R. W., Vecchiok, R. P., & Logan, J. W. (1989). Equity theory and interpersonal attraction. *Journal of Applied Psychology, 74*, 394–401.

Gueguen, N. (2008). The effect of a woman's smile on men's courtship behavior. *Social Behavior and Personality, 36*, 1233–1236.

Gueguen, N. (2010). The effect of a woman's incidental tactile contact on men's later behavior. *Social Behavior and Personality, 38,* 257–266.

Gueguen, N. (2010). Men's sense of humor and women's responses to courtship solicitations: An experimental field study. *Psychological Reports, 107,* 145–156.

Gueguen, N., Boulbry, G., & Selmi, S. (2009). "Love is in the air": Congruency between background music and goods in a flower shop. *International Review of Retail, Distribution and Consumer Research, 19,* 75–79.

Gueguen, N., & Delfosse, C. (2012). She wore something in her hair: The effect of ornamentation on tipping, *Journal of Hospitality Marketing and Management, 12,* 414–420.

Gueguen, N., Martin, A., & Meineri, S. (2011). Similarity and social interaction: When similarity fosters implicit behavior toward a stranger. *Journal of Social Psychology, 15,* 671–673.

Gueguen, N., Martin, A., & Meineri, S. (2011). Mimicry and helping behavior: An evaluation of mimicry on explicit helping request. *Journal of Social Psychology, 15,* 1–4.

Gueguen, N., & Morineau, T. (2010). What is in a name? An effect of similarity in computer-mediated communication. *Journal of Applied Psychology, 6,* 1–4.

Gunnery, S. D., & Hall, J. A. (2014). The Duchenne smile and persuasion. *Journal of Nonverbal Behavior, 38,* 181–194.

Guo, S., Ahang, G., & Ahai, R. (2010). A potential way of enquiry into human curiosity. *British Journal of Educational Technology, 41,* 48–52.

Hall, E. T. (1966). *The hidden dimension.* Garden City, NY: Doubleday.

Hancock, J., & Toma, C. (2009). Putting your best face forward: The accuracy of online dating photographs. *Journal of Communication 59,* 367–386.

Harnish, R. J., Bridges, K. R., & Rottschaefer, K. M. (2014). Development and psychometric evaluation of the sexual intent scale. *Journal of Sex Research, 5,* 667–680.

Hazan, C. D., & Diamond, L. M. (2000). The place of attachment in human mating. *Review of General Psychology, 4,* 186–204.

Hill, C., Memon, A., & McGeorge, P. (2008). The role of confirmation bias in suspect interviews: A systematic evaluation. *Legal and Criminological Psychology, 13,* 357–371.

Hunt, G. L., & Price, J. B. (2002). Building rapport with the client. *Internal Auditor, 59,* 20–21.

Kaitz, M., Bar-Haim, Y., Lehrer, M., & Grossman, E. (2004). Adult attachment style and interpersonal distance. *Attachment and Human Development, 6,* 285–304.

Kassin, S. M., Goldstein, C. C., & Savitsky, K. (2003). Behavior confirmation in the interrogation room: On the dangers of presuming guilt. *Law and Human Behavior, 27,* 187–203.

Kleinke, C. L. (1986). Gaze and eye contact: A research review. *Psychological Review, 100,* 78–100.

Kleinke, C. L., & Kahn, M. L. (1980). Perceptions of self-disclosures: Effects of sex and physical attractiveness. *Journal of Personality, 48,* 190–205.

Kellerman, J., Lewis, J., & Laird, J. D. (1989). Looking and loving: The effects of mutual gaze on feelings of romantic love. *Journal of Research in Personality, 23,* 145–161.

Kenrick, D. T., & Cialdini, R. B. (1977). Romantic attraction: Misattribution versus reinforcement explanations. *Journal of Personality and Social Psychology, 35,* 381–391.

Knapp, M. L., & Hall, J. A. (1997). *Nonverbal communication in human interaction* (4th ed.). New York: Harcourt Brace College.

Krumhuber, E., & Manstead, A. S. R. (2009). Are you joking? The moderating role of smiles in perception of verbal statements. *Cognition and Emotion, 23,* 1504–1515.

Lee, L., Loewenstein, G., Ariely, D., Hong, J., & Young, J. (2008). If I'm not hot, are you hot or not? *Psychological Science, 10,* 669–677.

Lewis, D. (1995). *The secret language of success: Using body language to get what you want.* New York: Galahad Books.

Lynn, M., & McCall, M. (2000). Gratitude and gratuity: A meta-analysis of research on the service-tipping relationship. *Journal of Socio-Economics, 29*, 203–214.

Macrea, C. N., Hood, B. M., Milne, A. B., Rowe, A. C., & Mason, M. F. (2002). Are you looking at me? Eye gaze and person perception. *Psychological Science, 13*, 460–464.

Mai, X., Ge, Y., Toa, L., Tang, H., Liu, C., & Lou, Y. J. (2011). Eyes are windows to the Chinese soul: From the detection of real and fake smiles. *PLoS ONE, 5*, 1–6.

Mantovani, F. (2001). Networked seduction: A test-bed for the study of strategic communication on the Internet. *Cyberpsychology and Behavior, 4*, 147–154.

Martin, A., & Gueguen, N. (2013). The influence of incidental similarity on self-revelation in response to an intimate survey. *Social Behavior and Personality, 41*, 353–356.

Mehu, M., & Dunbar, R. I. M. (2008). Naturalistic observations of smiling and laughter in human group interactions. *Behavior, 145*, 1747–1780.

Mittone, L., & Savadori, L. (2009). The scarcity bias. *Applied Psychology, 58*, 453–468.

Moore, M. (2010). Human nonverbal courtship behavior: A brief historical review. *Journal of Sex Research, 47*, 171–180.

Nadler, J. (2004). Rapport in negotiations and conflict resolution. *Marquette Law Review, 5*, 885–882.

Nahari, G., & Ben-Shakhar, G. (2013). Primacy effect in credibility judgments: The vulnerability of verbal cues to biased interpretations. *Applied Cognitive Psychology, 27*, 247–255.

Navarro, J., & Karlins, M. (2007). *What every body is saying: An FBI special agent's guide to speed-reading people.* New York: HarperCollins.

Nelson, H., & Geher, G. (2007). Mutual grooming in human dyadic relationships: An ethological perspective. *Current Psychology, 26*, 121–140.

Nelson, S. (2014). Woman checks [boyfriend's] phone, finds footage of him having sex with her Staffordshire bull terrier dog. *Huffington Post UK*, February 14.

Olff, M. (2012). Bonding after trauma: On the role of support and the oxytocin system on traumatic stress. *European Journal of Psychotraumatology, 3*, 1–11.

Opt, S. K., & Loffredo, D. A. (2003). Communicator image and Myers-Briggs type indicator extroversion-introversion. *Journal of Psychology, 137*, 560–568.

Patterson, C. H. (1985). *Empathic understanding: The therapeutic relationship.* Monterey, CA: Brooks/Cole.

Patterson, J., Gardner, B. C., Burr, B. K., Hubler, D. S., & Roberts, K. M. (2012). Nonverbal indicators of negative affect in couple interaction. *Contemporary Family Therapy, 34*, 11–28.

Pease, A. (1984). *Signals: How to use body language for power, success, and love.* New York: Bantam Books.

Radford, M. (1998). Approach or avoidance? The role of nonverbal communication in the academic library user. *Library Trends, 46*, 1–12.

Rogers, C. R. (1961). *On becoming a person.* Boston: Houghton Mifflin.

Smeaton, G., Byrne, D. M., Murnen, S. K. (1989). The repulsion hypothesis revisited: Similarity irrelevance or dissimilarity bias. *Journal of Personality and Social Psychology, 56*, 54–59.

Stefan, J., & Gueguen, N. (2014). Effect of hair ornamentation on helping. *Psychological Reports: Relationships and Communication, 114*, 491–495.

Stewart, J, E. (1980). Defendant's attractiveness as a factor in the outcome of criminal trials: An observational study. *Journal of Applied Social Psychology, 10*, 348–361.

Swann, M. (2013). The professor, the bikini model and the suitcase full of trouble. *New York Times*, March 8.

Toma, C. L., Hancock, J. T., & Ellison, N. B. (2008). Separating fact from fiction: An examination of deceptive self-presentation in online dating profiles. *Personality & Social Psychology Bulletin, 34*, 1023–36. The conference paper was later published as a journal article.

Vanderhallen, M., Vervaeke, G., & Holmberg, U. (2011). Witness and suspect perceptions of working alliance and interviewing style. *Journal of Investigative Psychology and Offender Profiling, 8,* 110–130.

Videbeck, S. (2005). The economics and etiquette of tipping. *Policy, 20,* 38–41.

Vonk, R. (2002). Self-serving interpretations of flattery: Why ingratiation works. *Journal of Personality and Social Psychology, 82,* 515–526.

Wang, C. C., & Chang, Y. T. (2010). Cyber relationship motives: Scale development and validation. *Social Behavior and Personality, 38,* 289–300.

Wainwright, G. R. (1993). *Body language.* Teach Yourself Books. London: Hodder & Stoughton.

Whitty, M. T., & Buchanan, T. (2012). The online romance scam: A serious cybercrime. *Cyberpsychology, Behavior, and Social Networking, 15,* 181–183.

Zunin, L., & Zunin, N. (1972). *Contact: The first four minutes.* New York: Ballantine Books.

ACKNOWLEDGMENTS

I would like to express my appreciation to Dave and Lynda Mills of Dave Mills Photography in Lancaster, California, for taking the photographs in this book. Both Dave and Lynda graciously contributed their photographic skills to provide accurate depictions of selected techniques presented in these pages. I would like to thank Andrew Cardone and my daughter, Brooke Schafer, for volunteering their time and talent to serve as models for the photographs in this book. I would like to thank Jenny Chaney, L. Michael Wells, Daniel Potter, Cory Garza, and Tony DeCicco for reviewing the manuscript and offering their comments and suggestions. I would also like to thank Randy Marcoz, whom I have worked with for many years teaching and developing new ideas to enhance people's communication skills. A special thanks to Mike Dilley, author and historian, whom I have worked with for many years developing and perfecting the many techniques presented in this book. He also reviewed and edited the manuscript and provided invaluable advice in crafting the final draft. I would also like to acknowledge the efforts of my English teachers throughout my educational career, who had the courage to identify the weakness in my writing and the patience to help me strengthen my writing skills.

JACK SCHAFER

I have been blessed with wonderful people who have provided me with encouragement, inspiration, and insight when I needed it most.

I would like to recognize them here—alphabetically—and thank each one for adding meaning and joy to my life. If I have inadvertently overlooked anyone, my sincerest apologies.

Lewis Andrews, Alan and Susan Balfour, Loretta Barrett, Ann and Steve Batchelor, Lyle Berman, Carole Bloch, Stephanie Boyer, Avery Cardoza, C. T. Chan, Grace Chock, Cynthia Cohen, Don Delitz, Alex DeSilva, Maurice DeVaz, Jim Doyle, Julio and Carmen Enriquez, Burt, Barbara and Daniel Friedman, Sally Fuller, Jean Golden, John Gollehon, Jan Gordon, David and Odean Hargis, Steve Harris, Phil Hellmuth, Paulette and Kevin Herbert, Tom Johnson, Grace Jones, Sandra Karlins, Miriam and Arnold Karlins, Robert Kindya, Jerry Koehler, Albert Koh, Freddie Koh, Ray Kuik, Jim Levine, Len McCully, Rob Mercado, Debra Miceli, Chad Michaels, Peter Miller, Joe Navarro, Jacqueline O'Steen, Fran Regin, Maryanne Rouse, John Russell, Wallace Russell, Harry, Jeannie, Libby and Molly Schroder, Steven Schussler, Mike Shackleford, Stan Sludikoff, Joan and Eric Steadman, Gary Walters, Annette, Jill and Michelle Weinberg, Robert Welker, Tom Wheelen, Ken VanVoorhis, and Anthony Vitale.

Finally, Jack and I want to extend a special thanks to Matthew Benjamin—our editor extraordinaire—and all the other wonderful people at Simon & Schuster who contributed mightily to making this manuscript all it could be.

MARVIN KARLINS

INDEX

ABOUT THE AUTHORS

JOHN R. "JACK" SCHAFER, PH.D., is a psychologist, professor, intelligence consultant, and former FBI Special Agent. Dr. Schafer spent fifteen years conducting counterintelligence and counterterrorism investigations, and seven years as a behavioral analyst for the FBI's National Security Division's Behavioral Analysis Program. He developed spy recruitment techniques, interviewed terrorists, and trained agents in the art of interrogation and persuasion. Dr. Schafer contributes online pieces for *Psychology Today* magazine, has authored or coauthored six books, and has published numerous articles in professional and popular journals. He is a professor with the School of Law Enforcement and Criminal Justice at Western Illinois University.

MARVIN KARLINS received his Ph.D. in psychology from Princeton University and is currently Professor of Management at the University of South Florida's College of Business Administration. Dr. Karlins consults internationally on issues of interpersonal effectiveness and has also authored twenty-four books, including two national bestsellers, *What Every BODY Is Saying* and *It's a Jungle in There*. He resides in Riverview, Florida, with his wife, Edyth, and daughter, Amber.